D0966991

The Party of Humanity

The Party of Humanity

Writing Moral Psychology in Eighteenth-Century Britain

Blakey Vermeule

THE JOHNS HOPKINS UNIVERSITY PRESS

BALTIMORE AND LONDON

© 2000 The Johns Hopkins University Press
All rights reserved. Published 2000
Printed in the United States of America on acid-free paper
2   4   6   8   9   7   5   3   1

The Johns Hopkins University Press
2715 North Charles Street
Baltimore, Maryland 21218-4363
www.press.jhu.edu

Library of Congress Cataloging-in-Publication Data

Vermeule, Blakey.
The party of humanity : writing moral psychology in
eighteenth-century Britain / Blakey Vermeule.
p.   cm.
Includes bibliographical references and index.
ISBN 0-8018-6459-3 (acid-free paper)
1. English literature—18th century—History and criticism.
2. Psychology—Great Britain—History—18th century.
3. Ethics—Great Britain—History—18th century.
4. Psychology—Moral and ethical aspects.   5. Self
(Philosophy) in literature.   6. Moral development in
literature.   7. Ethics, Modern—18th century.
8. Psychology in literature.   9. Psychology—Philosophy.
10. Ethics in literature.   I. Title.
PR448.P75 V47 2000
820.9'353—dc21   00-008288

A catalog record for this book is available
from the British Library.

To Emily, Cornelius, and Adrian Vermeule
and Lisa Freeman

What wonder then, that moral sentiments are found of
such influence in life; though springing from principles,
which may appear, at first sight, somewhat small and deli-
cate? But these principles, we must remark, are social and
universal; they form, in a manner, the party of humankind against vice or disorder, its common enemy.

—DAVID HUME,
Inquiry Concerning the Principle of Morals (1751)

It seems to me natural to think that art is more deeply
rooted in human nature than morality, and I am surprised that philosophers make little of the fact that,
though good art is more likeable than bad art, virtuous
people do not enjoy this same advantage over those to
whom we are drawn primarily for their charm, or their
gaiety, or their sweetness of temper, or their outrageous-
ness.   —RICHARD WOLLHEIM,
The Mind and Its Depths (1993)

Contents

Acknowledgments

A version of chapter 2 appeared as "Shame and Identity: Pope's 'Critique of Judgment' in *An Essay on Criticism*" in *1650–50: Ideas, Aesthetics, and Inquiries in the Early Modern Era* 4, ed. Laura Morrow and Anna Battigelli, 10–36 (New York: AMS,1995); chapter 3 appeared in *Modern Philology* 96, no.1 (August 1998): 16–41; chapter 6 appeared in *Modern Language Quarterly* 59, no.1 (March 1998): 1–32.

This book was written in Berkeley, London, Pasadena, New Haven, and Chicago. The staffs of the Harold Washington Library Center of the Chicago Public Libraries, the University of California Berkeley Library, the Newberry Library, the Huntington Library, the British Library, the Yale University Libraries, and the Paul Mellon Centre for British Art made every aspect of research and writing easier, often suggesting sources that became part of the fabric of the book.

Without financial assistance from many organizations—most notably the Mellon Foundation and the Morse and Griswold Fellowship funds at Yale—this book could not have been written. For practical help, I thank the administrative staffs of the Berkeley and Yale English departments, especially Diane Repak.

Many people have helped me with the ideas and style of this book. Charlie Altieri, Leslie Brisman, Paul Hunter, Marjorie Levinson, David Marshall, Claude Rawson, and George Starr contributed their thoughts and time. Paul Bloom, David Bromwich, Marshall Brown, Frances Ferguson, Larry Lipking, Jennifer Thorne, James Turner, Howard Weinbrot, and an anonymous reader turned their prodigious energies to some or all of the manuscript. They may not agree with the final version, but their suggestions have improved it. Maura Burnett and the staff of the Johns Hopkins University Press have overseen this project with professionalism and care.

Steven Knapp directed the dissertation from which this book evolved. Although our lives have taken us to different places lately, he should know how brightly his example of intellectual energy shines for me.

During the writing of this book, I have benefited from the wisdom of a wide array of cultivated, kind, and passionate seekers: Bob Applebaum, Terry Castle, Meenakshi Chakraverti, Alison Conway, Scott Dykstra, Judith Jackson Fossett, Michael Ghazi, Kevis Goodman, Laura Green, Lanny Hammer, Andrea Henderson, Nasser Hussain, Victor Luftig, Dolores Pigoni Miller, Tyrus Miller, Jim Noggle, Cyrus Patell, the Patterson family, Viv Redhead, gabby redwine, William and Betsy Sledge, Ed Stein, Simon Stern, Aidan Wasley, and Benj Widiss.

Squash players make the best company. For giving me a place to unwind, laugh, and have fun every day for over a year, I am grateful to my friends at the Lakeshore Athletic Club in Chicago, especially Imran Nasir, squash pro, wit, and consummate gentleman.

Sylvia Brownrigg, Jill Campbell, Elizabeth Fowler, Jonathan Freedman, Bill Jewett, Jeannine Johnson, Mark Miller, Ruth Nisse, Sean O'Sullivan, Eleanor Pepples, and Kathy Rowe have generously given of their best selves to me and sometimes gotten less from me in return; still they have endured, laughed, argued, gossiped, fortified.

Yun Soo Lim is a wonderful new presence in my family. Mom, Dad, and Roo know how much love goes along with the dedication to this book. They have watched me wander off and return too many times to count, always welcoming me home with a joke and a provocative idea or two. This book is also dedicated to Lisa Ann Freeman.

The Party of Humanity

Chapter One

Introduction

Some Paradoxes of Moral Psychology

This is a book about the pain, pathos, and pleasures of moralizing—a topic that works deep into the terrain of moral psychology and out into the field of social relations. The book explores the anxious moral postures adopted by three eighteenth-century writers: Alexander Pope, Samuel Johnson, and David Hume. While these writers would not have seen themselves as part of a coherent tradition, they are all moralists whose texts raise common questions about moral life: What is the relation between the self and society? Where do moral judgments come from? How do they motivate and become normative for us? What is the role of the arts in securing those judgments? How do we obligate other people, entering into their concerns and—occasionally, when we need to—resisting the obligations they impose upon us?[1] The answers their texts explore are at once both broad and narrow, reflecting general features of human nature and the contours of a particular historical period.

The term *moralist* is one that Hume and his circle in provincial Calvinist Edinburgh would be astonished and perhaps amused to see next to his name. For in marked contrast to his London contemporaries, the "great Infidel" took himself to be a "scientist of man," offering a description of the way human psychology works rather than recommending one particular course of action over another. For Pope and Johnson, description is a tool to be used for correction. Pope and Johnson ride the crest of a flood of public moral energy in London in the early part of the eighteenth century. Like many other writers of their time, they believed that literature is a moral instrument, a way of directly imposing obligation on other people.

The cultures of eighteenth-century Britain teem with moralists. In all spheres of human life and activity—from sexual relations and gender to art, finance, health, law, politics, and religious belief—moralists can be found proclaiming that things could or should be different from, and better than, the way they are.[2] Few of these proclamations—even in a single sphere—coincide with each other to settle on a common diagnosis of what is wrong and how it should change. Instead, moralism is a rhetorical stance, a general mode of address. Given the range of conflicting moralisms, the eighteenth century seems not so much the Age of Reason as the age of reasons; it is less a time of universal standards than a time for factions, groups, and persons to invoke standards in order to obligate one another. The voices of eighteenth-century Britons echoing down to us today are voices of *should* and *ought*. Many writers adopted the voice of obligation unquestioningly and greedily; others turned ironic in giving advice. Even persons burdened by intense self-doubt adopted it. It seems they needed to, in order to be heard at all.

I have used the word *moralist* to describe writers who gave voice to the culture of obligation, but it is not a precise term. A better word would fall somewhere in between persuader, evaluator, invoker of norms, and obligator: a moralist is any person who sees that things could be different or better and argues from the convictions of a general standard—whether that standard is God, virtue, tradition, the public, common sense, reason, or truth. I use the word *normative* to cover the work of all such persons; as a group they include almost anybody who wrote or spoke about anything at all during the early and middle part of the eighteenth century. We can restrict the word *moralist* to anybody who is concerned specifically with how *people* can be better, different, or more perfect than they are. But this is hardly to narrow the field at all. The first few decades of the eighteenth century saw a massive increase in social consciousness and in awareness of the concept of the public. Along with this newfound social consciousness came a passion for observing other human beings and characterizing them. We might say that giving meaning to the human face (prosopopoeia) is the eighteenth century's most common trope and that persons are its most common unit of interest. Even Hume is a moralist in this sense, although he directs his descriptive powers toward others while reserving his normative energy for himself.

The premise of this book is that Pope, Johnson, and Hume—the three moralists—are practical psychologists whose moral impulses are inseparable from their social aims, projects, and networks. A further premise is that moral psychology in general presents us with a paradox (and that this paradox, of which we are only fitfully conscious, is painful). Moral psychology is closely connected to reasoning about social life. Reasoning about social life is closely connected to reasoning for personal or collective advantage. Moral psychology is therefore closely connected to self-interest. Yet the lifeblood of moral ideals is the fiction that they can transcend the social. There are deep differences in the outlooks, temperaments, talents, and beliefs of the writers in this study; yet this paradox marks each of their intellectual lives. For the moment, I will put their specific differences aside to explain the method by which I hope to bring this paradox into focus. Most broadly, the method is naturalism, which in the field of ethics has revived self-interest theories of human motivation.

Ethical naturalism posits that our moral beliefs arise from facts about the way we are, not from a transcendental source. *Moral subjectivism*—the notion that there are features of our minds that give rise to moral behavior—is a late-seventeenth-century British invention; so too is the material theory of mind on which it rests. *Moral psychology* is the science of describing the features of our minds that are responsible for moral behavior; it developed as part of a broad empiricist philosophical outlook whose explanatory power has in recent decades become much greater. *Empiricist ethics* seeks to understand how psychology grounds different aspects of our moral lives, from our moral sentiments to our normative social codes; it seeks to understand how our norms and conventions of justice arise (or do not arise) from our intuitions about the right and the good. This larger project of moving from the mind to culture and back again has been the intellectual engine of empiricist ethics since the beginning: late-seventeenth- and eighteenth-century moral philosophers developed moral psychology in part to explain individual moral choices and broad social norms under a single framework. Something like this unifying project is the subject of the most fruitful work going on right now in the philosophy of culture.[3]

In the last two decades, bolstered by advances in cognitive science and evolutionary biology—especially the branches of it that treat humans: sociobiology and evolutionary psychology—empiricism has achieved a new authority and prestige. This new synthesis of evolutionary biology and the brain sciences has powerfully extended the naturalist revolution begun by Locke, Hume, and the British moral sense philosophers. There are profound differences between old and new empiricist cognitive psychology, but between eighteenth-century moral psychology and evolutionary ethics there are distinct continuities.[4] These continuities may be explained in several ways. British empiricists such as Hobbes, Boyle, Locke, and Hooker can lay claim to having invented the scientific study of the mind within whose framework moral psychologists operate; in one Kuhnian scenario, they invented the paradigm that allows moral questions to be articulated in the idiom inherited by evolutionary ethics. But I favor a different explanation. Rather than seeing the science of moral psychology as an effect of Enlightenment ideology, I would argue that it picks out deep facts about the sources of morality, facts that the evolutionary synthesis is now able to explain and contextualize. On this view, empiricism turns out to have the right account of the sources of moral life. This view informs the readings in this book in ways that I will explain. It gives rise to a host of questions, consequences, and objections. But in general, I mean not only to explain the theory but also to adopt it as a guide.

Some overview of evolutionary naturalism is in order. "Selection thinking" is a broad tent, housing many different kinds of projects and schools of thought. Evolutionary hypotheses about human psychology are emerging from a growing body of work by geneticists, ethologists, psychologists, biologists, linguists, anthropologists, archaeologists, and social historians. These hypotheses are being codified, popularized, and explained by science writers, philosophers, and journalists. Until now evolutionary psychologists have been unified by their opposition to the overwhelmingly dominant "Standard Social Science Model" (SSSM) (Cosmides and Tooby 1992, 23ff). The SSSM argues for relatively few innate principles, a small core of human nature, and domain-general cognitive capacities; human cultures are infinitely variable, and all behavior is learned. Evolutionary psychology, by contrast, argues for many innate principles, a large core of human nature, and domain-specific cognitive capacities (Mithen 1996, 13–14). Included in the mental modules proposed and analyzed so far are language, "cheater-detection," kin selection, reciprocal altruism, incest avoidance, color recognition, and many others. Now that evolutionary psychology is becoming more widely accepted in the social sciences, hypotheses about the content of these specific adaptive modules are proliferating and being tested.[5]

One set of questions has been central to evolutionary theory, as it was to the British philosophers: questions about the sources of our moral lives.[6] For both old and new empiricist traditions, enquiring into the sources of our moral lives runs the investigator directly up against some paradoxes of moral psychology. The main paradox is that morality seems to be closely connected to self-interest. This intuition can take many forms, some stronger and some weaker, some plausible, some ludicrous, some that seem to cut against the grain of our most deeply held values. The best way to explain it is to unravel some of the many threads that connect the two empiricist traditions of eighteenth-century moral thought and evolutionary ethics.

Let us begin with the first principle of empiricist ethics, the rejection of a transcendental source for morality and values. At the very beginning of his

Enquiry Concerning the Principle of Morals, Hume asks the question of which features of our psychologies give rise to moral actions and moral systems: "There has been a controversy started of late . . . concerning the general foundation of morals; whether they be derived from reason, or from sentiment; whether we attain the knowledge of them by a chain of argument and induction, or by an immediate feeling and finer internal sense; whether, like all sound judgment of truth and falsehood, they should be the same to every rational intelligent being; or whether, like the perception of beauty and deformity, they be founded entirely on the particular fabric and constitution of the human species" (E 170). Hume's answer is that the general foundation of morality is the moral sentiments, an answer almost identical to the answer offered by evolutionary ethicists. But Hume and these later empiricists diverge in choosing their level of explanation. Hume wants to know what the moral sentiments are, how they work, and especially how they can be encouraged; evolutionary ethicists come at those questions by a historical, indeed evolutionary, explanation of where they came from. Evolutionists tell a fascinating story about the prehistory of the moral sentiments, how they evolved via reciprocal altruism, kin selection, and perhaps even group selection.[7] What evolutionary ethics has done most powerfully is to coordinate commonsense reflections on familiar human moral dilemmas with a workable set of scientific hypotheses. Furthermore, evolutionary ethics reaches back in time to address such eighteenth-century-style questions about sympathy and altruism as How does sympathy arise between people? Why are people moral? Why do sympathy and altruism always seem so much more fragile than selfishness? What are the limits of sympathy? Are there any limits to selfishness? The obvious conundrum is that while morality does not necessarily seem to be in our best interests, as a species we have developed complex canons of moral norms, institutions, and obligations.

In recent decades evolutionary theorists have begun to work out ingenious answers to these familiar questions. They argue that even the most genuinely moral sentiments can evolve out of an extreme methodological individualism. Here is an overview of this approach, as described by Barbara Smuts:

Evolutionary theory predicts that individuals will behave in ways that, on average, increase their own reproductive success. From this perspective, all individuals are selfish competitors. Yet, paradoxically, the formation of cooperative relationships is sometimes the most effective way to increase individual reproductive success. However, the genetic interests of individuals are not identical, and conflicts of interest perpetually endanger the survival of these relationships, particularly when they involve unrelated individuals. This familiar tension between individual self-interest and the well-being of some larger social unit reflects the selection pressures that underlie all social life, both in humans and other animals. Thus, animals could not evolve stable, long-term, mutually dependent reciprocal, intimate relationships with non-kin without simultaneously evolving mechanisms to ensure that, on average, each member of the cooperating unit received benefits greater than she or he would receive if acting alone or in cooperating with others instead. (1997, 67–68)

Smuts is here referring to the selfish gene theory, as brilliantly popularized by Richard Dawkins (1976), and to its extension in moral theory by George C. Williams, Robert L. Trivers, William D. Hamilton, and Robert Axelrod. The selfish gene theory has spread rapidly over the last two decades, proving to be both successful and, for fascinating and important reasons, easily misunderstood. It is associated with a program of strict *adaptationism,* that is, the notion that genetic reproduction is an algorithm that has given rise to complex organismal design (Dennett 1995, 48ff). In moral theory, adaptationism has sponsored a set of arguments about how our moral systems arise from long-term self-interest through two mechanisms: kin selection and reciprocal altruism. These mechanisms are related but not identical. *Kin selection,* a theory first formulated by William Hamilton (1964), is the idea that genes can program their carriers to sacrifice themselves for other organisms who also carry copies of those genes—relatives, in short. If we take the "gene's eye view," we soon realize that genes do not particularly "care" about the organism that carries it. Nor do they care who spreads them. My genes are replicated just as efficiently if I sacrifice myself to save the lives of two siblings—each carrying roughly half of my genes—as they would be if I passed my genes to one child. They are also passed more effectively if I make sacrifices to ensure the well-being of that child. This is not to say, of course, that my survival is a matter of indifference to me or that the sacrifice is not hard: in an ingenious contribution to the theory of kin selection, Robert Trivers (1974) offered to explain why it is that parents and children, not to mention siblings, may experience profound conflicts and may overtly and subtly seek to manipulate each other to favor their own interests. But the very difficulty of the sacrifices and power of the conflicts may be tempered by the emotional compulsion I feel on behalf of relatives. The theory of kin selection suggests that morality gets started by piggybacking on family love (see Hamilton 1964; Wright 1994, chap. 7).

Meanwhile what compels us to cooperate with unrelated individuals? One well-known eighteenth-century answer, recently revived by James Q. Wilson (1993), is the moral sense. But this answer begs a further question: Where does the moral sense come from? The theory of *reciprocal altruism* suggests an answer. It describes how morality can extend even to people who are unrelated to us, while predicting that our moral feelings for others will diminish in proportion to our degree of relatedness. George C. Williams describes the theory in a general way:

Simply stated, an individuals who maximizes his friendships and minimizes his antagonisms will have an evolutionary advantage, and selection should favor those characters that promote the optimization of personal relationships. I imagine that this evolutionary factor has increased man's capacity for altruism and compassion and has tempered his ethically less acceptable heritage of sexual and predatory aggressiveness. There is theoretically no limit to the extent and complexity of group-related behavior that this factor could produce, and the immediate goal of such behavior would always be the well-being of some other individual, often genetically unrelated. Ultimately, however, this would not be an adaptation for group benefit. It would be developed by the differential survival of individuals and would be designed for the perpetuation of the genes of the individual providing the benefit to another. It would involve only such immediate self-sacrifice for which the probability of later repayment would be sufficient justification. (1966, 94–95)

The theory was developed with the help of two special tools—computer simulation and a thought experiment from game theory called "the prisoner's dilemma." Robert Axelrod, a political theorist, has devised a complicated way of testing the reciprocal altruism hypothesis in a computer simulation that he convincingly claims models evolution. He has discovered that while selfishness may be tempting in the short run, in the long run the optimal social strategy is to cooperate initially, to reciprocate both cooperation and selfishness, and to punish noncooperators but forgive them when they repent (Axelrod 1984; Wright 1994, 191–202). The theory of reciprocal altruism will be the topic of chapter 5.

To put it mildly, these theories have been controversial. For they are easily misinterpreted (even by some mischievous biologists) to say something unpalatable, namely that all moral emotions are really self-serving, indeed that we adopt them cynically and insincerely.[8] Yet this misprision is also uncomfortably plausible: moral emotions are often closely connected to moral self-advertising; and moral beliefs seem to track self-interest rather than departing significantly from it. And this empiricist insight, far from being merely cynical, is genealogically close to several Copernican revolutions in moral thought—such as Freud's system—that predict that our moral systems derive from immoral impulses. First among these Copernican revolutionaries we can place a number of seventeenth- and eighteenth-century British moral philosophers: Thomas Hobbes, Bernard Mandeville, Frances Hutcheson, David Hume, and Adam Smith. We can exclude Shaftesbury. To be a Copernican revolutionary is to be something of a moral antirealist, someone who thinks that morality arises from facts about the way we are, and someone who thinks that insofar as our ideas track the best or the truth, it is because those categories too can be traced back to our psychologies.

To early critics of sociobiology, the strong resemblance between the self-interest theories of altruism and eighteenth-century moral philosophy is evidence of flaw and ideological taint. This critique has been mounted most seriously by the philosopher Philip Kitcher, writing against what he calls "pop sociobiology" (by which he means not just its popular manifestations but the whole sociobiological enterprise) (1985, 396, 399). And indeed, the parallels are stunning. The following statement could have been written as a paraphrase of Richard Dawkins's *The Selfish Gene* (1976):

Men are naturally selfish, unruly creatures, what makes them sociable is their necessity and consciousness of standing in need of others' help to make life comfortable: and what makes this assistance voluntary and lasting are the gains on profit accruing to industry for services done to others, which in a well ordered society enables every body, who in some thing or other will be serviceable to the publick, to purchase the assistance of others. (Quoted in Horne 1978, xi)

On the other hand, evolutionary psychologists would probably reject the strong dualism of this next statement, for it misses the most important fact about human moral psychology, which is that people really are moral, altruistic, unselfish, and so on.

What renders [man] a sociable animal, consists not in his desire of company, good nature, pity, affability, and other graces of a fair outside; but that his vilest and most hateful qualities are the most necessary accomplishments to fit him for the largest, and according to the world, the happiest and most flourishing societies. (Mandeville 1989, 53)

Both are quotations from the writings of Bernard Mandeville. Meanwhile, evolutionary psychologists would strongly agree with both of the following statements, the first from Hobbes, the second the opening words of Adam Smith's *Theory of Moral Sentiments:*

I put for a generall inclination of all mankind, a perpetuall and restless desire of power after power, that ceaseth onely in death. And the cause of this, is not always that a man hopes for a more intensive delight, than he has already attained to; or that he cannot be content with a moderate power: but because he cannot assume the means to live well, which he hath at present, without the acquisition of more. (Hobbes 1991, 90)

How selfish soever man may be supposed, there are evidently some principles in his nature, which interest him in the fortune of others, and render their happiness necessary to him, though he derives nothing from it except the pleasure of seeing it. Of this kind is pity or compassion. (Smith 1982, 9)

The first passage exhibits a concern with status, whose importance evolutionary psychologists have uniformly emphasized: "Status is central to all complex mammal societies, humanity included. To say that people generally seek status, whether by rank, class, or wealth, is to sum up a large part of the catalogue of human social behavior" (E. O. Wilson 1998, 170). The second points to the striking paradox of moral psychology on the naturalist view, namely that selfishness and altruism are of a piece.[9]

Rather than becoming suspicious of this coincidence, we should perhaps see it as evidence of an ongoing human obsession with the scandal of self-interest. Perceiving ourselves to be self-interested is by turns troubling and liberating; perceiving others to be self-interested is just shocking. Evolutionary psychology can even help us understand these responses. Believing in our own disinterestedness is often a highly useful strategy: in order to pursue our own ends most effectively, we need to be able to convince other people that we are disinterested. But in a famous set of experiments, the psychologist Leda Cosmides (later with John Tooby) demonstrated that people reason most effectively about violations of the social contract when they suspect they are being cheated. She posits that we have a "cheater-detection" module by which we enforce social contracts (1992b, 163–228). So in the game of social contracts, successful players pursue a strategy in which they receive just a little bit more in benefit than they pay out in cost. But if our fellow social animals are scanning for signs of just such shady accounting, we should develop (evolve) ways of fooling their cheater-detection modules. And here a key evolutionary psychological use of the unconscious comes into play: the most effective way to convince our fellow social animals that we have their best interests in mind is to believe, whole-heartedly and without conscious guile, that we *do* have their best interests in mind. We thus relegate knowledge of our self-interest to our unconscious, where it cannot be exposed or unmasked by others. So prized is this suppression that unmasking it is risky, bringing either social benefit or social disgrace. On the one hand, we value people who can expose the self-interest of people who are more socially successful than we are. We are repeatedly scandalized to discover that other people are self-interested. Our shock is, of course, a social strategy. It suggests that we ourselves couldn't possibly be self-interested. On the other hand, those who too zealously or greedily expose other people are dangerous to us. Richard Alexander, a prominent

evolutionary biologist, has even proposed that we are evolved to resist thinking of ourselves as self-interested and will contemn theorists who offer such a
dismal picture of the human animal (1987, 31–32).[10] Finally, those who come
off the worst in all this are the morally self-righteous exposers who can be
shown to be self-interested. Alexander Pope is one such figure. He made a career out of exposing other people, yet an entire tradition of Pope criticism has
been devoted to unmasking his self-interest, with generation after generation
of critics newly scandalized.

We have now begun to sketch the outlines of moral psychology from an
empiricist standpoint: it is a psychology adapted to an environment in which
hardships are not natural objects but other people. It is also a psychology in
which values closely track personal and collective interests: values arise from
conflicts and confluences of interest, never becoming fully abstracted from
them. But now we must turn to a second tradition, that of ethics itself. This
tradition developed in response to the nascent empiricist program, and the
founding intuition of post-Kantian ethical theory is that ethics depends on a
strict separation of values from interests. On this dominant way of thinking,
ethics and moral psychology have nothing to do with each other; the field of
ethics has developed largely by cordoning itself off from all empiricist and self-
interest theories of moral psychology. In the early part of the twentieth century, G. E. Moore famously argued against the "naturalistic fallacy," claiming
that there is no relation between "what we ought to do" and "what we do do"
(May, Friedman, and Clark 1996, 1–2; M. Johnson 1996). Twentieth-century
moral philosophy has handled moral psychology by resolutely invoking the
fact/value distinction, separating the naturalist ("is") from the normative
("ought") and arguing that moral agency (the subject of ethics) consists solely
in the normative demands that we make upon ourselves. Of course this distinction was also drawn by Hume, who saw the problem set by moral sense
philosophy as being not so much how self-interest leads to altruism as it is how
the atomistic impressions in our head can recommend one course of action
over another (see T 469). The Kantian tradition has answered this empiricist
conundrum by asserting that facts do not and cannot give us an adequate purchase on values.

Such an argument has recently been forcefully made by Christine Korsgaard, who has produced the most intense and profound meditations on
Enlightenment philosophy since Ernst Cassirer. Like John Rawls, she has concentrated on updating Kant's moral philosophy. In her magnificent interpretation of Kant, moral obligation, and indeed all human values, arises from our
capacity for autonomous self-reflection. Autonomous self-reflection is a

product of human social life, a tenet that brings Kant so far into the mainstream of eighteenth-century moral philosophy, which holds that we regulate our conduct according to social norms. But Kant rejects what I call at points in this book "the spectator morality of the Enlightenment" and takes a crucial further step: we have the capacity to obligate ourselves through the process of reflection; the moral law may originate in sociability, but we make the law count for ourselves. A human being enters the domain of the moral law within by reflecting on the choices she faces.

Korsgaard repeatedly calls herself a "naturalist," a moral philosopher whose insights fit into emerging paradigms in evolutionary psychology.[11] She invokes the canonical moral philosophical distinction between facts and values, between the anthropology of morals and moral agency. But by naturalism she means only the former. The normative is quite a separate matter, and the fact that the source of moral obligation can be found in the natural world is little more than an irrelevant curiosity: "We are social animals so probably the whole thing has a biological basis" (1996, 9). The brief story she tells about how the roots of conscience can be found in our aggressive impulses turned inward resembles nothing so much as an eighteenth-century parable of civilization emerging from the state of nature:

The world of social animals is characterized by elaborate structures of hierarchy and domination. Although the ability to dominate does have to do with strength and prowess, it is not related to it in an obvious way. When two animals battle for dominance, the battle may be highly ritualized, and often the losing party is not at all injured. It is a battle of wills.

Both Nietzsche and Freud believed that morality and the special character of human consciousness emerged simultaneously in the evolution of our species. Since I have grounded morality in the special character of human consciousness—in particular, in its reflective nature—I take these accounts to be harmonious with my view. Both also believed that the special character of human consciousness arose when the impulse to dominate—the will to power, or the aggressive instincts—were deprived of any outlet and turned against the self. An intelligent, wilful animal, held captive and punished by others, was not permitted to be aggressive. And having nothing else to dominate it, it turned these instincts inward, and learned to dominate itself. And in that way reflective distance and the autonomy that goes with it came into being . (1996, 157–58)

For Kant, reason sets the laws of morality, just as it does the laws of mathematics; and the task for the rational individual is to find out what those laws are and to freely choose to be bound by them. The two tests that human beings should apply to moral choices to find out whether they meet the criteria of reason are the Categorical Imperative: "Act as if the maxim of your action were to become through your will a universal law of nature," (1981, section 421, p. 30), and the Formula of Humanity: "Act in such a way that you treat humanity, whether in your own person or in the person of another, always at the same time as an end and never simply as a means" (1981, section 429, p. 36). And here is the paradox of moral psychology in its most extreme form: elaborate theories of justice and fairness arise from the dominance behavior of intelligent, willful, aggressive animals. Pressed to a Kantian extreme, the paradox posits a distinct split between selfishness and altruism, between the needs of the individual and the demands of humanity.

Perhaps because of the reflective psychology that Korsgaard identifies as the ground of ethics, and perhaps because self-interest theories are uncomfortable, dualism underlies most ethical systems. We should consider the possibility too that dualism underlies some interpretive systems, especially when other people's motives are at issue. To understand the role of moral postures in the lives and works of these writers, we could take one of two approaches. We could either try to explore their values from the inside out, taking their testimony about what motivates them at face value, or we could override their testimony in favor of explanations they might reject. The first method would roughly correspond to historical reconstruction, the second to critical—especially psychoanalytic or deconstructive—exposure. Both approaches would yield limited but very real insights into the claims of social life. The first approach would look at experience from the first-person perspective, while the second would import an interpretive framework. This is a distinction, to use a distinctly modern vocabulary, between the phenomenology of morals and the anthropology of morals, between what compels us and the reasons that we are compelled, between the two questions "Why am I moral?" and "Why are people moral?"[12] The paradox of moral psychology is that both approaches could be true, but each would yield a vastly different result.

Let me try to convey what this distinction puts at stake. All human actions can be described under two aspects. Anger has both a phenomenological and a descriptive aspect. So do sexual desire, beauty, pain, pride, and guilt. Usually there is some distance between the two aspects, a distance that may trouble us when we become aware of it. Who among us likes to think that when we get married and have children we are marching lockstep with our generation to death, as Nietzsche said? What distinguishes moral psychology is that the distance is unusually wide and that we find it more than usually disturbing.

The theory of naturalism that I am outlining (and endorsing) here is, by contrast, antidualist. It seeks to locate moral psychology and ethics on a unified plane. Naturalism recognizes that humans need, for various psychological reasons, to posit a split between the feelings our values give us and descriptions of why our values motivate us. It presumes, nonetheless, that there is no such split, but rather that moral psychology and moral agency are unified. Because the normative and the descriptive seem to diverge, a naturalistic analysis seeks to bring them back together under a unified field. There are many complications, such as the fact that we are inclined to separate the normative "ought" from the descriptive "is" in our own case but to disallow that distinction in the case of others. On the naturalist view, even extreme self-sacrificing behaviors are in our long-term self-interest, but we have elaborate defenses against allowing our moral consciousness to be penetrated by thoughts of any motives other than the ones we set for ourselves. Naturalism refers to a hope, as much as a method, for uniting diverse aspects of moral psychology together under a single explanatory framework.

At most points in this book, especially in the three chapters on Pope, we will not have to go far to find evidence of the paradox of moral psychology. The people in my study—writers and their characters—confront familiar dilemmas in social life: sexual desire, gender identity, family relations, trade, patronage, friendship, cheating, ambition, cooperation, status, rivalry, shame, trust, betrayal, even insanity. They respond by developing a practical ethics, shaped in first-person questions about what is best for them to do, and a moral stance on why others too should conform. Often their moral beliefs are drawn from wider religious or moral doctrines. Yet even then they can be explained naturalistically. From the perspective of naturalism, moral postures are not abstract—human beings use them as frequently as they use their senses of sight and hearing—but they can only be grasped in relation to specific social situations and other people. We can locate the moral sentiments—and their close cousin, moral aggression—in some practical need and in the deep self-interest from which those emotions grow. Naturalism helps us treat moral stances as social strategies: by following their track, we can explore the web of social practices and relations, and the way some people have found to navigate this web by obeying the practical demands of their social identities.

Moves in the game of moral objectivity, a game played ferociously and reverentially by Pope and others, can be placed in a broader social context of the desire for status and conflict over the control of resources. Pope repeatedly adopts postures of moral objectivity to extend his interests, using those postures as moves in a game of social domination. Yet even as he asserts the power to obligate, this moralist guiltily conceals the traces of his manipulations. A moralist fitfully and ambivalently identifying with a correcting perspective on his own impulses is a familiar and remarkable figure in post-Augustinian sacred and secular moral writing (including psychoanalysis). While in much homiletic literature the moral stance is self-reflexive, in the eighteenth century it becomes assimilated to the genre of satire: at those moments when the moralist identifies most fully with a corrective power, he claims the right to peer into the naked soul of man. The moralist both points towards the stringency of normative ethics and strips the fictions from the social world.

Naturalism, too, would seem to be a stripper of fictions.[13] In its popular modes, it holds out that very hope. It flirts with cynicism and reductionism; it is exhilarating and dangerous; it opens the possibility of a comically melancholy style at the same time that it threatens to lapse into mere raving. And in this it resembles nothing so much as that dark twin of Enlightenment moralizing, eighteenth-century satire. Consider a widely read book by Robert Wright called *The Moral Animal* (1994). Wright takes familiar facts of social life, namely that we are animals caught in a cross weave of status hierarchy and reciprocal altruism—status-seeking, debt, trade, friendship, and trust—and explains the evolutionary logic behind them. At its worst, the book tells "just-so" stories outlandish enough to garner tremendous press attention for the book. His procedure: take any "feature of human nature" and look for the evolutionary logic behind it. If you can think of environmental circumstances in which adopting that behavior would maximize genetic fitness, you've got yourself a neat evolutionary explanation. Many writers have published lists of "features of human nature," but Wright's has an undeniably sensationalist cast. He nominates the tendency of men to see women as either virgins or whores, infidelity in both sexes but especially in men, status-seeking, lying out of self-justified motives, infanticide, sibling rivalry, rape, low self-esteem among criminals, and an intense thirst for gossip.

All of these phenomena can be grouped under the heading of dominance relations.[14] Under this heading too, Wright places moralizing itself. Much as Nietzsche did in the *Genealogy of Morals* (1887), Wright locates the origins of morality in competition over the control of resources. From conflicts of interest come moral self-righteousness, along with a tendency to deceive ourselves about our own moral failings; from confluences of interest come moral approval. Moral realism, the notion that our moral views correspond to the way things really are, is itself a powerful tool in the game of moral objectivity. Wright's thesis is a familiar one in the evolutionary analysis of human moral life. As he puts it succinctly elsewhere, "Our moral evaluations of people are often subordinate, by design, to our social agendas" (Wright 1996). In fact, Wright's prose owes much of its rhetorical life to eighteenth-century satire, from his inviting us to get an overview of our crazy species by adopting the detached pose of an alien anthropologist from Mars, to the attempt to think through human nature in terms of animal nature. Surely here he is thinking of Book IV of *Gulliver's Travels* and of Mark Twain's *Letters from the Earth:*

In a small group (a group, say, the size of a hunter-gatherer village), a person has a broad interest in deflating the reputations of others, especially others of the same sex and similar age, with whom there exists a natural rivalry. . . . Expect [this derogation of others] to reach high volume when two people are vying for something that there's only one of—a particular woman, a particular man, a particular professional distinction. . . . The keen sensitivity with which people detect the flaws of their rivals is one of nature's wonders. It takes a Herculean effort to control this tendency consciously, and the effort must be repeated on a regular basis. Some people can summon enough restraint not to talk about their rivals' worthlessness; they may even utter some Victorian boilerplate about a "worthy opponent." But to rein in the perception itself—the unending, unconscious, all-embracing search for signs of unworthiness—is truly a job for a Buddhist monk. Honesty of evaluation is simply beyond the reach of most mortals. (1994, 268–69).

But now a certain familiar double vision sets in. We can admit to finding an explanation powerful while also standing back from it to investigate the cultural interest it provokes at a particular moment in time. The naturalist thesis about moral life has a definite form with a distinguished history in both sacred and secular thought. The urge to get outside of human moral systems and to anatomize them has been intellectually sanctioned in different periods of history. It has also been forcefully condemned (this dialectic has played out most recently in the public opposition between the "two cultures" of science and the humanities, between proponents of the scientific method and inventors of "Science Studies"). Evolutionary naturalism is only the latest in a long line of attempts to socialize the transcendent while transcending the social: a naturalist—since the seventeenth century an experimenter, but once, perhaps, a prophet—looks down on human society from a great height and finds that human ideals have a strongly social character. He hopes for a Pisgah sight. Since the Enlightenment, judgments with this form have been an effective instrument of secularization, wielded most trenchantly by David Hume, *"le bon David,"* who on his deathbed prided himself on being almost "more detached from Life" than it is possible for any person to be (1932, 1:7). Judgments with this form are also a standard satirist's tool.

This study, in short, is in the peculiar methodological position of offering up a naturalist explanation of writings by people who themselves offered up their own (eighteenth-century versions of) naturalist explanations of the world around them. It should be clear by now that this is no coincidence, for there are at least two resonances between evolutionary psychology and eighteenth-century rhetoric. From Enlightenment moral philosophy, evolutionary psychology inherits a unifying ethos, addressing the relation of the individual to social norms; of sub-individual, to individual, to supra-individual entities; of genes to gene complexes, to modules, to persons, to culture. And from eighteenth-century satire, it inherits a passionate, rebellious, disruptive way of talking about the self in society and about the complicated motives of human moralizing. Both resonances help us understand how in the small, personal culture of British letters in the early eighteenth century, moralism came to be twinned with its opposite, cynicism.

The Normative Power of Art

These are some of the themes that will recur in the following chapters. But the texts in this study insist on a second order of concern: besides being psychologically and morally complex, they are aesthetically complex, a fact that at once makes naturalism more appealing and sets powerful limits on it. Let me take each of these claims in turn. The aesthetic complexity of these texts makes naturalism more appealing because eighteenth-century aesthetics, like evolutionary psychology, gropes toward a theory of the unity of moral psychology while claiming to transcend mere intuition about the relationship between an individual and culture. In their philosophically explicit forms, moral psychology, the aesthetic, and social theory are eighteenth-century European inventions; to trace the origins of one concept is to find it entangled, at its roots, with the other two. Historically, aesthetics stands in a foundational relationship to the other two concepts: eighteenth-century British culture assigned the task of making sense of human social life to its emerging aesthetic sphere. Artists and theorists met this challenge with gusto, transmuting the raw material of social life into innovative narratives and new media. The most sophisticated stories about human sociability, including such diverse topics as gender, nation, rank, unequal distributions of wealth and power, and what Wordsworth called "the increasing collection of men in cities," were handled in poems, paintings, novels, and by prose nonfiction writers using the language and idiom of art.

Meanwhile every British moral philosopher, including Hobbes, Locke, Mandeville, Shaftesbury, Hutcheson, Kames, Hume, Burke, and Smith, was obsessed with a single question: how to reconcile private interest with public benefits, two points of view seemingly in conflict with each other. Increasingly, they turned to aesthetics as the best explanatory tool, making it an instrument—as the scientific method has since become—of both reduction and of synthesis, a way of traveling into the human psyche and out again into the world. To borrow a term coined by E. O. Wilson (1998), aesthetic theory was their instrument of consilience. Through these developments, aesthetic culture became the primary forum for social abstraction, the means by which concepts of society were represented back to its members. Perhaps in some other time and place the main forum would have been religion or science, but to use John Barrell's phrase, the "value-languages" (and indeed the political languages) of Georgian culture were spoken in the idiom of art (Barrell 1986, 12).[15]

The analogy to evolutionary psychology lies not only in the fact that evolutionary psychology is suffused with Enlightenment explanatory idealism. Nor does it lie, entirely, in the fact that analyses in evolutionary psychology are, for the time being, more aesthetic than scientific; that is, they are narratively compelling but explanatorily vague. The analogy encompasses these two facts but goes beyond them. Both eighteenth-century aesthetics and evolutionary psychology are conceptual modes of inquiry that attempt, in E. O. Wilson's words, "to explain phenomena by webs of causation across adjacent levels of organization" (1998, 189). Adjacent levels of organization comprise everything from the inner workings of the mind to the most complex social forms. Both methods are instruments of reduction and of synthesis, preoccupied by the question of the relationship between the individual and culture and by the hope of finding underlying regularities in human nature. Both methods purport to help us understand the way human beings characteristically react to their surroundings, especially when their surroundings include other human beings reacting to them. They promise to help us trace feelings and actions back into the minds of the people who experience them and to piece together a story about large-scale social formations, especially, perhaps, in the eighteenth century, when people believed that such moral emotions as sympathy were the cement of society. Both come into being in response to an earlier order of mystification and credulity against which they proclaim themselves to be instruments of demystification, detachment, and objectivity. Finally, and most importantly, both are centered on the problem of self-interest.

The very strength of the analogy, however, points to the limits of naturalism. For to some extent, naturalism hopes to deliver on promises first made by eighteenth-century moral philosophy to establish the unity of moral psychology and to find a ground from which to explain the individual in relation to the group. Yet as David Bromwich writes, works of art in this period draw sustenance by putting these questions always into play: "A motive for great writing throughout [the modern period] has been a tension, which is felt to be unresolvable, between the claims of social obligation and of personal autonomy. That these had to be experienced as rival claims was the discovery of Burke and Wordsworth. Our lives are lived today and our choices are made in a culture where any settlement of the contest for either side is bound to be provisional. There is nothing to approve or regret in such a situation; it is the way things are; and in a time like ours, it is what great writing lives on" (1989, vii).

In practice what this means is that individual works of art often contradict and falsify aesthetic theory. All of the authors in this study seek to obligate other people, but they confront the limits of art as an instrument of obligation, indeed of social explanation. They share the concerns of aesthetic theory but resist its mandate to clarify, discovering how intransigent and opaque their medium can be. This is a practical rather than a metaphysical claim: I am not claiming on behalf of aesthetic formalism that eighteenth-century art should not be read as an instrument of moral instruction or sociological explanation; indeed, some of these authors would like nothing better than for their art to be so read. There is nothing essential to art that makes it fail in these ways, but it repeatedly does so anyway. It fails, most poignantly, despite a powerful promise made by the very moral philosophical tradition that invented ethical naturalism: perhaps to ease the burden of having unlocked the secret of human self-interest, these moral philosophers promise that art can soothe conflicts between aggressive social animals by binding individuals to the group. Art, this tradition claims, is the first among instruments of moral obligation, and the most effective. This tradition will be most familiar to readers of work in eighteenth-century studies as "the culture of politeness"; I will call it the "Party of Humanity," adapting a phrase from David Hume's *Enquiry Concerning the Principles of Morals* (1751) in which he articulates its key elements.

In late twentieth-century Britain and America, the idea that art has a normative power has become commonplace and obviously politicized. The range of competing claims is breathtaking. Art refines, ameliorates, and cures diseases of the body and soul. Art can make us more tolerant and liberal; it can gladden us and challenge us to expand our emotional capacities. Art can provide a sense of identity for politically marginalized groups. Alternatively, art can give rise to politically marginalized groups in the first place by corrupting our common heritage. It can lead people astray. It can make us lose control of our bodies and emotions; it can ruin our symbols and ironize our values. So pervasive is the idea of art's normative power, so deeply entrenched in the collective psyche of the dominant classes, that we are only fitfully aware of its power over us.

While many other cultures, especially the Greek, have held strong views about art's normative power, the idea first became commonplace in England of the eighteenth century. What did the idea of art's normative power mean then? Thanks to a massive effort in scholarship by such English and American writers as John Brewer, Catherine Gallagher, Terry Castle, John Barrell, Jill Campbell, Ann Bermingham, Michael McKeon, Frances Ferguson, Jonathan Lamb, John Mullan, Ann Van Sant and many others, we can begin to specify. "Our modern idea of 'high culture' is an eighteenth-century invention," writes John Brewer, and I might add that high culture as a separate sphere of activity and influence supports self-conscious reflection about art's normative power (1997, xvi).[16] The idea took many forms, but up until speculations on the sublime initiated by Edmund Burke, one narrative was dominant: art fits the individual to the social order by playing on her moral sentiments to render her more virtuous, sympathetic, and altruistic. (My choice of the female pronoun is deliberate here, since this tradition resolutely genders its subject of obligation female.)

This story about the moralizing power of the aesthetic originated with Shaftesbury and Addison, who rebelled against the rationalism of such neoclassical theorists as Boileau and Rapin to center aesthetic theory on human psychology.[17] Art, or anyway the experience of art, has a normative power that, when directed towards society, fosters public virtue. Shaftesbury wrote: "The admiration and love of order, harmony, and proportion, in whatever kind is naturally improving to the temper, advantageous to social affection, and highly assistant to virtue, which is itself no other than the love of order and beauty in society. In the meanest subjects of the world, the appearance of order gains upon the mind and draws the affection towards it" (1964, 1:279). Certain genres like the heroic painting and the epistle were thought more likely to have these beneficent moral effects; others, like the conversation piece and the novel, were initially suspected of playing on the wrong sentiments; still others, like satire, were thought to laugh or lash people into a social mood.

The effects on subsequent aesthetic theory have been massive. Theorists of the sublime acknowledged this narrative by reversing the priority it gave to the collective over the individual: "The essential claim of the sublime is that man can, in feeling and in speech, transcend the human," wrote Thomas

Weiskel ([1976] 1986, 3). Kant and Coleridge inherited the tradition and rejected its practical morality, arguing that our cognitive responses to art are interesting for what they can tell us about human psychology quite apart from
their ethical, moral, or political effects (the Kantian view will be discussed in
greater detail in chapter 2). Formalist new critics of the twentieth century inherited the Kantian tradition through Coleridge, but it has now all but died
out under the pressure of critique from the followers of Raymond Williams,
Pierre Bourdieu, and Jurgen Habermas. Some of these followers have revived
the idea of art's moral efficacy in the service of (small-l) liberal moralism; others have accused the Kantian tradition of smuggling (large-L) Liberal bourgeois universalism into a doctrine of aesthetic disinterest; still others have
concentrated on reconstructing the true (negative) effects of aesthetically induced social pressure on people in the past.[18] More generally, these theorists
have found stories about the moralizing power of art congenial to their
methodological collectivism, their emphasis on the pressure society puts on
the individual.

An example will illustrate the Shaftesburian tradition. Joseph Wright of
Derby's "Three Spectators Viewing a Gladiator by Candlelight" (1765) (fig. 1)
is one of a set of "moral pictures" in which Wright experimented with the conventions of history painting by privatizing them, making contemporary civic
and national virtues the topic of self-consciously aesthetic reflections (another is the "Academy by Lamplight" [1769]). In his excellent book *Painting for
Money,* David Solkin presents the "Three Spectators" as an orthodox example
of the empiricist position that "the central mission of culture itself" is the civilizing process (1993, 169). Solkin quotes Hume, but he might have quoted anybody from Shaftesbury to Kames to Adam Smith: "'A cultivated taste for the
polite arts,' [Hume] had written in the early 1740's, '. . . improves our sensibility for all the tender and agreeable passions'—passions that elsewhere
Hume described as those of 'generosity, humanity, compassion, gratitude,
friendship, fidelity, zeal, disinterestedness, liberality, and all those other qualities which form the character of the good and benevolent'" (1993, 169). A cultivated taste for the polite arts, in other words, is normative from the perspective of the group, becoming an instrument through which culture exerts
its hold on us.

The moralizing power of the aesthetic depends on an empiricist psychological tradition going back to Locke and Descartes in which the boundary between aesthetic perception and ordinary perception is especially thin. To the
empiricists, perception is a two-stage process: a person perceives some object
and brings it under a concept or judgment. To take a very short line, empiri-

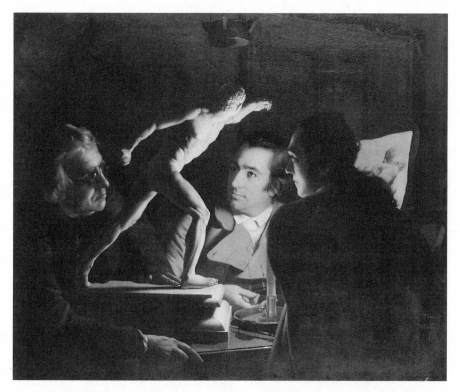

Figure 1. Joseph Wright of Derby, *Three Persons Viewing "The Gladiator" by Candle-light* (1765). Private collection; permission to reproduce conveyed by Tate Britain, London. Photo courtesy of Ashmolean Museum, Oxford.

cists often use theatrical metaphors in their epistemology, describing subject/object relations as relations between a beholder or spectator and a multiplicity of objects. Hume makes this theatricality explicit in his famous "the mind is a kind of theater" metaphor. Descartes in his treatise *Of the Passions of the Soul* (1649), Smith in the *Theory of Moral Sentiments*, and Burke in his treatise on the sublime and the beautiful, all assume it. Descartes saw wonder *(l'admiration)* as the first of the passions and the most simple. Other passions, such as hatred and love, are complex, involving some judgment of the object at hand. These complex emotions depend causally on the prior passion of wonder, which is a distinctly amoral passion, not involving judgments of good and bad. He describes *wonder* as something unwilled, a feeling that just jumps up and catches at you: "When the first encounter with some object surprises us, and we judge it to be new, or very different from what we knew in the past or what we supposed it was going to be, this makes us wonder and be astonished at it. And since this can happen before we know in the least whether this object is suitable to us or not, it seems to me that wonder is the first of all the passions. It has no opposite, because if the object presented has nothing in it that surprises us, we are not in the least moved by it and regard it without passion" (1989, 52). Descartes limited his remarks to facts about our cognitive capacities, so how and why in the eighteenth century were there so many attempts to derive the moral part of human social life (values, in short) from this first, minute aesthetic transaction?

To answer this question, we need to revisit the question of how Enlightenment philosophers, particularly empiricists, conceived of obligation. When Enlightenment philosophy invented the view that moral obligations arise from features of our psychology (ethical naturalism), they set off a debate that continues until this day about which features and how morality arises from them. Hume was the first full-blown ethical naturalist. He rejected reason as a source of moral values, finding instead that our moral values spring from our sentiments:

Take any action allow'd to be vicious: Willful murder, for instance. Examine it in all lights, and see if you can find that matter of fact, or real existence, which you call vice. In which-ever way you take it, you find only certain passions, motives, volitions, and thoughts. There is no other matter of fact in the case. The vice entirely escapes you, as long as you consider the object. You can never find it, till you turn your reflexion into your own breast, and find a sentiment of disapprobation, which arises in you, towards this action. Here is a matter of fact; but 'tis the object of feeling, not of reason. It lies in yourself, not in the object. (T 468–69; quoted in Korsgaard 1996, 50)

Hume thought that our peculiar disposition of sentiments made us especially vulnerable to moral manipulation; being an empiricist, the metaphors he used for how this manipulation works on us were overwhelmingly audiovisual. Christine Korsgaard explains:

Hume compares the theoretical philosopher to an anatomist and the practical philosopher to a painter. The business of the anatomist is to explain what causes us to approve of virtue; the business of a painter is to make virtue appealing. And Hume styles himself a theoretical philosopher: his aim is to reveal the elements of the mind's 'anatomy' which make us approve and disapprove as we do. . . . The practical philosopher is a preacher or a Mandevillian politician. His task is to get people to behave themselves in socially useful way, and he is prepared to use "all helps from poetry and eloquence." (1996, 52; quoting E 5)[19]

The best way to understand Hume's stance is to sketch the Kantian revision of it. For both Hume and Kant, norms arise from facts about the way we are, especially the deep fact that we are social animals. Most words and concepts for virtue are "other directed," encouraging altruism towards others; here again is Hume's list of the "agreeable passions": "generosity, humanity, compassion, gratitude, friendship, fidelity, zeal, disinterestedness, liberality." The Kantian, we recall, looks at how these norms are generated by a process of reflection within the individual consciousness. The Humean sees norms as given by society, and sees them as penetrating us through our senses, getting all the way into us. By society we are encouraged to practice greater kindness, selflessness, and so on, to join what Hume calls the "party of humankind, against vice and disorder" (E 275). But resistance has shadowed the Party of Humanity since it was formed. Korsgaard's reference to the Mandevillian (i.e., cynically manipulative) politician is fascinating. For it reminds us that there have always been politicians who have encouraged people to add their help to the general pool (their spokesman might have been the third Earl of Shaftesbury). But just as surely there have been others, like Mandeville, who have been inclined to expose those appeals on the grounds that seemingly altruistic politicians can use them as a cover for their self-interest.[20]

These philosophical concepts are sketchy and imprecise, but they give some insight into questions people were asking about the psychology of obligation. When we turn to the texts in this study, the picture of an intense personal and artistic struggle emerges. All of its themes are linked, and to separate them, as we must, is to create false oppositions. In the foreground of this struggle are local issues about obligation, and in the background are vast problems about sociability: since none of the writers in this study faces these questions in the form given by moral philosophy (except Hume, whose personal struggle yields surprising results for his theoretical reflections), answers to these questions will come from interrogating their practical moral identities. Their moral identities take concrete rather than abstract forms: these sorts of questions arise because these writers face social conflicts. The rhetoric of the Party of Humanity raises questions about moral and social identities in a form that people have found deeply compelling, if not binding, even to the present. Yet it is too limited, because it seeks to foreclose quickly on the answers, failing to account adequately for people's resistance to it. Testimony from the writers in this study will show that they are drawn to the form of the questions but find, often against their will, that they cannot easily settle them.

What makes the rhetoric of the Party of Humanity most compelling is that it articulates a troubling and exhilarating division between the rationally reflective self and the pressures of a social role; what causes it to fail is that it pretends illegitimately to have healed that division and made it less troubling. For the moralists in this study, the intuition that there is a split between the reflective self who chooses "between the rival claims of rival desires" and the social role that people seem to inhabit more blindly becomes, at many points, ironic, satiric, sentimental, discursive, anxious, and pleasurable—but never easy (MacIntyre 1984, 48). The form of moral reasoning this division suggests is, as Alasdair MacIntyre has argued, the canonical form that moral reflection takes up until today: "It is in this capacity of the self to evade any necessary identification with any particular contingent state of affairs that some moral philosophers . . . have seen the essence of moral agency. To be a moral agent is, on this view, precisely to be able to stand back from any and every situation in which one is involved, from any and every characteristic that one may possess, and to pass judgment on it from a purely universal and abstract point of view that is totally detached from all social particularity (1984, 31–32).

In some of the chapters that follow, the disparity between rationally reflective self and the social role will express itself as comic play, in others as a stubborn posture against the pressures of religious fanaticism, in still others as a conduit to economic and emotional reciprocity. Although the split may be rooted in epistemology and even theology, its branches are social and moral.

How does the Party of Humanity claim to resolve these questions? What shape has that resistance taken? Let us return to Joseph Wright's painting. Solkin has good cause to read the painting as a straightforward statement of the moralizing power of the aesthetic. Wright was a follower of Shaftesbury's, and he represents things largely from the empiricist point of view, seeing values as something art puts into us. The painting's narrative unfolds over time, moving from the Gladiator to the drawing of him on the right. The narrative progression follows the path of enlightenment, at least for the two fashionably, though conventionally dressed gentlemen sitting over the candle (Solkin 1993, 224). For surely their gaze has produced the drawing as an objective correlative of their aestheticized perception. They are artists not by any sublime or unsociable action, but by being imitators: while they have not created the Borghese Gladiator, they have re-created him by the simple and passive act of perceiving. An empiricist aesthetic is committed to the aesthetic position that meaning resides not in the object but in its viewers, who make up the meaning of the work as they encounter it. Yet as many critics of the empiricist aesthetic, including Kant, have noticed, its radical relativism smuggles in an ideal

viewer, or standard or norm of taste, a standard that must go beyond empirical observation. Here the ideal viewer is created by his encounter with ancient
art and by extension with the painting of it. He is unsublimed, demasculin-
ized, attentive, kindly, cooperative, and self-effacing, living the aesthetic
"dream of reconciliation" (Eagleton 1990, 25). There is no Samuel Johnson
"talking for victory" among this group of men.

There is another candidate for ideal viewer, in a more Kantian sense: the
only one who seems shut out of the circle of light is the older man sitting to
the left. Solkin writes, "From his position the elderly gentleman hardly seems
capable of seeing anything at all of the statue that rests on the table between
his arms—yet surely he knows it already, as an image clearly fixed within the
storehouse of his mind. Paradoxically, then, his impaired vision . . . implies a
degree of enlightenment greater than that yet possessed by his two companions, who seem determined to profit from his guidance. If he is giving them a
lesson on the principles of art, he is also leading them along the well-worn
path of custom—teaching them to embrace the values sanctioned by the authority of experience, and to know themselves as part of an established social
order" (1993, 220). He teaches, in short, less about the gladiator than about the
social value of self-consciousness and of reflective distance from the very
object that gives rise to their train of associations. He moves the source of
authority from outside to inside, from experience to reflection.

The recent critical synthesis of the Shaftesburian tradition suggests that it
relies on a moral version of epistemological induction, deriving the general
from the particular.[21] But if we look closely at the painting, it begins to seem
less a propaganda sheet for the Party of Humanity than an allegory of the individual's conflicted relation to the group. There are some uncomfortable aspects of the painting that should raise doubts about the moralizing power of
the aesthetic to override the individual's insistence on his uniqueness and in-
violability. Subtle signs of distinction begin to emerge. On the face of it, we
can't tell which of the two younger men on the right has done the drawing,
but we might guess that it is the one with his back to us. Why? Two reasons:
first if spectators are supposed to "identify-in" to this painting, as the force of
culture argument demands, we would probably identify most closely with the
person who most mimics the stance of the beholder. Tellingly, this figure's face
is the most obscured, a fact that points us in the direction of Catherine Gallagher's influential argument, loosely in the Party of Humanity tradition,
about how fictions invite us to identify with characters: by referring to "nobody," they become an invitation to "imagine in detail" (1994, esp. 167–74).

More importantly, this beholder is also the only figure whose right hand is hidden from us. All the other figures hold some long object, such as a sword, a candle, or a table edge, so we can only imagine that he holds his own long object, perhaps a pencil or pen.

The fact that we credit his right hand with the drawing leads us to reconsider the whole problem of hands. They are instruments of individuation, indeed of the division of labor: scientist, artist, soldier, and—as the hand on the table might suggest—property owner or merchant. Left hands, too, are important. Only two appear, and one is conspicuously missing: the rationalist elder statesman or merchant with the hooded eyes has arranged his two hands in a pose that mimics that of the gladiator. His left hand is raised and placed in a territorial way on the pedestal, imitating the strong thrust of the gladiator's left hand into space. But now that we see the left hand as an instrument of aggression, territoriality, assertion of dominance, we see that the artist on the right has not shown the gladiator's left hand in his drawing; he has either deleted it altogether, or he has chosen to draw the statue from the only perspective from which it would be impossible to see the thrust into space, namely the odd angle just below the statue's right shoulder. It is almost as if the artist figure is resisting the older man's claim on him; in fact, the painting looks less like what Solkin calls an experience of "that sense of fellow-feeling which is the basis for society" (1993, 216) and more like an allegory of the ways that people resist each other's pressure.

As the writers in this study attest, joining the Party of Humanity is hard. And the reasons they give are diverse. Hume, like Joseph Wright, sees maleness as an obstacle, or at least that seems to be the meaning of a passage in which he specifically excludes from the realm of the moral any feelings of rivalry, vanity, avarice, or ambition, and self-love. He does think, however, that if people can render their rivalrous judgments in a sufficiently neutral tone, they "touch the principle of humanity" and get to join its party:

When a man denominates another his enemy, his rival, his antagonist, his adversary, he is understood to speak the language of self-love, and to express sentiments, peculiar to himself, and arising from his particular circumstances and situation. But when he bestows on any man the epithets of vicious or odious or depraved, he then speaks another language, and expresses sentiments, in which, he expects, all his audience are to concur with him. He must here, therefore, depart from his private and particular situation, and must chuse a point of view, common to him and others: He must move some universal principle of the human frame, and touch a string, to which all mankind have an accord and symphony. If he means, therefore, to express, that this man possesses qualities, whose tendency is pernicious to society, he has chosen this common point of view, and has touched the principle of humanity, in which every man, in some degree, concurs. (E 272)

Having synthesized an emerging aesthetic and moral tradition, Hume needed to find a way to make it stick. Hume the anatomist, the scientist of man, offers some free advice to the painter, to the Mandevillian politician, and most especially to the satirist. What the painter, the Mandevillian politician, and the satirist learn, however, is that touching the principle of humanity by finding the right objective tone in which to express universal judgments is just as hard as joining the Party of Humanity. The drive toward disinterestedness is an aesthetic problem that refers to a deep moral problem.[22] Pope and Johnson, especially, intuit the moral problem underlying the aesthetic one. But here naturalism diverges from its eighteenth-century moral philosophical predecessor, for if art helps us see that joining the Party of Humanity is hard, naturalism can help us sort out why. Evolutionary psychologists speculate that humans have evolved to resist general calls for indiscriminate beneficence: such calls are manipulative, putting pressure on us to make altruism mistakes by paying out a little more than we get back (Alexander 1987, 102–3). The more general principle is bound to be controversial.[23] But again, nothing normative follows from it: joining the Party of Humanity is hard because the person, if left free to choose, will draw the limits of collective identity at the edge of her own reflective individuality.

Outline of Chapters

Charles Simic has written "Poetry proves again and again that any single overall theory of anything doesn't work. Poetry is always the cat concert under the window of the room in which the official version of reality is being written" (quoted in Burt 1998, 6). At the center of this book is Alexander Pope, a poet for whom reality is the cat concert under the window, and poetry the official version trying to get itself written. The first three chapters of this book form a complete section, loosely under the rubric of the art of obligation, and can be read on their own. The purpose of these chapters, which focus intensely on *The Dunciad* and on early and late character sketches, is to reinterpret moral authority as a set of social strategies. Pope's poems can best be read as a social record—a record of debt, obligation, and beyond all else, the desire for status. Pope designed his poems to circulate socially in order to record grievances, reward friends, undermine enemies, and generally get his side of the story out there. His poems are acts of gossip, revenge, self-justification, patronage, flirtation, alliance building, and debt repayment.[24] But in seeking to obligate people in and around his social world, Pope repeatedly runs up against the limits of art's normative power.

From the single author focus of the first three chapters, chapters 4, 5, and 6 broaden out to consider local aspects of a problem in Enlightenment thought that I call "spectator morality," or the way tropes of exposure govern social regulation and moral agency. Chapter 5, on Samuel Johnson's *Account of the Life of Mr. Richard Savage,* examines Johnson's quest to find a way to secure obligation through, alternatively, sympathy and the moral command. The *Life of Savage,* which Johnson's friend James Boswell called "one of the most interesting narratives in the English language" (1934, 1:165), raises certain questions about moral life: What is virtue? What is vice? Can they ever be wholly separated? What can we do to be more moral? Is there such a thing as opting out of the system of morality altogether? Is it possible to be an amoralist?[25] This chapter argues that Johnson develops a standard of morality for Savage that is quite different, more naturalistic, and far less demanding than the one he develops for himself and promotes in his moral writing elsewhere. The minimal standard he invents for Savage is that morality comes from having to take other people's interests into account, which means that insofar as we admit the perspective of other minds, we are already moral. All we have to do to admit the perspective of other minds is to take part in an economic system of exchange. Savage, meanwhile, seeks to frustrate even these minimal requirements, leading Johnson to press home the psychological question: What does it take to be *homo economicus?*

The concept of spectator morality is spelled out more fully in chapter 6, on Hume's theory of pride and its relation to eighteenth-century theories of motivation and inwardness. Finally, chapter 7 examines testimony from three writers, Hume, Thomas Warton, and William Cowper, about religious feeling in an increasingly secular age. Across the century, these writers pose versions of a single question: Can intensely private, even painful beliefs be penetrated by social forces?

Part I

Alexander Pope
The Art of Obligation

Moral talk is often rather repugnant. Leveling moral accusations, expressing moral indignation, passing moral judgment, allotting the blame, administering moral reproof, justifying oneself, and above all, moralizing—who can enjoy such talk? And who can like or trust those addicted to it? The most outspoken critics of their neighbors' morals are usually men (or women) who wish to en-sure that nobody should enjoy the good things in life which they themselves have missed and men who confuse the right and the good with their own advancement.

—KURT BAIER, *The Moral Point of View*

Chapter Two

Formalism, Criticism, Obligation

The notion that people could be different, better, or more perfect than they are gripped Alexander Pope at an early age and became his ruling passion. His first poem was a satiric character sketch directed against an older male, a schoolteacher who had punished him. Details of the incident are sketchy, and Maynard Mack (1985) cautions us not to make too much of them.

The shreds of evidence are collected by Pope's first biographer, Joseph Spence: "Mr. Pope . . . was sent to the school at Twyford when he was about eight, stayed there only one year. . . . [He] was but a little while under his master at Twyford. He wrote extremely young, and among other things a satire on that gentleman for some faults he had discovered in him." Spence then quotes Mrs. Rackett, Pope's half-sister: "My brother was whipped and ill-used at Twyford School for his satire on his master, and taken from thence on that account" (1966, 1:10). Other details are supplied in a letter from the fictitious E. P. (Pope himself) to his enemy, the bookseller Edmund Curll: "It was a libel of at least one hundred verses, which a fellow-student having given information of, was found in his pocket, and the young satirist was soundly whipp'd, and kept a prisoner to his room seven days; whereupon his father fetch'd him away, and I have been told, he never went to school more" (*Corr.* 3:360; 27 March 1733).

Despite warning us not to read this episode as proleptic, Mack seems drawn to the details of the pocket and the schoolfellow: "The episode may have added its farthing's worth of caution to what eventually became in Pope a distinctive taste for secrecy, dissimulation, and surreptitious action" (1985, 49). At the tender age of eight, Pope wrote a secret satire that was discovered when he was betrayed by a schoolmate. Already moralistic, he became secretive and shadowy, obsessive and vengeful.

This story bears all the hallmarks of Pope's future career. Almost everything Pope wrote for close to fifty years afterward involved sketching characters. Many of his sketches, especially the early ones, were directed against people he knew, by whom he felt wronged. His later characters are disturbingly abstract and general, almost cubist in their intricacy. Meanwhile, much of his writing life passed in a frenzy of grievance: one poem was a "Bill of Complaint" (TE 4:95); another was a "PROTEST against that insuperable corruption and depravity of manners, which he had been so unhappy as to live to see" (TE 4:327 n). It is significant that the target of his first satire was an older male authority figure: Pope was deeply attuned to the personalities of older men in his vicinity, so much so that he could whip off a satire exposing their inmost flaw in an instant.

Pope's character sketches are so dazzling and difficult that we can make few, if any, general claims about them, other than that they are central to his art (see Boyce 1962). There is, first of all, the sheer number of characters who appear. Sometimes the narrative of a poem—the *Essay on Criticism* is an excellent example—progresses through a train of half-shadowed persons—a briefly glimpsed "you," a stray "critic," wit, judge, or financier. Sometimes a full-blown personification ("Black Melancholy" in "Eloisa to Abelard") intrudes into an otherwise realistic poetic space, figuring human psychology as a gothic battle between personifications. The most famous later portraits—Wharton, Atossa, Sporus—inhabit center stage like singers in opera seria. Reference is always a question: criticism from Pope's time to the present day has raised questions of whether Pope meant to refer to real people, and if so to whom.

But one general claim we *can* make. All of Pope's character sketches develop a moral stance, invoking some standard and explaining why the person meets it—or more usually, fails to meet it. The aesthetic questions raised by the moral stance are complex, especially in the later satires. When they record a real encounter with someone in Pope's circle or in public life, the portraits are meant as practical interventions: they seek to obligate either the person in the sketch or some group of people reading it, fashioning the very social fabric they record. They have the power to demand, make claims, pay debts. Pope was aware early of his enormous poetic gifts and used them to get what he wanted from other people. The social record is deeply embedded in every verse essay and epistle, and in his very sense of what a poet does; his verses are a guide to the small, homogenous, personal literary and political cultures of the first few decades of eighteenth-century London. As a guide, his poems are more partial and fragmentary than the diaries of Pepys, Boswell, Thrale, or Burney; angrier than the comically melancholy letters of Walpole; less narrative than the great progresses of Hogarth. They are, by turns, prophetic and pedantic, brilliant and blazing. They are, most of all, evidence of a mind trying to hook itself onto the world by imagining that the world can be better.

The following three chapters on Pope are devoted to teasing out some of the strands of his moral and aesthetic approach to obligation, especially in his representations of persons. They are by no means an exhaustive or even partial taxonomy. Much excellent scholarship has been devoted to the historical, material, social, and economic significance of Pope's portraits; these chapters will take a consciously aesthetic and psychological tack. The problem of obligation changes significantly from poem to poem, from genre to genre, from Pope's early to his late poems. But in one way or another, it is central to his whole career. Obligation, I will suggest below, even informs much Pope criticism from the early eighteenth century to the present day.

What is *obligation*? A useful, if open-ended, definition is that it is a normative stance taken toward the world of imperfect objects and creatures, a stance from which the moralist proclaims that people, institutions, circumstances an be better, different, more perfect than they are. This definition is provisional; it will change and grow as Pope's own interest in the topic becomes clearer.

Since at least the antididactic turn of the English Romantics, art and obligation have been enemies, both fascinated and repulsed by each other. They inhabit different spheres. A very shorthand way of describing their differences is to say that values can be explained, while art cannot. This claim, on its surface, is highly abstract and formalist: it suggests that art possesses some ineffable quality that transcends the rational. And it seems so obviously false. We are led by the promise that we can spell out everything about a work of art: its creator, origins, referents, provenance, materials, sellers, buyers, collection history, ideological motivation, cultural meaning.[1] Each component of a work of art can be similarly anatomized: where did Milton get the words "Amphisbeona dire"? What did Hogarth intend by the hail of straight lines in "Midnight Modern Conversation"? We can situate the artist in a circle, group, school, academy, movement. We can find intertexts for a work of art in the political, medical, legal discourses of the day. As the philosopher of aesthetics Richard Wollheim has suggested, we can always hope to learn more about an artwork, constantly increasing—to use his metaphor—our cognitive stock (1993, 132–43). Explanation is endlessly inventive, urgently restless; it rushes like a strong river along ever-widening channels.

Yet despite explanation's promises, some division between explanation and meaning has persisted in most aesthetic speculation in the West in the last two centuries. Pope certainly faced this division in his poems, and his poems have long been associated with a certain canonical form the division has taken in Anglo-American criticism. Readings of Pope's poems from his time to ours have been marked by a striking consensus about the grounds of interpretation. The consensus is that criticism proceeds from an act of division, although few critics have agreed about what to divide. High from low culture, text from context, intention from meaning, style from content, sincerity from insincerity, ancient from modern, brave moral purpose from dirty personal attack, "a nasty little view of human nature or a nobly stern one" (to quote William Empson [1964, 213])—each division marks an era in critical history and a phase in the history of the Anglo-American academy. Pressed hard enough, these divisions will resolve themselves into one: the division of author from poem. There are good reasons why this division founds the rest, reasons that range from the history of eighteenth-century authorship and the intimate frustrations Pope faced in his writing, to the invention of criticism as a discipline and the strictures of twentieth-century theory.

But now a question may arise: if critics have disagreed about what to divide, why should we concern ourselves with finding an overarching pattern of division? Each distinction may only meet some critic's provisional need. Does the distinguishing impulse itself merit investigation? One answer is that the divisions that structure Pope criticism can be read back into the poems themselves. Another is that they can be read outward into literary theory. I will return at the end of this section to the antithesis between art and explanation, because it is arguably the one with which Pope struggled most intensely. In the meantime, I will take up the perspective of Pope criticism to outline some of the issues at stake. Modern literary theory has been profoundly dualist: it understands literary language as different in kind from ordinary language, and it understands authorship as an activity different in kind from other activities. The relevance of Pope's poetry to the dualisms of literary theory cannot be overstated. He wrote his poems during the period when these dualisms were becoming codified, and many of the people who later systematized them considered Pope's poetry to be the epitome of the literary itself. Pope thus plays a foundational role in modern literary theory, and that theory has been most dualist when responding to Pope's poetry.

These last sentences seem anachronistic. For when Pope's poetry was considered the epitome of the literary, twentieth-century Pope critics were at the zenith of academic power. Yet Pope studies are now distinctly marginal within American departments of English; his poems are read, taught, and discussed less frequently than those of other canonical English poets. This displacement may be ultimately beneficial: Pope critics are now disinherited from any structures of power that could ever have made interpreting the poems a comfortable activity. Relevant to this history are Richard Rorty's views on cultural change, which come under the heading of "pragmatist functionalism." Rorty argues that some works of literature are great because they inspire people rather than inspiring people because they are great (1996, 8–17). Pragmatist functionalism holds an "evolutionary" view of cultural change: certain formations and ideas become more popular than others because they appeal to more people, and the losers must either adapt to the new formation or become more persuasive. The thought behind pragmatist functionalism is central to the history of arguments about taste: taste can be molded, but it cannot be dictated.

Pragmatist functionalism has not been the dominant paradigm in Pope studies. For two and a half centuries, the field of Pope studies has been marked by a stunning commitment to evaluation and polemic, divided (naturally) into two camps, pro- and anti-Pope. The pro-Pope critics have long argued that Pope has been the victim of historical misunderstanding and would be more popular if we could only clear away the tissue of misreadings imposed by Johnson, Wharton, Wordsworth, Arnold, and others (see Greene 1988; R. Griffin 1995). The anti-Pope camp has been driven by the hope of exposure (more on this below). Both camps assert the normative "ought" against the pragmatist functionalist's "is," an assertion that is bound to fail unless it is backed up by institutional pressure (see McCrea 1990).

Relevant, too, is the fate of a canonical linguistic formalism. The history of Anglo-American criticism in the twentieth century could be written as a long war, sometimes cold sometimes hot, over the control of resources. Even the restricted and specialized subdiscipline—twentieth-century Anglo-American writing about eighteenth-century British culture—has a strong political history in just this sense. Conflicts and confluences of interest within institutions and between them have shaped how that criticism has been written. More importantly, these conflicts and confluences have governed what counts as an acceptable critical contribution to the field. Norms have obviously shifted in the past two decades as the field has witnessed a massive transfer of resources from one group of people to another. This transfer of resources has been largely, though not exclusively generational, and as with any such transfer, there has been the predictable complaining about decline and demise. The thrust of these complaints is that a generational shift has caused a net loss of cultural capital to eighteenth-century studies, but the situation is potentially more complicated and interesting than that. It seems that what has happened is a two-pronged movement: first, the dispersal of cultural capital out of the hands of a few literary critics at a few historically prestigious English departments; and second, a general move away from a top-down model of value toward a more pluralist and democratic one. The democratization of the field does not mean that there are no longer conflicts over such tangible material resources as jobs, access to journals, conferences, publishers, tenure, and so on. It does mean that such resources are no longer automatically concentrated in a few hands and that conflicts are not resolved a priori in favor of an elite group.

Formalism has played a central role in this struggle for control of resources. Why should it have done so? By *formalism,* I refer specifically to a set of theoretical propositions about poetic language. But before offering a provisional account of these propositions, let me rehearse a familiar narrative about the role it has played. The most familiar version of the narrative is this: formalism was a set of doctrines that implicitly served the interests first of white male agrarian southerners, and later of white male (and some female) Ivy League critics who made the close reading of poems a tool in the service of (small-l) liberal values of education, cognitive expansion, and the fashioning of gentlemen and women. On this view, theoretical propositions are locked down to the ambitions of a particular class. For both formalists and the antiformalists, the institutional project (either of protecting the interests of a ruling class or of supplanting them) is linked to formalism's theoretical project (though of course both sides need to specify what they take this theoretical project to be).

A definition can be found in a highly influential ten-year-old manifesto: Laura Brown and Felicity Nussbaum's introduction to *The New Eighteenth Century* (1987). Not having read it in some years, I was struck immediately, when I read it again, by its clear, large voice, its bold vision. But I was struck too by something else: Nussbaum and Brown are willing to extend this familiar narrative in a surprising direction. Formalism, they claim, "represents an identification with the elite culture of the eighteenth century" and its putative values, including "the stereotype" (challenged in the twentieth century) of "a political stability linked to an image of equivalent social and cultural coherence, to a sense of an unchallenged class hierarchy represented and perpetuated in a literary culture where aesthetics, ethics, and politics perfectly mesh" (5). Their startling assertion, in other words, is that the ideologues of a twentieth-century class formation served their own interests by identifying with a two-hundred-year-old elite and its putative values. That is certainly a heavy load for any theory of poetry to bear, especially one whose best-known slogan, as adapted by Cleanth Brooks (1947) from Archibald Macleish's "Ars Poetica," is that "a poem should not mean, but be."[2] Or, as Douglas Mao has recently diagnosed it, New Criticism tended "to treat the text . . . as though it were a self-contained object" (1996, 227).

Both Brooks's and Mao's formulations are too benign, for New Criticism's program was more radical than that. It subscribed to set of doctrines that I will call *methodological realism*—the notion that there are objective or agent-neutral values, and that we can pick those values out by finding methods that track the truth (an anti-methodological realist, by contrast, might believe that there are objective values but that we humans have no way of figuring out what those values are).[3] Formalists are methodological realists with a special set of beliefs about poetic language. They think that there are agent-neutral values and that human beings have the ability to capture such values in certain patterns of words known as poems that, unlike ordinary patterns of words, can transcend their spatio-temporal point of origin. They are, in short, verbal realists who believe that language has its own agency apart from any human intending agent. Verbal realists have always found support in the objective aesthetic of Alexander Pope. An impressively clear example of verbal realism is given by William Wimsatt in a brief analysis of a couplet from *The Rape of the Lock:* "Whether the nymph shall break Diana's law / Or some frail China jar receive a flaw." Wimsatt writes: "In the first line the breakage, the fragile thing (the law), in the second another fragile thing (the jar) and then its breaking (the flaw). The parallel is given a kind of roundness and completeness; the intellectual lines are softened into the concrete harmony of 'law' and 'flaw.' The meaning is locked into a pattern of inevitability" (1954, 162).

Few writers have the power to harmonize fully their practical criticism of poems with their theoretical assertions about them, but Wimsatt was one. He wrote three important theoretical pieces—"The Intentional Fallacy," "The Affective Fallacy," and "The Concrete Universal"—all of which preached the doctrines of anti-intentionalism and the immanent transcendence of poetic language. Pope's small couplet is a perfect example of both. Once the couplet gets going, a greater logic takes over. It becomes impossible to stop this logic, and the meaning is "locked into a pattern of inevitability" (Wimsatt 1954, 162). Pope's couplet looks as though it has been designed by language itself, its outcome inevitable from the beginning.[4] Pope's hand was forced. A greater logic set into motion an unstoppable process, in much the same way a Christian metaphysics holds that history assumes certain patterns by divine intervention. What Nussbaum and Brown help us to see is that the New Critics were not just methodological realists—which might be innocent enough—after all, one could be a methodological realist about, say, laws of mathematics—but that they were methodological *moral* realists, who thought that the values their methods picked out corresponded to moral bestness (perhaps the clearest example can be found in Tillotson 1966).

It might be easy to conclude that formalism is a quaint and superannuated set of beliefs, somewhat like phrenology or theosophy, except that elements of its program keep popping up in the most unexpected places. Moral realism goes deep and is very hard to shake, even when verbal or methodological realism is debunked. For even criticism that claims to be antiessentialist can become a haven for parts of the formalist program, typically moral obligation and a certain tendency to identify aspects of an agenda with values people held in the eighteenth century. If these didn't make much sense when formalists practiced them, we should continue to be skeptical of them now.

Most of the suspicion about a formalist resurgence has been directed, appropriately enough, against a recent trend in eighteenth-century studies sometimes called "new formalism." The new formalism is nothing like the old formalism; in fact, it may be its methodological opposite. A new method is taking root in the challenging work of our best critics. The method is to examine a technique exhaustively, describing how it works in texts carefully selected to contain the richest examples. Only after elaborating a technique do critics help us to see what it can have meant. A technique can usually have meant many different things and have been pressed into a wide range of ideological services in a culture. Among the best examples are Michael McKeon's exhaustive study of the prehistory of novelistic modes (1987) and Catherine Gallagher's story about how techniques of fiction were especially well-adapted to the kinds of cognitive pressures young female novel readers faced as they entered the marriage market (1994, esp. chap. 3). These critics helps us to appreciate a crucial point: a technique can mean many things, but it cannot be inherently meaningful. It can be useful, but that is a different matter. As J. Paul Hunter has shown, a technique is not inherently meaningful even when it comes to us encrusted by layers of value and tradition—instead it is a tool of meaning. Hunter's example is the couplet. Using the analogy of a list, he rejects any procedure that would conflate form with meaning: "One simply cannot tell from a list per se just what kind of comparison is going on; lists mean one kind of thing in a recipe and quite another in a political pamphlet" (1996, 261). Hunter forcefully rejects the kind of methodological realism I have been describing: "What genre and verse form really are, are merely frozen moments in the historical process of ideational and aural organization, rather than some kind of essential category described by Plato but ultimately set in the mind of God" (1996, 259).

Thus new formalism is both intentionalist and methodologically relativist: a form or genre may be associated with certain values, but it cannot mean something apart from what its author made it mean. The new formalism recognizes that even apparently objective techniques are tools in a larger scheme whereby different groups seek to control resources. This is a little bit like what Wittgenstein called "moves in a language game"—except, on the view I am developing, language is one of those tools, and a better name for such relativism would be "moves in the game of moral authority." A key move in the game of moral authority is concealing the grounds of interest on which claims of disinterest rest.

Pope has been associated with this game of moral authority since the eighteenth century—indeed, he was one of its inventors. In Pope's world, and the world of his critics, the game of moral authority has two principal players: the moral author and the cynic or exposer. These two characters are locked together in a dance of blindness and insight in Pope's career, and they have danced together in Pope criticism since the eighteenth century, the former setting out idealizing claims and the latter constantly unmasking those pretensions. In literary history, Pope has been one of the authors most closely associated with the normative power of art, for both good and bad. No other author except Samuel Johnson has so often been called "moral," and with that weighty moniker a long train of associations comes into play. Authority, classicism, canonicity, imitation, a late-Renaissance sensibility, anticommercialism, retirement, *hortus conclusus, concordia discors*: the list may sound old-fashioned, but it has resonated with generations of critics.

A different set of values are invoked in Byron's claim that Pope "is the moral poet of all civilization" (1898–1904, 5:560), a set of values that Pope himself might have endorsed. Now Pope is the avenging satirist, boldly expressing our collective outrage at deceitful friends and hypocrites. In fact, Byron invoked Pope's moral power mostly to avenge himself against the Lake Poets, whom he viewed as self-promoting overreachers (Chandler 1984, 216–18). But this particular episode of male rivalry seems not to dampen the larger point. Pope is moral, he himself tells us at length, because vice disgusts him and virtue delights him: "Yet think not friendship only prompts my Lays; / I follow Virtue, where she shines, I praise" (TE 4:318). And if the charge of a certain rigidity is laid at his door, Pope has his answer: "Yes I am proud," he says, "I must be proud to see / Men not afraid of God afraid of me" (TE 4:324).

In this vein James Winn writes, "Much of Pope's poetry is concerned with moral questions. The ideal qualities praised in that poetry—moderation, generosity, tolerance, humility—appealed to Pope not only because of his grounding in classical and Christian ethics, but because they were qualities he saw and admired in some of his friends" (1977, 86). Winn, Mack, and Aubrey Williams are firmly on the side of the moral author. I once traveled to Twickenham to visit St. Mary's Church, where Pope and his parents are buried. Twickenham is a nondescript suburb of London, more working-class and hard-edged than its splendid neighbor Richmond. Signs of Pope are nowhere to be found in Twickenham. Richmond Council runs a walking tour along the banks of the Thames, where visitors can stop to sample the eel pie. Pope's villa is now a convent school, its grotto a tunnel beneath the highway that divides the building from its garden. Down the road is the Pope's Head pub, but the area's main tourist attraction, two kilometers away at Strawberry Hill, is Horace Walpole's lavishly preserved gothic revival castle. Elsewhere in England, literary tourism is booming: Dickens, Wordsworth, Austen, Shakespeare, Beatrix Potter are commemorated. St. Mary's Church is old, small, and cold. Its parishioners have gray hair and pinched cheeks. Pope is buried in the floor beneath the memorial he erected to his parents. He stands vertically, the spot marked by a modest P carved in the stone. Below the P is a large plaque of shining gold: "Here lie the mortal remains of Alexander Pope. Qui nil molitur inepte. This tablet was placed by three members of the Faculty of English of Yale University 1962".

Other people have been disinclined to divert their attentions to a lofty view of the ground of classical and Christian ethics over which Pope strides: John Dennis, Edmund Curll, Lady Mary Wortley Montagu, and Colley Cibber in the eighteenth century; the Reverend Whitwell Elwin and Leslie Stephen in the nineteenth century; Laura Brown, Felicity Nussbaum, and many other feminist literary critics in the twentieth. Suspicion and dislike of Pope have a long critical provenance, stretching back to the Dunces, and to the other eighteenth-century figures I have mentioned. The grounds of attack have shifted, but the strategy remains the same: to expose the illegitimacy of Pope's cultural position. Alexander Pope was a hypocrite. Often nasty and underhanded in his business dealings, he preached virtue without practicing it. His calls to virtue often went hand in hand with aristocratic exclusion and cliquishness. He could be brutally misogynist even while claiming to sympathize with the plight of women victimized by his culture's rigid sex/gender system. He acquired cultural capital by manipulating a system that favored the classical learning of aristocratic males while excluding women and the lower classes. He took credit for other people's work, even plagiarizing some of it. He was apolitical. He wrote protocapitalist poetry at a time of Britain's expanding empire. He celebrated Britain's gaining the asiento, the right to trade slaves in the North Atlantic. He challenged some of the foibles and practices of particular monarchs but never the status quo of monarchy or feudalism. When young and powerless himself, he kicked people who were down; when older and more financially independent, he began to kick those in power, not out of firmly held convictions but because the group of friends he sought to please were in the political opposition. He castigated his contemporaries for currying favor with the great while concealing his own sycophantic tendencies. He widely broadcast his generosity while cheating those to whom he owed money. In short, in his "insatiable vanity," territoriality, social climbing, moral hypocrisy, self-absorption, and desire for status, he was deeply and utterly flawed (Stephen [1880] 1888, 210).

I take this exaggerated tone in order to raise some skeptical questions. The first is why it should matter that the man who wrote such intricate, funny poems was such a frustrating human being. Why should it matter to our reading of those poems who the person was who wrote them? My question arises from formalist skepticism, yet it is closely, though not obviously, related to a second question, this one arising from antiformalist skepticism: Why should we feel obligated by knowing that Pope acquired cultural capital through sneaky and perverse means? What does having this knowledge motivate us to do? By asking this question, we seem to be resisting a certain moral pressure. For in the accounts I have sketched above, moral authority—the authority to obligate us—has shifted from Pope (or the set of values he was supposed to exemplify if not embody) to the very critics who call Pope immoral. It has shifted from the moral author to the debunking exposer. But if the life of Pope contains any lesson, any one moral, it is this: when you claim moral authority, some people will find your claim compelling and meaningful, and others will resist, meeting it with skepticism and even downright hostility. This is the pathos of moralizing, and it provoked in Sir Leslie Stephen a decidedly harsh response: "It is difficult to say what will be the final element in our feeling about the man. Let us hope that it may be the pity which, after a certain lapse of years, we may be excused for conceding to the victim of moral as well as physical disease" (1888, 210).

If critics risk facing skepticism and hostility when they seek to obligate us, what would compel them to bother? The question seems particularly stark when what is at stake is Alexander Pope's cultural authority. For his cultural authority seems, at this late date, minuscule. As a comparison, let us examine an instructively different case of cultural authority, recently imperiled. According to a growing chorus of revisionists, Sigmund Freud was a plagiarist, a liar, and a fraud who strove mightily to construct and preserve a reputation as a fearless crusader for scientific truth. Frederick Crews (1997), Frank Sulloway (1979), Adolf Grunbaum (1984), and others have waged an energetic and successful campaign to debunk the legitimacy of Freud's claims to cultural authority. Why? Not, presumably, to anger Freud himself or to lessen the value of his estate for his heirs. Surely the revisionists' motive is to lessen the force of Freud's authority in the present insofar as he represents a "charismatic legitimater" for doctors who charge hundreds of dollars an hour selling cures that may not work (Jay 1993, 168).

But what comparable purpose is served by showing how Pope often illegitimately gathered and husbanded cultural authority? One purpose may be to expand the number of voices available to us when we listen to eighteenth-century British culture; another may be to teach us a lesson about cultural change while at the same time pushing an agenda for change—an agenda such as challenging Pope's lingering canonicity, thus creating room on syllabi for new voices. Or, finally, the purpose may be to reflect generally on the process by which cultural capital is produced and acquired. Even though the real target is our own practices and values rather than Pope's, this target is (mysteriously) hit by giving us a more realistic assessment of Pope's practices and values. The broadest point, again, is to obligate us: revisionists may give us a set of reasons strong enough to make us reflect on our current practices and change them.

Idealism and suspicion are both moralistic; they are modes of obligation. They are therefore vulnerable in similar ways. When we turn to Pope's life and writing, we find that rather than "steering betwixt the extremes of doctrines seemingly opposite," as he puts it in the preface to the *Essay on Man*, he is driven to both extremes at once, often painfully.[5] As Pope grows older, the urge to project an idealized self-image grows stronger and the shadow marring that ideal grows thicker. As a young man, his fascination with other people expresses itself mostly as hero worship; later on, when he becomes the disillusioned wasp of Twickenham, it mutates into a burning desire to expose. Pope's idealizing mode and his exposing one repeatedly pick out the single person. He kept the portraits of older males around him all the time: Dryden and Shakespeare, and Milton "to keep him humble" (*Corr.* 1:120; 25 June 1711). Keeping him humble was not their only effect. He once complained, chillingly, that "many people would like my ode on music better if Dryden had never written on the subject. It was at the request of Mr. Steele that I wrote mine, and not with any thought of rivaling that great man, whose memory I do and have always reverenced" (Spence 1966, 1:28). He began early on to read the European humanists, Erasmus and Montaigne, both of whom became lifelong heroes, according to Maynard Mack (1985, 81–82). Later, when he took up painting, he mostly drew portraits of his friends: "I find my hand most successful in drawing of friends and those I most esteem; in so much that my masterpiece has been one of Dr. Swift and one Mr. Betterton" (*Corr.* 1:189; 31 August 1713). In 1735 Frederick Prince of Wales paid Pope a deliciously complicated tribute and gave him a fitting gift: "Frederick commissioned the Amigoni portrait . . . showing him deeply engrossed in a copy of Pope's Homer translation; he later presented Pope with some urns for his garden and four marble busts of Spenser, Shakespeare, Milton, and Dryden for his library," writes Christine Gerrard (1994, 83).

Pope's writing is motivated by certain moral passions—passions for revenge, justice, honor, status. These feelings go far beyond his private phenomenology, carrying with them a sense of obligation. They confer objectivity, normative authority. Can the twin drives to idealize and to expose be traced to a single source? Most biographers of Pope describe the development of a person who, as a child and adolescent, suffered intense social and physical deficits. Born with unusual mental powers, he soon found out how to use them to control the people around him. He became visibly socially anxious at a very young age, pursuing fame with what he once described as a "frenzy." Because he was handicapped socially and physically, he risked having his status permanently lowered. This risk Pope was never prepared to accept.

The story continues: Pope's anxiety translated directly into his peculiarly controlling aesthetic. Readers have long connected Pope's bodily deformity to the elegance of his writing and to his aesthetic obsession with managing his readers' experience. The commonest insult for Pope's enemies to hurl at him was that his poetry was so precise, coupletted, and refined precisely because his body was so grotesque and deformed. Pope was ambitious enough to translate all of Homer's *Iliad* when he was in his mid-twenties—so the line went—to compensate for his physical shortcomings, for being as he once said about himself "that little Alexander women laugh at."[6] Helen Deutsch revives this tradition in an elegant and simple phrase, "a couplet of form and deformity" (1996, 4–5). One of Pope's earliest biographers makes much the same point, although in 1769 the explanatory trappings are different: "Perhaps too the uncomeliness of his person might not be without some effect. It has been well remarked by Lord Bacon, that whoever hath anything fixed in his person, that doth induce contempt, hath also a perpetual spur within himself, to rescue and deliver himself from scorn. This consideration, therefore, might render our poet more assiduous to cultivate his mental faculties, that he might atone for the defects of an ungraceful figure, by the accomplishments of an elegant and polished mind" (Ruffhead 1769, 29).

Why does Pope so obsessively target the figure of the person? Even though his social anxiety seems intensely personal, the answer to this question may paradoxically come from the broader culture. Gordon S. Wood offers a penetrating analysis of the penchant of early eighteenth century Englishmen to think in terms of conspiracies. Social paranoia, he claims, is the dark side of the recently enlightened mind:

The conceptual worlds of many individuals were being broadened and transformed. The more people became strangers to one another and the less they knew of one another's hearts, the more suspicious and mistrustful they became, ready as never before in Western history to see deceit and deception at work. Relationships between superiors and subordinates, rulers and ruled, formerly taken for granted, now became disturbingly problematical, and people became uncertain of who was who and who was doing what. Growing proportions of the population were more politically conscious and more concerned with what seemed to be the abuse of power and privileges of ruling elites. Impassioned efforts were made everywhere to arouse 'the vigilance of the public eye' against those few men 'who cannot exist without a scheme in their heads,' those 'turbulent, scheming, maliciously cunning, plotters of mischief.' (1982, 410–11)

Wood's insight opens up the most interesting question of all: How does a particular culture shape an individual's psychology? Pope's desire to expose the plotter and the hypocrite was certainly enforced by this cultural tendency. His most intensely personal characteristics are relative to the social condition into which he was born and against which he struggled for so long.[7]

The game of moral authority is becoming clearer. The moral author and the cynic are still the two principal players; their names may change, but they always move in tandem. The object of the game is to acquire status. The players move around a small social circle fraught with conflicts of interest—a world of deceitful social climbers, dangerous friends, cunning enemies. The smiler with the knife is everywhere. Of course there was a Golden Age called antiquity, when writers were magically able to turn social conflict into cultural capital, eventually retiring, like Horace, from the world of plots and flattery. But now dangers lurk in Grub Street and Whitehall: in both worlds—one east, one west; one poor, one rich—ambition is naked, cutthroat, desperate. For the virtuous, moral, learned writer, recognition is fleeting and poverty is always near at hand. Yet this writer has some trump cards to play, such as the Corruption of Culture card, against which all other players are suddenly powerless. All of the conflicting elements of Pope's career and writing can be brought under the unifying perspective of the social poet navigating his world. Satire,

epistle, character sketch, couplet, painting, garden, grotto: these are all instruments to reduce the world to a manageable size, to reorient its ever-ex-
panding scope to the human scale.

What, then, of the post-Romantic intuition that art transcends the merely
instrumental? Wordsworth, of course, hated Pope's art, associating it with
"false thoughts, languid and vague expression, unmeaning antithesis, and la-
borious attempts at discrimination" (1974, 150). And Keats, remarking of the
Augustan poets in general but thinking particularly of Pope, wrote slightingly,
"With a puling infant's force/They sway'd about upon a rocking horse,/ And
thought it Pegasus" ("Sleep and Poetry" ll. 185–87; [1978] 1982, 42). After all
the other dualisms are reduced to a unified field, does this final one—art versus obligation—survive? To answer that question, here and in the next two
chapters I will look closely at Pope's moral stance, particularly at the way it is
structured by aesthetic choices.

The Duke of Wharton

Many of the themes of Pope's career, such as the way moral feelings arise from
social life, the ways humans find to obligate each other and to resist each
other's pressure, the tactics and reach of the moral emotions, can be compressed into a single line from Horace: *"Et mihi res, non me rebus, submittere
conor"* (I attempt to condition the things of the world to me, not myself to
those things). The line had acquired a rich history by the time it found its way
to Pope, for whom these questions were, as time went on, increasingly a source
of artistic and personal torment. Expressing his longstanding desire to master the social world by transcending it, Pope aggressively mistranslated the
line, turning it into (among other things) a meditation on St. Paul's words to
the Corinthians: "Even as I please all men in all things, not seeking mine own
profit, but the profit of many, that they may be saved" (1 Cor. 10:33).[8] Here is
the full passage, from Pope's first *Horatian Imitation,* a set of topical satires he
wrote in the 1730s:

> But ask not, to what Doctors I apply?
> Sworn to no Master, of no Sect am I:
> As drives the storm, at any door I knock,
> And house with Montagne now, or now with Lock,
> Sometimes a Patriot, active in debate,
> Mix with the World, and battle for the State,
> Free as young Lyttleton, her cause pursue,
> Still true to Virtue, and as warm as true:

> Sometimes with Aristippus or St. Paul,
> Indulge my Candor, and grow all to all;
> Back to my native Moderation slide,
> And win my way by yielding to the tide. (TE 4:281)

Pope's late satires are typically filled with proper names, some of which refer to his enemies, friends, and associates, others of which refer to more distant figures. His poems describe a densely populated social world. Horace had mentioned only Aristippus, a Cyrenean hedonist who lived from 435 to 366 B.C.E. Aristippus thought that people should be adaptable and should learn how to turn people and circumstances to advantage (*Encyclopedia Britannica* 1973, 2:387). His motto, "I possess, I am not possessed," allowed Horace to dream of finding his pleasures close at hand, of "conditioning the world" to him. Yet Pope expands this social register. Many people—men mostly, but sometimes women—become the markers by which Pope navigates his world: St. Paul, who seeks satisfying relations with others in the service not of his own interests but of all people; Michel de Montaigne and John Locke; George Lyttleton, secretary to the Prince of Wales and prominent member of the Patriot Opposition to Prime Minister Robert Walpole. With these men Pope dances a social minuet, entering into their spirit in order to pursue his ends more effectively.[9] He conditions himself to the world in order to condition the world to himself; he wins his way by yielding to the tide.

In reversing Horace's line Pope preserves its spirit, allowing the bold assertion of social mastery to stand but disguising it as social carelessness. Perhaps Pope wants to mask the intensity and direction of his desires, to put his contemporaries at ease about his motives, and to make winning his way seem a relaxing and easy prospect. He hardly disavows winning as such; rather he goes limp with respect to such familiar facts of human social life as power, status, ambition, and dominance. He is passive too with respect to the needs, desires, and beliefs of other people. Later in the century (later too in the life of the culture that Pope knew), the painter Joshua Reynolds could write, "I go with the great stream of life," as though the great stream of life had made him passive with respect to his own desires (quoted in Wendorf 1996, 7).

Pope develops a distinctive way of reading other people that is based on technique: Sporus, most famously, is "himself one vile Antithesis." Yet Pope's way of reading moves beyond rhetorical terms, though they go deep in it, to constitute an ethos that I will call Pope's formalism. Like the twentieth-century formalism that responded so profoundly to his poems, Pope's formalism is realist, but it is realist in a peculiarly psychological way. Pope's portrait of Philip, Duke of Wharton from the Epistle to Cobham (1732) illustrates his formalism. Cobham is the first of the "epistles to several persons," a series of four written, as Pope thought, to complete his magnum opus. In a general way it concerns the characters of men, particularly, in the Montaignian tradition, the inconstancy of their actions. As Frank Stack so movingly describes this tradition, it responds to "deep inconsistencies in desires and action, and the perennial human inability for people to know, or be happy with, who they are, or what they are doing" (1985, 220). Pope's portrait of Wharton is, puzzlingly, one of his sources for the self-portrait I quoted above.

Pope's formalism is a social attitude that seeks to provide a solution to the practical problems posed by "deep inconsistencies in desires and action." This may seem counterintuitive, for surely the main doctrine of any formalism, whether critical dogma or aesthetic mode, is its separation from the social sphere, a separation that Bourdieu and many others have taught us to regard with suspicion. Twentieth-century formalists have embraced the charge. As William Wimsatt so perfectly put it, "Poetic symbols—largely through their iconicity at various levels—call attention to themselves as symbols and in themselves invite evaluation. What may seem stranger is that the verbal symbol in calling attention to itself must also call attention to the difference between itself and the reality which it resembles and symbolizes. . . . In most discourse we look right through this disparity. . . . But poetry by thickening the medium increases the disparity between itself and its referents. Iconicity enforces disparity" (1954, 217). Wimsatt is talking about the texts of poems. But iconicity in a different, though related sense is—so I will argue—one response to a set of psychological problems posed by obligation.

Philosophy's Judgment of Poetry

Let me offer an analogy to a theoretical topic, the relationship between theory and poems. Of all the stories to tell about the relationship between philosophy and literature, by far the most familiar is a story involving mutual hostility and suspicion. A philosopher approaches a poet and demands that she tell what she knows; the poet responds that poetic knowing and philosophical knowledge are two different matters. The philosopher cries "mystification" and subjects the poet's intention, meaning, and language to logical scrutiny, looking first for repeating structures, then seeking to classify, and finally taking his own classifications metaphysically. Symbol, allegory, concrete universal: all these have become pure concepts abstracted from heteroglossic texts.

After abstraction comes explanation. But here the poet is able to put the philosopher back on the defensive: the philosopher is unconscious of the way his explanations lapse into theatricality, often betraying more than they say. As many defenders of poetry have intuited, philosophical "explanations" of poetry are expressive of a wish that poetry would just disappear. If philosophy begins in wonder, it ends in murder.

A spate of works have recently appeared that offer just this view of relations between poetry and philosophy, from a perspective hostile to the latter. Among them are Arthur Danto's 1986 book, *The Philosophical Disenfranchisement of Art*; Mark Edmundson's 1995 *Literature Against Philosophy: Plato to Derrida*; and a brief piece by Richard Rorty in *Raritan* (1996). Rorty argues that the rise of cultural studies in English departments is analogous to the earlier rise of analytic philosophy in philosophy departments: in both movements, writes Rorty, an attitude of hard-eyed "knowingness"—the refusal to be impressed—is driving pleasure, awe, inspiration, and genius out of the literary academy. Edmundson's book takes the largest target, not just philosophy narrowly, but criticism broadly. New criticism, deconstruction, and new historicism all turn out to be versions of the same impulse to govern literary interpretation by an appeal to method, which, in Edmundson's view, is the only necessary move in the disenfranchisement of poetry.

But what then, one wants to ask, is the alternative? It is typical of diagnoses like Edmundson's not to offer an alternative to criticism, or to offer one like this: "The only contexts [of reading] that matter . . . are the present and the future. And the only way to know these contexts . . . is to know yourself" (1995, 17). In fact, we can all think of better alternatives, practical alternatives that would center on the historical explanation of literary effects or the patient reconstruction of a poet's intentions. Without disenfranchising poetry, I might, for instance, wonder what Wordsworth meant by *human* in the line "I had no human fears"; my target of explanation would then be Wordsworth's intentions.[10] But—and this is my second objection—it is almost impossible for me to stop there. In order to understand what Wordsworth meant by *human,* one wants to know what literate English people generally meant by *human* circa 1800. But as soon as one wants to know that, one transfers one's attention from the poem to its context, perhaps asserting some general claim about the relationship between Wordsworth's poetic intentions and the beliefs widely held in his culture. Suddenly one finds oneself in the territory marked out by Socrates, who worried that the poem and its referents compete with each other in an irrational way. Yet Socrates—like many historicist critics—also thought that it worse if the poem's referents fail to compete with the poem for our attention because then we become absurdly dependent on the poet for knowledge about what the poet depicts—soldiering, sailing, and governing among other examples.[11] Edmundson's worry, though, is not that we will find ourselves more interested in the poem than in the poem's referent, but that the direction of explanation chosen will be from referent to poem. If we make that basic historicist move, on Edmundson's view, we have disenfranchised poetry.

Yet despite these objections, Edmundson's diagnosis of philosophy's impulse to take poetry metaphysically, to abstract pure concepts while simultaneously staging a demonstration of its feeling about literature, seems to me right on the mark. We will call this structure philosophy's judgment of poetry. We immediately notice that what philosophy claims poetry does to its referents—strips them of knowledge content and creates an emotional field around them—philosophy does also to poetry by constructing such judgments. Indeed, metaphysical judgments of any kind have traditionally been ripe for some enterprising logician to step in at the end of the line to show how someone else's philosophy is really only poetry. Arthur Danto neatly makes this point:

Not so terribly many years ago, the latest thought on the relationship between philosophy and art would have been found . . . in the writings of Rudolph Carnap, a leader of the Logical Positivist school of philosophical analysis. Carnap wrote: "Many linguistic utterances are analogous to laughing, in that they have only an expressive function, no representative function. Examples are cries like 'Oh, Oh!' or, on a higher level, lyrical verse. Metaphysical propositions are . . . like laughing, lyrics, and music, expressive." . . . There is a delicious justice in Carnap's suggestion that Plato himself, that crafty designer of a prison house for art, in fact is one of its inmates, since the theory of Forms belongs in the same family of utterances as the lyrics of Archilocus: it but expresses the feelings of the philosopher (= hatred of poetry): he might as well have written verse. "Metaphysics is but a substitute, albeit an inadequate one, for art," Carnap wrote . . . his thought being that metaphysicians use the forms of meaningful discourse (science) to create the illusion of meaning when it is in fact only the philosopher's feelings that are being expressed *en travestie*, and for which the structures of literature would be more suitable and less misleading. (1986, 163–66)

The comparison I am suggesting, that philosophy is to poetry as poetry is to its objects, seems even more apt when we recall that since Plato's *Ion* philosophers have accused poets of fostering irrational dependence on their art. And yet the charge goes both ways. We can all think of examples of combing through a dense piece of theory to discover its payoff—that literary language always means more than it says; or that, to quote an influential and persuasive definition, "[the literary is] any linguistically embodied representation that tends to attract a certain kind of interest to itself; that does so by particularizing the emotive and other values of its referents; and that does *that* by inserting its referents into new 'scenarios' inseparable from the particular linguistic and narrative structures of the representation itself"—only to be left in the position of wondering what critics can do next (Knapp 1993, 2–3). Are we to repeat the formula while pointing out that this or that poem has it too? An intriguing notion not explored here is whether some of the causes of discipleship in literary studies are internal to the theoretical impulse itself.

Philosophy's judgment of poetry, as I have described it, bears a strong resemblance to judgments of taste as characterized by Immanuel Kant in the "Analytic of the Beautiful" section of the *Critique of Judgment* (1952); it is practically equivalent to high formalist aesthetic judgments. I will briefly review here what Kant says about judgments of taste—the most complete explanation of this complex topic can be found in *Kant and the Claims of Taste* by Paul Guyer (1979). Judgments of taste have the apparently paradoxical quality of being "subjectively universal"—that is, I reflect on the pleasure I take in an aesthetic object and at the same time judge that my pleasure is universally valid. Kant famously asked how a feeling of aesthetic pleasure in an object can entail a judgment that such a feeling ought to be universally valid. He sharpened the question by rejecting cognitive *interest* as having any part in aesthetic judgments, arguing instead that an aesthetic judgment consists of a feeling of pleasure in the free play of the faculties and a simultaneous judgment that our pleasure is universally communicable, and hence *ought to* possess universal validity. This is a massive departure from two traditions, the empiricist and the realist, that place cognition—and hence knowledge—at the center of aesthetic judgments. In the empiricist account, as I mentioned, one is struck by a feeling of pleasure in an object and then one brings it under some concept and begins to fill out explanations about it. In the realist account, one's judgment is universally communicable because it is identical to ordinary categorical judgments of reason and of the understanding (Guyer 1979, 2–10). The two peculiarities, or counterintuitive aspects, of Kant's account are, first, that there is nothing inherent in the object that causes the "free and harmonious play of the faculties"; and second, that it is because of the subjective feeling of pleasure that I take in the "free and harmonious play of the faculties" that I can lay down my judgment as a rule universally binding on others.

In some of Pope's literary portraiture, and more generally in the representation of persons, Pope mobilizes what looks to a nonphilosopher essentially like Kantian aesthetic judgments in the service of moral and political ends. To say that Pope mobilizes aesthetic judgments in the service of moral and political ends is immediately to avoid saying something crude about how Pope anticipated Kant or about how Kant systematized eighteenth-century aesthetic theory, although historical reconstruction of influence is warranted. For the hallmark of the Kantian aesthetic is its essential separateness from the sphere of morals and politics, or so Kant claimed. There has been a great outpouring of recent work in recent years seeking to demystify that claim (see, for example, Lloyd 1989, 1990). But advocates of Kantian aesthetics should agree on one point if nothing else, namely, that aesthetic judgments, because they lack any specific representational content, differ in kind from moral and political ones (Ginsborg 1991). Pope's aesthetic is grounded, by contrast, in the world. For him aesthetic judgments are not only reducible to moral and political judgments, but also they are an oddly inescapable feature of our moral lives. They arise when we, or in any case Pope, encounter others who impose their sublime or terrifying natures on us. Yet crucial to Pope's response is the Kantian denial of cognitive interest as any part of the production of impartial aesthetic judgments. He develops an attitude of disinterestedness primarily by denying that the content of an object has any bearing on the relationship we form to it. The object itself is thus, in the strictest sense, irrelevant to our apperception of it.

Transcendence, however, is a social attitude and not a metaphysical fact. Let me offer a brief, speculative, and strictly ahistorical account of why we might allow a formalist strain to inflect our relations with one another. One thing we gain is an inability to comprehend. Yet this is strange: under what conditions would one want to enter into a relation with an object, to the extent of having an extensive poetic concern with it, and yet also remain uncomprehending of it? The very short answer is satire, in which one would want to maintain a poetic ethos of disinterestedness toward a person while at the same time producing harsh invective about him. Satire, a literary mode with a distinctive history and an elaborate set of conventions, may in fact pick out something distinctive about human moral psychology. The elements of satire may constitute a deeply ingrained habit of thought. The reasons have to do with the way people respond to conflicts of interest. Conflicts of interest arise when resources are disputed; in those disputes, we can sometimes judge other people, keeping meticulous accounts of their moral failings, reducing their motivations to caricature, turning them into flat characters and thereby explaining them away—while scrupulously maintaining and defending our own objectivity to ourselves and others.[12] This is the corner of our moral lives where fiction making and moral aggression converge: we have a tendency to make other people less real to us than we are to ourselves. It is possible to reject the essentialism and universalism of this account and still to accept that judgments with this form are a tool for the expression of moral aggression.

If even this formulation is unacceptably ahistorical, we can narrow the scope of the claim to Pope, who strips his character portraits of interest in the empirical or representational sense to signal his lack of interest in the ethical sense. A paradigmatic example is Pope's extended meditation on Wharton, "the scorn and wonder of our days":

> Search then the Ruling Passion: There alone,
> The Wild are constant, and the Cunning known;
> The fool consistent, and the False sincere;
> Priests, Princes, Women, no dissemblers here.
> This clue once found, unravels all the rest,
> The prospect clears, and Wharton stands confest.
> Wharton, the scorn and wonder of our days,
> Whose ruling Passion was the Lust of Praise;
> Born with whate'er could win it from the Wise,
> Women and Fools must like him or he dies;
> Tho' wond'ring Senates hung on all he spoke,
> The Club must hail him master of the joke.
> Shall parts so various aim at nothing new?
> He'll shine a Tully and a Wilmot too.
> Then turns repentant, and his God adores
> With the same spirit that he drinks and whores;
> Enough if all around him but admire,
> And now the Punk applaud, and now the Fryer.
> Thus with each gift of nature and of art,
> And wanting nothing but an honest heart;
> Grown all to all, from no one vice exempt,
> And most contemptible, to shun contempt;
> His Passion still, to covet gen'ral praise,
> His Life, to forfeit it a thousand ways;
> A constant Bounty which no friend has made;
> An angel Tongue, which no man can persuade;
> A Fool, with more of Wit than half mankind,
> Too quick for Thought, for Action too refin'd;
> A Tyrant to the wife his heart approves;
> A Rebel to the very king he loves;
> He dies, sad out-cast of each church and state,
> And (harder still) flagitious, yet not great!
> Ask you why Wharton broke thro' every rule?
> 'Twas all for fear the Knaves should call him Fool. (TE 3.2:28–31)

This portrait is significant in Pope's work in all sorts of ways. Five years later, Pope adapts it into his first sustained self-portrait: "I condition myself to the world." But this, too, would seem to be Wharton's motto, and therein lies a paradox. Why does Pope rewrite himself as a version of Wharton, both, in the most conscious echo of St. Paul, "grown all to all"? These two portraits and some others constitute an extended meditation on aspects of sociability—how we submit to the pressures of others, how we get what we want from them, how we oblige them and are obliged in turn, how we manipulate and are manipulated.

Wharton's father was an influential Whig politician, an early and tireless supporter of William of Orange. He held various posts in government, including the Lord-Lieutenancy of Ireland under Queen Anne, but died shortly after the Whigs came to power. His son, renowned for remarkable speaking ability, came very early to the attention of the Lords, and after he had visited France and sworn a loyalty oath to the young pretender, he returned repentant to England. The Whig government granted him a dukedom at the age of nineteen to ensure his future loyalty to them. It didn't work. Wharton soon began to attack the government in speeches and print. An anonymous biography written after he died poor, drunk, and destitute in Spain at the age of 32 had this to say:

The Duke of Wharton did not confine this spirit of opposition to the House of Lords; but exerted it both in city and country, promoting it in all kind of elections, persons who were suppos'd to be no favourites of the court; he push'd himself into the metropolis, invested himself with the rights and privileges of a citizen, and was received a member of the wax chandlers company, in virtue of which he appeared at all meetings, charmed all societies, and voted in his own right upon all occasions. His grace's turning himself on all sides, and exercising his rare talent to all ranks of men, was still not so sufficient as he desired, to infuse the same spirit into every one: He could not be in all places, in all companies at once. As much an orator as he was, he could not talk to the whole nation, and therefore he wrote and printed his thoughts twice a week, in a paper called the *True Briton;* several thousands of which being weekly dispersed, the duke was pleased to find the whole kingdom giving attention to him, and admiring his fine style and writing (*Memoirs* 1731, 13).

Wharton's anonymous biographer represents *The True Briton* as his supplement, helping "his grace to turn himself to all sides" and "to infuse the same spirit into everyone." But what exactly is the spirit Wharton seeks to infuse? Wharton provides an answer of sorts in the first paper of *The True Briton*. He wants to be praised for his independence, for avoiding factions, for showing self-determination, for inventing, as Blake would say, his own system: "The first essential ingredient necessary to form a patriot, is, *impartiality;* for if a person shall think himself bound by any other rules but those of his own reason and judgment, or obliged to follow the dictates of others, who shall appear the heads of the party he is engaged in, he sinks below the dignity of a human creature, and voluntarily resigns those guides which nature has given him to direct him in all spheres of life" (Wharton 1723, 1: 2; Monday, June 3).

Wharton seems to want to resist the pressure of belonging to the Party of Humanity seeking instead to become a party of one. Caught up in waves of admiration, Wharton achieves social universality by restlessly particularizing, by growing "all to all," as Pope says in the strongest misapplication yet of St. Paul's words to the Corinthians. Here Pope renders the Pauline sense of potential action into an action already comically complete in Wharton—an ideal Wharton only passively attains by actively pursuing his vices. The completeness of Wharton's action (Philip, Duke of Wharton had been dead for four years when the poem was composed) encourages Pope to survey the opposites of which he is composed. He even devises a method for us ("search then the Ruling Passion") that requires that we define Wharton as a series of oppositions: "there alone / The wild are constant, and the cunning known." The absolute adjectival phrase "cunning known" suggests that the play of opposites comes to rest in the reader, conferring an advantage to us: using the method of the ruling passion, we "condition the things of the world to us, not us to the world." If Wharton is the "wonder" of his days, the readers are the concept or judgment under which he is subsumed. Wharton is practical and accommodating: he becomes whatever object, concept, profession, or role will win him praise. It does not matter what he is, "Enough if all around him but admire, / And now the Punk applaud, and now the Fryer." Yet ultimately he is incomprehensible, says Pope, because he is "too quick for Thought." It is hard to detect any content to his character at all, so driven is he to extremes by his "lust of praise."

Just as Wharton is no character, his portrait is not a portrait in any recognizable sense—all conventional features of literary portraiture have been suspended, including narrative, motivation, time, and internal coherence. As many readers have remarked, Pope undermines his flagship example of the ruling passion by his choice of example. Yet Spence's notes on Pope's conversation during the period show that Pope explicitly meant his theory to disrupt our habit of drawing inferences from the attributes to the character. He seems to have intended his theory to be contradicted by any case that comes under it. If anything, the opening lines of the portrait explicitly bear out Pope's theory. He begins by invoking the ruling passion as a space or place ("a prospect") that seems almost theatrical in the division between the devious types who are exposed and corrected and the audience who are invited to subject them to this procedure.

Although we do not realize it, we are looking for a clue; we happen upon the clue accidentally. Suddenly the "prospect clears" and "Wharton stands confest"—perhaps he was one of the priests lurking about in the previous lines. Yet as soon as Wharton comes clearly into the center of our prospect, Pope begins to confer attributes on him, extending them out over the length of a verse paragraph: "the scorn and wonder . . . Whose ruling Passion was the Lust of Praise; / Born . . . " Pope here gives us a modified version of a Theophrastan character, which typically begins by definition, positing a type (the coward, the drunkard, etc.) and filling in the type's characteristics. Pope undoes this procedure by first positing the concrete name of the person and deferring the abstraction "Lust of Praise" by interposing a few other characteristics. When we discover that "Lust of Praise" has no particular content (there is nothing that Wharton wants to be praised *for*), we have realized that inferring the attribute (lust of praise) from the person (Wharton) is impossible. And yet, far from wanting to teach us a benign lesson about making assumptions, Pope underlines in two ways that the refusal to make inferences from the particular to the general is a Whartonian procedure. Wharton becomes "all things to all men" by adopting their characteristics.

So forceful is the disparity between the overall theory of the ruling passion and its particular instance in the "Lust of Praise" that it creates a disruption in the portrait's first lines between Wharton and his attributes. It is for his desire to stand outside attribution, to achieve reflective autonomy, that Pope mocks Wharton: the problem with being a party of one is that you have to be at once the general concept and the particular instance of it, at once the ruler and the ruled. Wharton's self-reflection becomes an empty formalism; his dream of transcendence is unmasked, again, as a social attitude particularly connected to the desire for status. Between what I have been calling Pope's formalism— a formalism of hoping to stand outside the social—and Wharton's formalism, there is of course little to choose. Both are stages in the evolution of the Enlightenment self. Pope's notion, like Wharton's, is that one can step outside of the Party of Humanity, classifying another's appeal as "the scorn and wonder of our days." Pope's formalism is intimately related to Wharton's formalism, the sense in which he wants to participate in the Enlightenment project of self-determination.

Pope's formalism may not, however, be totally negative. While I have been concerned to expose the logic behind Pope's formalism, I have also claimed that it has deep affinities with features of our moral psychology. So let me end by answering Mark Edmundson's call to address our present contexts by asking what the ethical consequences might be of formalist judgments of the kind I have been describing. The general question is, what is gained for the self when we suspend our understanding of others? Of course it seems like hubris, yet we may find ourselves newly liberated from the tyranny of having to impute meaning to people who may never fully live up to our expectations of them. Hume once said that we "spread ourselves" onto objects. By contrast, in the formalist, Kantian tradition, what we lose for the understanding we perhaps gain by checking our impulse to spread ourselves onto things—the Kantian tradition oddly builds the moral values of accountability and personal circumspection directly into its aesthetics. The movement I am describing, the denial of content, the stripping away of allegorizing and obligating detail, is a basic movement of the sublime. Thus the most powerful benefit we may derive from the relationship to persons that Pope advocates is that we may be relieved to find ourselves safe from having to admire persons whom we can't understand.

Another more abstract and difficult possibility is suggested by Christine Korsgaard, summing up the Kantian tradition of conditioning one's self to the world. It is in the spirit of this possibility that Pope's desire to master the world by transcending it can be read. Obligation, writes Christine Korsgaard, is "the imposition of value on a reluctant, recalcitrant, resistant matter" (1996, 4). She argues that the materialist "metaphysics of the modern world" raises difficult questions about the source of obligation. We no longer think, like the Platonists, that excellence inheres in the form of objects, nor do we believe, with the Christian metaphysicians, that its source is otherworldly. For modern Westerners, an antithesis between matter and value poses a conundrum that, Korsgaard writes, art alone can solve: "If the real and the good are no longer one, value must find its way into the world somehow. Form must be imposed on the world of matter. This is the work of art, the work of obligation, and it brings us back to Kant. And this is what we should expect. For it was Kant who completed the revolution, when he said that reason—which is form—isn't in the world, but is something that we impose upon it. The ethics of autonomy is the only one consistent with the metaphysics of the modern world, and the ethics of autonomy is the ethics of obligation" (1996, 5).

Chapter Three

"To Virtue Only and Her Friends, a Friend"

A Sequence of Early Portraits

> As I was sitting by Sir Godfrey Kneller one day, whilst he was
> drawing a picture, he stopped and said, "I can't do so well as I
> should do unless you flatter me a little; pray flatter me, Mr. Pope!
> You know I love to be flattered."
>
> —ALEXANDER POPE

One aspect of the psychology of friendship has especially appealed to late-twentieth-century advice writers: friendship means confirming other people's delusions about themselves. A famous example, Dale Carnegie's massively best-selling book of salespersons' etiquette, *How to Win Friends and Influence People,* counsels that we get what we want from people by telling them what they want to hear. Carnegie only makes explicit what we suspect about flattery, namely, that it is a currency. We expect to be paid back for confirming people's high ideas of themselves. This is because—we think—we can see our friends more clearly than they can see themselves, and lying takes energy.

All this raises questions. Most of us are highly susceptible to flattery because, as Henry St. John Bolingbroke wrote to Lord Essex, "Self be the most artful flatterer of self in the whole world."[1] Most of us, therefore—unless our status is very high—are in the position of having to shade the truth with our friends and of paying social debts to people who shade the truth with us. Both of these practices seem, from some rational point of view, undesirable. Why don't we see ourselves as clearly as we see other people? If we did, we could avoid entering into a social contract of unspoken narcissism. We could pay social debts as we incur them, rather than building long-term alliances in which we have to keep finely calibrated track of whether we pay out more than we receive. We could also avoid the high emotional cost of betrayal. Betrayal usually means that our friend has, for whatever reason, stopped confirming our self-delusions either by his noncommittal attitudes toward our grievances or (much worse) by agreeing with other people's grievances against us.

Our elaborate emotional architecture—including the ability to detect and punish those who betray us—suggests what we already know: we are creatures who enter into long-term alliances despite the potential costs. Yet we rarely enter into them ironically, detaching ourselves by calculating in advance how much all this will cost us. Most of the time we confirm our friends' delusions about themselves because we love them, and we entertain no doubts about the justice of their cause. The feelings that get us into these alliances are as powerful as those that get us out of them again: love leads us to perceive our friends selectively, while a sudden compulsion to be honest leads us to betray them.

Of Pope's long and intimate friendship with Henry St. John, Viscount Bolingbroke, in which the betrayal happened after Pope's death, Maynard Mack writes: "Pope had many heroes. . . . It was Bolingbroke alone, however, who inspired in Pope an intensity of admiration almost uncanny. That lord, he told Spence, 'is something superior to anything I have seen in human nature'" (1985, 507). Pope fell deeply in love with Bolingbroke. For over two decades, he was willing to support two mutually contradictory beliefs that Bolingbroke held about himself. The first is that, after being exiled from government for his Jacobitism and stripped of his title, he was voluntarily living in Horatian retirement on his Sabine farm. The second is that he would soon sweep back into power and unseat the hated Walpole and his Whig government. Bolingbroke's concerns, grievances, friends, and enemies—even the themes he chose to govern his life—saturated Pope's poetry.[2] Pope was capable of teasing Bolingbroke about some little vanities, like having the inside of his house painted with "Trophies of Rakes, spades, prongs, & c. and other ornaments merely to countenance his calling this place a Farm" and about his womanizing; but his aggression (according to one view of the betrayal) lay carefully hidden underneath ever more sublime professions of love, gratitude, and obligation (*Corr.* 2:503; to Swift, 28 June 1728).

Even these professions did not prevent the notoriously jealous and rivalrous Bolingbroke from thinking he found evidence of Pope's suppressed aggression. In 1739 he gave Pope the text of his political pamphlet *The Idea of the Patriot King* and authorized him to print a limited number of copies. Pope made some corrections to the text and secretly printed 1,500. He had, his biographers speculate, either the basest or the purest of motives: either he hoped to profit, or he hoped to disseminate Bolingbroke's ideas in an improved form. Horace Walpole describes the betrayal: "Pope, who loved money infinitely beyond any friend, got 1,500 copies printed privately, intending to outlive Bolingbroke, and make great advantage of them; and not only did this, but altered the copy at his pleasure, and even made different alterations in different copies. . . . What seems to have made Bolingbroke most angry, and I suppose does, is Pope's having presumed to correct his work" (quoted in Johnson 1967, 3:193 n. 3).

Walpole may be recalling that when Pope was much younger, he had lost an important friend because he presumed to correct the friend's work; why couldn't he apply the lesson he learned from his rupture with Wycherley to his friendship with Bolingbroke? One answer—Bolingbroke's answer—is that he did. When, late in their friendship, Pope wrote letters like the following, he may have felt obliged to flatter:

My dear Lord,—Your every word is kind to me, & all the openings of your mind amiable. Your communicating any of your Sentiments both makes me a happier & a better man. There is so true a fund of all Virtue public & Social within you, I mean so right a sense of things as we stand related to each other by the Laws of God, and indebted to each other in conformity to those Laws, that I hope no partic: Calamity can swallow up your care & concern for the General. (*Corr.*, 4:260; 3 September 1740)

Perhaps Pope nurtured dissident feelings toward Bolingbroke—competitiveness, for example—and experienced the need to flatter as burdensome. His self-representations as a "little bark attendant" upon Bolingbroke's "name/ Expanded" may have been designed to soothe his friend's suspicions (TE 3[1]:165). We have no evidence. We do know that Pope was becoming increasingly famous in Bolingbroke's own sphere—Opposition politics—as Bolingbroke's influence waned.[3]

We know something else about the period of their friendship that leads us to suspect that its normative bonds eventually became stronger than its emotional ones. We know that normativity itself became the quasi-hysterical focus of their collective rhetoric. From being merely friends, Pope and Bolingbroke became Friends to Virtue, the abstraction all-consuming. Both men had a penchant for the conspiratorial and paranoid alliance. For instance, Sir William Trumbull, the secretary of state, wrote to Bolingbroke when the latter, his protégé, was in Italy on his Grand Tour, explaining how he wants to "be revenged upon the world and use it scurvily, when we are alone" (quoted in Hammond 1984, 25). And both were able to calculate, to a hair's-breadth of accuracy, degrees of status and power in those whose friendships they solicited. But together they fantasize about contemning the world so absolutely that they seem to make it disappear under their conviction of mutual virtue. There is constant rhetoric, in their letters, of each man being abstracted from the crew—too good for a nation that does not appreciate him. There is language too of personal insufficiency, of each man shriveling up in the face of the great abstractions he worships. Here is one of Pope's most famous tributes to their friendship, in Satire 2.1 of the *Imitations of Horace*:

> Hear this, and tremble! you, who 'scape the laws.
> Yes, while I live, no rich or noble knave
> Shall walk the World, in credit, to his grave.
> TO VIRTUE ONLY and HER FRIENDS, A FRIEND
> The world beside may murmur, or commend.
> Know, all the distant din that world can keep
> Rolls oe'r my Grotto, and but soothes my sleep.
> There, my retreat the best companions grace,
> Chiefs, out of war, and statesmen out of place.
> There St. John mingles with my friendly Bowl,
> The Feast of Reason and the Flow of Soul:
> And He, whose Lightning pierc'd th'Iberian Lines,
> Now, forms my Quincunx, and now ranks my Vines,
> Or tames the Genius of the stubborn Plain,
> Almost as quickly, as he conquer'd Spain.   (TE 4:17–19)

The languages of threat (toward the world) and protectiveness (toward his friends) mix in these lines, which perhaps subtly diminish Bolingbroke as well as Peterborough, the retired warrior who appears at the end of them. Both men have been displaced by worldly forces, by corruption and accident; now Pope repatriates them in places that metonymically signify his proprietary largesse. St. John "mingles with my friendly Bowl," and Peterborough seems comically challenged by recreating his victories in Spain against the plants in Pope's garden.

Pope's subtly reductive metonymies imply that he is a world complete, wrapping up his partial, perhaps damaged friends. On the one hand, Pope's stance shows how powerfully he absorbed Bolingbroke's political philosophy, which preached the absolute continuity of private with public virtue. On the other hand, it shows how strongly he misinterpreted and revised it to make himself the center of a doctrine of local transcendence. The cornerstone of that philosophy was "the idea of a patriot king" from whose personal and private conduct good government was supposed to flow. I am not going to undertake here a direct study of Bolingbroke's complicated civic humanism, but some themes are of special interest.[4] *The Idea of a Patriot King* has been seen as a treatise on rulership in which transcendent and abstract values arise from the person of the ideal king, eventually leading to "panegyric without the prince," writes Howard Erskine-Hill (1981, 139). Bolingbroke argued for sociable exchange as the foundation of good government; by direct analogy, Pope sees his friendship with Bolingbroke as the center of an ever-widening circle of virtue that eventually consumes them both. A complicated letter from George Lyttleton, Secretary to the Prince of Wales and prominent member of the Patriot Opposition to Pope, captures the rhetoric of the group of men for whom Pope and Bolingbroke were in 1737 the moral center:

I wish [Bolingbroke] was in England upon many accounts, but for nothing more than to Exhort and Animate you not to bury your excellent talents in a Philosophical indolence, but to employ them, as you have so often done, in the service of virtue. The corruption, and hardness of the present age is no excuse; for your writings will last to ages to come, and may do good a thousand years hence, if they can't now; but I believe they would be of great present benefit; some sparks of publick virtue are yet alive, which such a spirit as yours might blow into a flame, among the young men especially; and even granting an impossibility of reforming the publick, your writings may be of use to private society; the moral song may steal into our hearts and teach us to be as good sons, as good friends, as beneficent, as charitable as Mr. Pope, and sure that will be serving your country, though you can't raise her up such ministers, or such senators as you desire. In short, my dear friend, though I am far from supposing that if you don't write, you live in vain; though the influence of your virtues is felt among all your friends and acquaintance, and the whole circle of society within which you live, yet as your writings will have a still more extensive and permanent influence, as they will be an honour to your country at a time when it has hardly anything else to be proud of, and may do good to mankind in better ages and countries, if not in this, I wou'd have you write till a decay of your parts, or at least weakness of health shall oblige, and authorise you to lay down your pen. (*Corr.* 4:368–69; 7 November 1741)

The letter is complicated because, as Christine Gerrard points out, Lyttleton was actively trying to bring about certain ends of his own: Pope should turn from writing satire to writing Patriot epic, perhaps even celebrating in verse Frederick, Prince of Wales, the Patriots' royal ally against Walpole and the King (1994, 81–82). Lyttleton brings this subtle pressure to bear on Pope by a flattering rhetoric utterly congenial to Pope's odd self-image. This rhetoric holds Pope to be the synecdoche of virtue. Ideally virtue ripples outward from his person ("the moral song may steal into our hearts and teach us to be as good sons . . . as Mr. Pope") to "private society" to "the publick" to "ages to come" "a thousand years hence." But of course each level may prove intractable, "corrupt" and "hard." The merely personal and fallible may "decay" (like Pope's "parts") as the abstraction becomes more distant, permanent, and abiding. Like the patriot king himself, Pope is the source of a virtue that eventually obliterates him. Lyttleton cannily notes that the whole process begins in Pope's bond with Bolingbroke. As one writer has noted in a puzzled tone: "Almost osmotically, a kind of moral idealism permeates the concept of friendship" in Pope's world (Davidow 1977, 154). The male bond, at the center of the male group, becomes the source of virtue.

Western culture has been profoundly ambivalent about the notion of the male bond as a source of virtue. On the one hand, we think of brothers and warriors as exhibiting the virtues of loyalty and self-sacrifice; on the other, our history demarcates kinship bonds as criminally nepotistic and male friendships as potentially homosexual, decadent, and corrupting. Male bonds are as often a source of violence as of virtue; sometimes violence and idealism run together in a frightening way, as when male-dominated groups become divisive and morally self-righteous, denying that their moral laws apply to the Other.

Pope's life and writings have been a lightening rod for such ambivalence, in part because his male friendships are so obviously part of his plan to advance his own interests. At one stage in his life, "Pope's powerful friends were constantly lending him coaches and chariots, putting him up for weeks at a time, voting for his candidates for various professorships and positions, and sending him items for his garden and grotto. Not only did these powerful men constantly do favors for Pope, but they did so with little or no grumbling," marvels James A. Winn. Pope's requests for favors were "written with great psychological insight and skill," he explains, carefully tailored to appeal to the deepest interests of his famous correspondents. In a telling elaboration, Winn apologizes for what might be taken as a slur:

I am not seeking to impugn Pope's sincerity. On the contrary, I am suggesting that he knew himself and others well, and recognized in others, because he felt it himself, the almost universal human need to be thought generous. He appealed to great men, not by toadying or obvious flattery, but by the more subtle means of understanding their "ruling passions" and special interests. To each of them, he presented a fitting side of himself: if Bolingbroke fancied himself a philosopher, Pope could be serious with him; if Oxford was proud of his library, Pope could play scholarly games with him; if any great man relished his power, Pope could provide him a chance to exercise it. Most important of all, he never presumed to ignore their "greatness," even while effectively overcoming the distances that greatness supposedly imposed. (1977, 84)

Winn's elaboration is telling for a few reasons. First, it suggests that Pope's psychological acuity, perhaps even his theory of the ruling passion, has its origins in his intense scrutiny of other men—a scrutiny born not out of disinterested fascination with human beings or from a desire to be the sort of person on whom nothing is lost, but born rather of a deep practical need to reason and calculate to his own advantage. Winn seems to find such calculation embarrassing: he thinks his readers might worry that he impugns Pope's sincerity by unmasking disinterest as interest. In fact, writers have impugned his sincerity since 1711 precisely by bringing into focus the doubleness of his motives. And if Winn *had* been impugning Pope's sincerity, he could have claimed to have anticipated by about ten years the major development in Anglo-American Pope criticism. Winn's gesture, in fact, is highly relevant to that long schism in Pope criticism that I sketched in the previous chapter.

Pope, it has often been said, is the "poet of friendship." The number of times that Pope refers to friendship in his poetry has been estimated at seven hundred (Stephanson 1997, 162).[5] Owen Ruffhead, Pope's first biographer, calls him "the soul of friendship." He then quotes Mrs. Arbuthnot as saying that he "was a perfect male-bawd in promoting friendship" (Ruffhead 1769, 496). George Sherburn says in his introduction that in his letters, Pope made "almost a cult of friendship" (*Corr.* 1: ix). Of this cult, centered on Pope's villa at Twickenham, Maynard Mack writes:

If [the interior of his villa] had a particular emphasis, that emphasis was on friends. Their portraits by Jervas, Kneller, Richardson, and many more constituted the decoration of his rooms, some four dozen in all. "Mihi & Amicis," he told Fortescue in 1736, "and indeed Plus Amicis quam Meipsi" [More for my friends than for myself] would be a proper motto over his gate, and five years later he informs another friend and frequent visitor that he is now indeed "putting over my door at Twitnam, Libertati & Amicitiae." In no small house of which we have records is there found such concentration on a single theme. Pope's villa, in other words, could increasingly seem to him, and to others, expressive of his deepest values as man and poet. (1985, 359–61)

"Plus Amicis quam Meipsi" and "Libertati & Amicitiae" are powerfully guiding ideals that Pope seems to need to inscribe, to make concrete. Twice— in letters five years apart—he chooses a gate as the medium of inscription, as though it were his constant idea. His gate marks the Horatian ideal of retirement and garden; it also marks the boundary of his private property. It is thus a peculiar symbol of "plus amicis quam meipsi" and of liberty, a metonymy even more obviously double-edged than those he uses to represent his relation to friends in the "to virtue only and her friends a friends" passage. Those critics seeking to point to the self-interest underlying Pope's claims of virtue need look no farther than his gate. How blatantly he inscribes these high ideals on a marker of ownership! Pope's moral self-advertisements and the sign of his self-interest stand in the same relation to each other as the duck and the rabbit in Wittgenstein's famous picture. The two pictures are so closely inter-woven that Pope cannot be said to be actually duplicitous, as he would be if he were concealing one of them.

Another of Pope's frankly ambidextrous images uniting virtue and self-interest is his own face. Consider two Horatian portraits, one of the Roubil-iac busts from the late 1730s, whose inscription is "Uni Aequis Virtuti atque eius Amicis" (fig. 2) and Jonathan Richardson's etching of Pope from 1736 (fig. 3). In the first, Pope's gaze is averted as though in concentrated humility; in the second, Pope stares out at us with a frank and open expression. The caption reads "Amicitiae Causa" (cause of friendship). Pope printed this etching as the frontispiece to his 1737 edition of letters, telling Richardson, "That excellent etching in my title page . . . will be the most valuable thing in the book" (*Corr.* 4:58; 3 March 1736, 7). Edmund Curll perceived the etching's value too, printing it as the frontispiece to his pirated edition. Having been repeatedly abused and double-crossed by Pope, Curll felt no need to underscore the irony of his gesture. *That* face as "cause of friendship" does all the work of pastiche that Curll needed it to do.

We are still far from the iconographic center of Pope's cult of friendship, however. As Mack makes clear, Twickenham centered on portraits of other males, the face of the beloved obsessively repeated. In this gallery of friends, levels of self-interest become undetectable; "plus amicis quam meipsi" is suddenly a plausible self-description. Or is it? Morris Brownell writes that for Pope and his contemporaries, portraits were "valued for their associations rather than their artistry." They were "one of the sacraments of friendship, exchanged in much the same way as letters . . . as much documents as works of art" (1977, 37–38). Brownell's distinction between the social value of the portraits and their content could surely be questioned in the case of those portraits of friends by artists such as Richardson, Jervas, and Kneller that Pope collected. In the portraits Pope drew, that distinction—or more precisely its collapse—becomes their special point. For something about collapsing the use/meaning and form/content distinctions helps Pope create social portraits adequate to the normative command and complexity he wants them to possess.

The purpose of this chapter is to trace the evolution of that normative complexity. "I find my hand most successful in drawing of friends and those I most esteem," Pope explained to Caryll in 1713 (*Corr.* 1:189; 31 August 1713). If love

Figure 2. Louis-Francois Roubiliac, Alexander Pope, (bust), 1741. Permission
to reproduce granted by Yale Center for British Art; gift of Paul Mellon in
memory of the British art historian Basil Taylor (1922–1975).

made Pope a better realist, his quest for status ("fame" is his word) made him
a better moralist. Pope's satirical powers came into view during same period
of his life as his deep concern for friendship and reputation. This is the period
of his late adolescence, from 1704 when he was sixteen, to 1711 when he published the *Essay on Criticism*. That poem is the fullest record we have of Pope's
social ascent. Recorded there are his friendships and enmities, his debts and

Amicitiæ causa.   *J. Richardson f. 1736.*

Figure 3. Jonathan Richardson, Alexander Pope (etching), 1736. Print Collection,
Miriam and Ira D. Wallach Division of Art, Prints, and Photographs; the New York
Public Library, Astor, Lenox, and Tilden Foundations. Permission to reproduce
granted by the New York Public Library.

obligations, and his growing resentment at the high social cost of overt ambition. Two of the three portraits I will focus on here—those of Dennis and Walsh—can be found in that poem. The third portrait, of Joseph Addison, though written a few years later, directly mirrors the Walsh portrait and is drenched in the themes of Pope's early career.

One of these themes concerns the relative status of Pope's male acquaintances. Even when Pope was quite young and in a very unpromising social position—prematurely "retir'd" to Binfield, thanks to his father's growing suspicion of the world—he was gifted at soliciting caring investment from older males. George Sherburn has said it best: "In many respects the most interesting fact concerning Pope's life at Binfield is that in this retired spot he acquired a circle of friends both numerous and distinguished. From the extreme of obscurity he 'arrived' at the pinnacle of fame in less than a decade, and his friends as well as his genius aided his success" (1934, 45).

A curious aspect of this pattern is that Pope selected friends who were just *past* the "pinnacle of fame." Winn has commented on this too: "The 'great' men with whom Pope corresponded were rarely men in real power. He had quarreled with Addison by the time Addison became Secretary of State, and while he attended dinners with and solicited favors from Robert Walpole, their relationship has been accurately called a 'wary armed truce.' By the early 1730's that truce was broken, and Pope was engaged in open literary warfare with Walpole; a consequence of his more frankly political position was a new group of friends, also out of power, the 'Patriot' Opposition typified by Lyttelton" (1977, 76). Wycherley was an old lion; William Trumbull, a retired secretary of state; Swift and the Scriblerians were alienated from public culture in various ways; and by the time Pope befriended the Tories, they had begun their forty-year exile from government. Men at the peak of their powers—Walpole, for instance, or Addison—were more likely to find themselves in sharp conflict with Pope than to find themselves praised and flattered. Men whose powers had never really been all that strong, like Dennis, would be passed over. Instead, Pope chose Wycherley, whose considerable powers were in decline. That friendship, too, will play a considerable part in my reading of Pope's early character sketches.

Shaming Dennis

Alexander Pope's personal attack on the literary critic John Dennis in the third section of the *Essay on Criticism* (1711) is a glaring interruption of the high and markedly general tone of the rest of his poem. The poem proceeds by portraiture, yet its negative characterizations are usually general, while its specific characterizations are usually positive. (There are a few exceptions: Blackmore and Milbourn are named enviers of Dryden [l. 464]). Strikingly wedged between such nonreferential formulations as "some praise at morning what they blame at night" (l. 430) and such epideictic set pieces as "Horace still charms with graceful negligence" (l. 653) is a brief sketch of the remarkable Appius:

> But Appius reddens at each Word you speak,
> And stares, Tremendous! with a threatening Eye,
> Like some fierce Tyrant in Old Tapestry!   (TE 1:306–7)

The attack is surprising because it subverts the poem's doctrines: Pope's exuberant Longinianism seems marred by aggression towards Dennis, the best-known of Longinus's English disciples and the one who had recently attempted a modernization or "completion" of Longinus.[6] In fact, the passage is a Longinian attack on Dennis for being insufficiently Longinian—for being too little his own author. Whereas "bold Longinus" is

> An ardent Judge, who Zealous in his Trust,
> With warmth gives Sentence, yet is always Just;
> Whose own Example strengthens all his Laws,
> And is himself that great Sublime he draws   (TE 1:316),

Pope identifies Dennis not with his critical achievements—his interpretations of Milton, his defenses of the neoclassical rules, or his views on poetic justice—but with a character in a failed play. (Dennis's final tragedy, Appius and Virginia, ran for only four or five nights before being withdrawn).

Pope's attack raises a number of biographical and conceptual questions. By 1710 Dennis had "retir'd from the world," and, as he pointedly remarked in the preface to his *Reflections Critical and Satirical upon a Late Rhapsody, call'd An Essay Upon Criticism*, he felt that Pope had attacked him "at a time when all the world knew that I was persecuted by fortune" (1939–46, 1:396). He had become a barely tolerated old joke among the crowd at Will's coffee house, his former place of glory. Pope had probably never met him. Dennis's biographer describes him thus: "His short figure, broadening with the years, his great scowling face, the large eyes that stared from beneath their shaggy brows, these with a slovenliness of dress that grew more noticeable with the passing of time, formed a marked contrast with the slender youth of the town" (Paul 1911, 55–56). What led Pope to attack a paranoid old man whose powers were failing and whose friends were dead? This puzzle is related to a puzzle in the portrait's iconography: why should Dennis's Longinianism sever his rhetorical excesses from his judgment rather than uniting them, as Longinus's own combination of these qualities does? And the answer to both questions, the biographical and the conceptual, lies in the kind of norm Pope seeks to impose.

Pope is careful not to attack Longinian theory but to deploy some of the tenets of that theory—as it was construed in the first few decades after the late-seventeenth-century European rediscovery and translation of Longinus's *Peri Hupsous*—against its chief popularizer. One tenet is that an author's identification with his characters and his themes is one of the sources of the sublime. Longinus's example is Homer identifying with the madness of Ajax: "These are truly the feelings of an Ajax. . . . Here indeed Homer breathes in the inspiration of the fray" (1965, 112). Longinus does not distinguish between Homer's identification with fully autonomous agents and his identification with "the sublimity of his heroic themes" or a "closely-packed profusion of the passions" (1965, 112, 113). Many different kinds of identification—with a person, with a theme, or even with a bundle of passions—point to Homer's "nobility of soul." Longinus could elide the difference between persons, themes, and passion sequences in a way that Pope, writing at a very different moment in the history of individuation, could not.[7] The principal reason that Longinus allows themes, passion sequences, and persons to count equally as sources of authorial identification is that sublime effects consist of a shock of surprise when content turns into form. The content of authorial identification is irrelevant: Longinus might as well say that Homer can show his nobility of soul by turning his identification with a foot or a tree into a source of the sublime.[8]

Other key Longinian concepts are those of self-reference and exemplarity. Longinian self-reference consists in being subject to the same effect you produce, whereas Appius's self-reference consists in being humiliated by your own bad play. In Longinus's treatise, the sublime orator achieves exemplarity by experiencing transport as a means of inducing it in his audience. Pope seems to want to show that this process is absurd in a case where the exemplary oscillation between source of poetic effects and their end (the audience) takes place at a second remove from the source of the sublime. An obvious difference between Longinus and John Dennis is that one is original, the other an imitator. Pope's praise of Longinian self-reference simply does not extend to other people behaving like Longinus.

In deploying Longinus against John Dennis, Pope revises Longinian doctrine to make his treatment of Dennis into a source of his own power. We can discern the following structure of effects. First, the well-known Longinian transfer of emotion from one person to another (which Neil Hertz has called the "sublime turn") allows Dennis to identify with Longinus and to feel empowered by his connection with the source of transport (1985, 6). In the normal course of events, Dennis should become a new source of transport by restarting the effects he has just witnessed. However, Pope blocks this orderly transfer of emotion and stuffs the transport Dennis is about to export to others back into himself, thus in one stroke grotesquely completing the circuit of self-reference and flattening transport into humiliation. Staring and reddening are not signs of transport but of violent shame and unwilling submission. Pope intends his portrait to shame Dennis for a public failure, thus doing to Dennis in a direct and satirical way what the Longinian orator does to his audience in a sublimely self-referential way.

Imagine for a moment that Pope had read Kant's "Analytic of the Sublime" in the *Critique of Judgment* (1790) and decided to give a parodic account of the "fascination" or, to use a more theatrical term, mesmerism of the sublime (Hertz 1985, 52). The sense in which Pope looks as if he is parodying Kant can be brought out by noticing that Pope's revision of Longinus parallels a psychoanalytic argument about the role of reason in the Kantian mathematical sublime. This argument, whose two main proponents have been Thomas Weiskel and Neil Hertz, is a structuralist revision of the Kantian picture, explaining the power-like conflicts (the characteristic "blockage" and "exaltation") of the sublime as having both linguistic and oedipal motivations (Weiskel [1976] 1986, 38–41, 99–100; Hertz 1985, 53). On the Kantian account, the imagination tries to grasp an infinity of magnitude, yet fails to synthesize enough particulars to complete the infinite series. Imagination's failure leaves the way open for reason to intervene and save the imagination in its identification with the sublime. Yet in saving the imagination, reason also humiliates it, identifying more closely than the imagination is able to with sources of sublime power. I quote part of Kant's account of the imagination's "delight in the sublime"—a delight whose limitation, negativity, and ambivalence have proved a starting point for later readings of the aesthetic power of mixed affect:[9]

It is a feeling of imagination by its own act depriving itself of its freedom by receiving a final determination in accordance with a law other than that of its empirical employment. In this way it gains an extension and a power greater than that which it sacrifices. But the ground of this is concealed from it, and in its place it *feels* the sacrifice of deprivation, as well as its cause, to which it is subjected. ([1790] 1952, 120)[10]

In Weiskel's and Hertz's revision of this passage, reason's saving humiliation of the imagination resembles the saving humiliation of male oedipal identification—that is, a boy must "renounce the aggression and turn himself into—

be swallowed by—the image, now an ideal, with which he is identifying" (Weiskel [1976] 1986, 93). In our imagined precursor sketch, Pope willfully toggles a literary elder between humiliation and transport.

Pope's attack on Dennis seems like a version of Kant's sublime written for an audience more interested in power and status than in the aesthetic, or interested in aesthetic principles as they are affected by worldly problems. Pope's satirical sublime looks like a political version of Kant's. It demands the poet's full and immediate identification with the source of power rather than the reason's embarrassingly late appropriation of it as in the Kantian and psychoanalytic versions. Power is conceived of as a human contest for dominance rather than as a contest sponsored by some supersensible agent between personified human faculties. In the satiric portrait, the relations between affect and effect are externalized, so that the self-consciousness that will later characterize the Kantian aesthetic is split up between two agents. In this respect Pope seems to be striking specifically ancient—Longinian—aesthetic postures: Pope is Homer; Dennis is either Ajax, a foot, a tree, or a bundle of affects—in short, an object devoid of self-consciousness. Dennis's status as mute object of power is confirmed in the following ways: while he is being toggled about by his satiric master, he seems unaware of the meaning of his emotion. His affect is misplaced. The character Appius in Dennis's play is a Roman tyrant notable for the thunder that accompanies his self-dramatizing emotional outbursts. (For this production, Dennis had suggested an innovation in the making of stage thunder: "Upon hearing thunder employed at a performance of Macbeth after his own play had been withdrawn, he caused a commotion in the theatre by denouncing the proceedings of the Managers, who, he alleged, stole his thunder but refused to act his plays."[11]) Pope's Appius is only metaphorically a tyrant, and a tyrant stitched into an old tapestry at that. He experiences the wrong emotion, thundering in anger at "your" words. He should be feeling shame—his red face betrays him, even if his experience is faulty. Other people—the audience—have got the right idea about his emotional state even if he himself does not.

Some moral psychologists have recently revisited the topic of shame. They claim that shame is an exceptional passion because it is caused by consciousness of others rather than by self-consciousness—caused, that is, by external rather than internal forces. Shame is as an emotion of moral motivation when the person for whom shame is a regulating ideal or moral emotion takes herself as her own example from the perspective of others. Feeling shame is connected both to self-consciousness and to an audience. Gabriele Taylor writes that "the person feeling shame feels exposed: he thinks of himself as being seen through the eyes of another" (1985, 57). Yet, she goes on, feeling shame does not require an actual audience, only the possibility of imagining what an audience would be like: "It is certainly true that to feel shame about his inferior work a craftsman need not think, i.e., either believe or imagine, that there is another craftsman looking at his work. He need not imagine an actual observer, and that there is such an observer need not be part of the content of his thought. All that seems necessary is that he shift his viewpoint from that of the creator of the work to that of the critical assessor, and he himself can fulfill both those functions" (1985, 58).

Bernard Williams (1993) has recently countered Taylor's view that shame feels the same whether there is an external agent or the shamed person only feels *as though* there is an external agent. In Williams's view, shame is not an emotion motivated by imagination. It is rather an emotion connected directly to the experience of a spectator. In fact, shame precisely does not have to connect to *internal* motivations in order to be morally effective, in the way that some Kantian moral philosophers argue that guilt or a sense of "Achtung" does. But there are other characteristics of shame that need to be emphasized, Williams thinks. Between the beholder and the beheld there is usually a difference in status. Shame is an especially effective moral emotion within the social sphere (1993, 89, 220).

Dennis does not, of course, experience shame—at least not directly. As a normative occasion, the portrait is rather convoluted. Its thought might be this: Dennis ought to be ashamed. The portrait shows him unaware that he ought to be ashamed. Instead it shows him angry. But—in truth—Dennis *is* angry, not ashamed, and so the logic goes round. By embodying this logic, Dennis finally becomes worthy of the Longinian exemplarity that Pope denies him in his own right: his exemplarity consists of his shame displayed for another person—but not directly experienced.[12] Pope thus offers his contemporaries the final revision or "completion" of Longinus that Dennis had first unsuccessfully attempted.

Pope and Wycherley

Pope's attack on Dennis is a late episode in a long saga of shifting alliances between male writers. At Will's coffee house in Covent Garden in the 1690's Dryden held suspicious and senescent court in exile, having been stripped of his official position as poet laureate upon the accession of William III. William Wycherley and William Congreve were princes in waiting; John Dennis stood a distant third in line to the throne. Shaftesbury describes the scene at Will's:

They are his guards ready to take arms for him, if by some presumptuous critic he is at any time attacked. They are indeed the very shadows of their immediate predecessor, and represent the same features, with some alterations perhaps for the worse. They are sure to aim at nothing beyond or above their Master, and would on no account give him the least jealousy of their aspiring to any degree or order of writing above him. From hence the harmonious and reciprocal esteem, which on such a bottom as this, cannot fail of being perfectly established among our poets. (1964, 2:327)

Among Dryden's supporters Dennis was the lap dog, roundly abused by the others. Congreve is said to have remarked that "of two evils, it was better to have Dennis's flattery than his gall" (quoted in Paul 1911, 11). Dennis's flattery was indeed effusive. He published a collection of familiar letters in 1696 to prove how intimately he was connected to Dryden, Congreve, and Wycherley. What strikes us in these letters is how often his high-flown and awkward compliments are met by the cool and ironic response. In one letter Dennis has written Wycherley, who is in the country, to praise him and lament his absence. Wycherley responds: "My dear friend, I have no way to show my love to you in my absence but by my jealousie. I would not have my rivals in your friendship the C——s, the D——s, the W——s, and the rest of your tavern friends who enjoy your conversation while I cannot; tho I confess, 'tis to their interest to make you dumb with wine, that they may be heard in your company" (Dennis 1696, 15). Dennis answers by rhetorically lowering himself, imagining as he often does in the letters that he is a woman spurned and abused by a powerful man: "You see I am as reasonable with my friend, as a Russian spouse is with her husband, and take his very raillery for a mark of esteem, as she does a beating for a mark of affection" (1696, 19).

The rhetorical jockeying at Will's in the 1690s reached a fever pitch around the charismatic figure of Dryden. Dropping broad hints about the role Dennis should play in publicizing his virtues, Dryden used Dennis as a coalition partner to ward off threats to his moral and literary reputation: "For my morals, betwixt man and man, I am not to be my own judge. I appeal to the world if I have deciev'd or defrauded any man: and for my private conversation, they who see me every day can be the best witnesses, whether or no it be blameless and inoffensive" (quoted in Winn 1987, 474).[13] Dennis performed his role as Dryden's moral propagandist admirably, stepping in even decades after Dryden's death to defend him at the slightest hint of a challenge. "Practically all of our author's critical writings before 1700 were directed against those who had opposed his master," writes Dennis's biographer (Paul 1911, 8). Perhaps for that reason Dryden never suspected Dennis of plotting against him. Dennis flattered Dryden, too, by adopting the posture of a lover: "Since

I came to this place I have taken up my pen several times in order to write to you, but have constantly at the very beginning found my self damp'd and disabled; upon which I have been apt to believe that extraordinary esteem may sometimes make the mind as impotent as a violent love does the body, and the very vehement desire we have to exert it, extremely decays our ability" (1696, 46). And again, "You may see too, that a friend may sometimes proceed to acknowledge affection, by the very same degrees by which a love declares his passion" (1696, 49). Dryden often responds frostily to these effusions: "When I read a letter so full of my commendations as your last, I cannot but consider you as the master of a vast treasure, who having more than enough for your self, are forc'd to ebb out upon your friends" (Dennis 1696, 53).

By the end of the first decade of the eighteenth century, power in literary circles had shifted from Will's to Button's coffee house across the street, which Addison had anointed as his place. Will's remained the haunt of Dryden's friends, now old and culturally impotent. Wycherley and Dennis were throwbacks to Restoration wit culture. Now perhaps Dennis expected to be repaid for his years of service to Dryden by similar deference from a younger male. Imitating Dryden, Dennis wrote elaborate self-justifications when his plays went unappreciated. Yet he grew increasingly marginalized—his patrons less generous, his finances more precarious, laughter about his slovenly appearance less guarded (Paul 1911, chap. 3).

Dennis's first meeting with Pope seemed auspicious enough, as the twenty-year-old Pope made a show of playing up to him and seeking his patronage. Mack speculates that Dennis verbally roughed Pope up, just as he had been hazed by Dryden. But imagine Dennis's surprise then—"indignation" is his word—when Pope refused the honor of becoming his satellite:

At his first coming to town he was very importunate with the late Mr. Henry Cromwell to introduce him to me. The recommendation of Mr. Cromwell induced me to be about thrice in his company, after which I went into the country and never saw or thought of him, till I found myself attacked by him in the very superficial Essay on Criticism, which was the effect of his impotent envy and malice, by which he endeavor'd to destroy the reputation of a man who had publish'd pieces of criticism, and to set up his own. I was mov'd with indignation to that degree, at so much baseness, that I immediately writ remarks upon that essay, in order to expose the weakness and the absurdity of it; which remarks were published, as soon as they could be printed. (1939–43, 2:370)

Pope's attack must have driven home to Dennis his newly marginal place, though perhaps it made him feel important again, reviving as it did the elaborate verbal displays of aggression of the Restoration wits. Dennis, after all, rediscovered his voice, spending the last twenty-five years of his life fighting back with short, sharp, ad hominem blows.

Pope seems, for much of the rest of *his* life, to have felt intensely guilty. Years after his ascent, Pope once again became obsessed with questions of flattery, subservience, servility, and the way power is exchanged within a tightly knit group of people. His fullest meditation on these themes is *An Epistle to Dr. Arbuthnot* (1734–5). In that dialogue with his restrained interlocutor, he worries about the way social pressures deform the human voice, his own and others. The terrain he works in is familiar to many poets and philosophers as the relation between essence and accidents, between condition and degree. For Pope, the sign of social infection ("plague," he calls it) is having rhythms, couplets, poems, and proper names inside his head. His idea is almost Wittgenstinian: language is the sign of social obligation; to have language is to be socialized; to be socialized is to be conditioned and fixed by the world. To get free of obligation is to strip the self of its accidental features. He seeks to strip his conscience of proper names; and the name most deeply fixed there is Dennis:

> Above a Patron, tho' I condescend
> Sometimes to call a Minister my Friend:
> I was not born for Courts or great Affairs,
> I pay my Debts, believe, and say my Pray'rs,
> Can sleep without a Poem in my head,
> Nor know, if Dennis be alive or dead.   (TE 4:114–15)

Pope's friendship with Wycherley mirrored in reverse his relationship with Dennis. Pope might have chosen either man as a friend, I've suggested, but he looked Dennis over and rejected him. He chose Wycherley instead, and even so found himself involved in an increasingly troubled relationship from which it would take him over two decades after Wycherley's death to disentangle himself. Meanwhile, Dennis followed him like an angry ghost clanking his chains in public. The lesson of both friendships applies to many of Pope's projects during this early ambitious phase of his life: there is no free ride to fame. Pursue status too openly and soon you'll find yourself paying a high social cost. The farther along the road to fame Pope traveled, the tighter the social net drew around him. Pope was the first person to draw this lesson from his own early career. Wycherley was old, rivalrous, and jealous, a *senex iratus* bent on bringing Pope down, the personification of unwanted obligation.

At first the cost of Wycherley's friendship seemed light, and its benefits great. Pope approached Wycherley by recalling the scene at Will's. It helped that he was awestruck: "It was certainly a great satisfaction to me to see and converse with a man, whom in his writings I had long known with pleasure: but it was a high addition to it, to hear you, at our very first meeting, doing justice to your dead friend Mr. Dryden." He had never had the good fortune to meet the great man, Pope declares, but "Virgilium tantum vidi" (I saw Virgil himself there). Pope then goes on to lay out an elaborate compliment to Dryden. The tenor of the compliment is thick with passive aggressive complication, praising Wycherley but also needling him about his age: "Had I been born early enough, I must have known and lov'd him." Throughout their correspondence, Pope seizes every opportunity to remind Wycherley of how precociously young he is, even calling the older man a "tree past bearing" in the guise of thanking him for his unexpected support of a younger writer: "Most men in years, as they are generally discouragers of youth, are like old trees, that being past bearing themselves will suffer no young plants to flourish beneath them. But as if it were not enough to have out-done all your coevals in wit, you will excel them in good nature too. As for my green essays . . ." and so on (*Corr.* 1:5; 25 March 1705).

Pope ends the first paragraph of his first letter to Wycherley by at once dropping the names of Congreve and Sir William Trumbull, sticking up for Dryden against the calumny of his envious detractors, and opining that "those scribblers who attack'd him in his latter times, were only like Gnats in a summer's evening, which are never very troublesome but in the finest and most glorious season; (for his fire, like the sun's, shin'd clearest towards its setting)" (*Corr.* 1:1–2; 26 December 1704). The meaning here too is clear: Wycherley's *Miscellany Poems* had just been published, to critical disdain.

In the early correspondence there is language of debt and obligation. Pope clearly felt himself indebted to Wycherley for the favor of his friendship, and Wycherley soon made that debt real by extending material help. In the midst of a correspondence with Wycherley that Thomas De Quincey said reminded him of "village cocks from neighboring farms, endeavouring to overcrow each other" ([1889–90] 1968, 4:255–56; quoted in Mack 1985, 838), several amazing documents follow each other closely. The first is a letter from William Walsh to Wycherley thanking him for showing the manuscript of Pope's *Pastorals*:

I have read them over several times with great satisfaction. The Preface is very judicious and very learned; and the verses very tender and easy. The author seems to have a particular genius for that kind of poetry, and a judgment that much exceeds the years you told me he was of. He has taken very freely from the ancients, but what he has mixt of his own with theirs, is no way inferior to what he has taken from them. 'Tis no flattery at all to say, that Virgil had written nothing so good at his age. I shall take it as a favor if you will bring me acquainted with him. (*Corr.* 1:7; 20 April 1705)

Mack points out that it is no flattery indeed: Virgil had written nothing at all by the age of sixteen (1985, 98). Each time Pope reprinted this letter, he included a footnote pointing out the source of Walsh's qualifications to judge Pope's early poems. Walsh is identified as "Of Abberley in Worcestershire, Gentleman of the Horse in Queen Anne's reign, Author of several beautiful pieces in Prose and Verse, and in the opinion of Mr. Dryden, (in his postscript to Virgil), the best critic of our nation in his time" (*Corr.* 1:7; 20 April 1705).

Soon thereafter, Jacob Tonson solicits Pope in highly flattering terms, apologizing for having ignored him once before and asking if Pope will do him the favor of allowing him to print the poems:

Sir,—I have lately seen a pastoral of yours in Mr. Walsh's & Mr. Congreves hands, which is extreamly fine & is generally approved off [*sic*] by the best judges in poetry. I remember I have formerly seen you at my shop & am sorry I did not improve my acquaintance with you. If you design your poem for the press no person shall be more careful in the printing of it, nor no one can give a greater incouragement to it; than sir your most obedient humble servant Jacob Tonson. (*Corr.* 1:17; 20 April 1706)

From his pastoral retreat, Pope had spread his net and drawn in some of the most influential patrons around. Like the *Essay on Criticism*, Pope's pastorals are a record of the social aspects of his quest for fame. The poems record, in turn, debts gleefully incurred and then ungracefully paid. The pastorals are a ledger sheet on which Pope writes his debts to older males: "These pastorals were written at the age of sixteen, and then past thro' the hands of Mr. *Walsh*, Mr. *Wycherley*, G. *Granville*, afterwards Lord *Lansdown*, Sir William *Trumbal*, Dr. *Garth*, Lord *Halifax*, Lord *Somers*, Mr. *Mainwaring*, and others. All these gave our author the greatest encouragement, and particularly Mr. *Walsh*, (whom Mr. Dryden, in his postscript to Virgil, calls the best critic of his age)" (TE 1:59n). By now he has become heavily leveraged and has done nothing to pay his patrons back except to dedicate each pastoral to one of them—spring to William Trumbull, summer to Samuel Garth, Autumn (fittingly) to Wycherley, and Winter to Mrs. Tempest, a deceased friend of William Walsh's. Wycherley thanked Pope for publicizing their connection: "I am pleas'd with the good news of your going to print some of your poems, and proud to be known by them to the publick for your friend" (*Corr.* 1:41; 27 February 1707/8).

Wycherley soon began to call in his debts, and Pope found he would have to offer aid more material than loud flattery, hero worship, and free publicity. Their transactions began amicably enough, with Pope reading Wycherley's "Epistle to Mr. Dryden," an elaborately witty praise poem (Pope 1935). The path of their friendship can be traced in miniature from this transaction to the next: from triangulating their friendship through the figure of Dryden, they begin to negotiate directly with each other. The net of obligation begins to tighten around Pope as the third figure of Dryden drops out, leaving him to negotiate with Wycherley directly, unmediated through the ancients. Soon Wycherley "laid a penance" upon Pope, asking him to "look over that damned Miscellany of Madrigals of mine to pick out (if possible) some that may be so altered that they may yet apeare in print again I hope with better success than they hitherto have done" (*Corr.* 1:15; 22 March 1705/6). Pope may have taken his charge a bit too literally, and found himself engaged in the burdensome task of "correcting" Wycherley's verses. Soon he began to complain that Wycherley failed to appreciate him. His sense of awe evaporated.

Years after Wycherley's death, in a letter to the reader anonymously prefaced to volume two of the *Posthumous Works of William Wycherly* (1729), Pope explained why the whole editing project had taken so long and proved so fruitless. His reasons included "the known inability of Mr. Wycherley in versification, added to the decay of his memory; the impossibility which his friend at last found of rendering them perfect pieces of poetry, even tho' he should have entirely new-written them; the conviction by several instances, that the more he should bring them to approach to it, the less he should obtain the end proposed of having them pass for Mr. Wycherley's; and lastly, his sincere opinion that they would make a worse figure as verses unequal and undigested, without ornament method or musick, than as single maxims or apothegms of good sense in prose" (1986, 311).

"Never was more friendly advice, or a truer judgment given," Pope concluded, wondering why the giving of it had only made Wycherley suspicious and guarded (Pope 1986, 311). And he may well have wondered: his habit of elaborate self-justification had allowed him to erase his part in it from his own mind. Years earlier, as the extent of Wycherley's aggravation was becoming known, Pope pronounced himself free of obligation because of the very Christian passivity with which he bore the old man's complaints: "Wheareas I must otherwise have been a little uneasy to know my incapacity of returning his obligations, I may now, by bearing his frailties, exercise my gratitude and friendship more, than himself either is, or perhaps ever will be sensible of" (quoted in Ruffhead 1769, 47).

Walsh, unlike Wycherley, had the good fortune to die before calling in Pope's debts to him. He thus merited a long epideictic set piece at the end of the *Essay on Criticism:*

Such late was Walsh—the Muse's judge and friend,
Who justly knew to blame or to commend;
To failings mild, but zealous for desert;
The clearest head, and the sincerest heart.
This humble praise, lamented shade! receive,
This praise at least a grateful Muse may give:
The Muse, whose early voice you taught to sing,
Prescrib'd her heights, and prun'd her tender wing,
(Her guide now lost) no more attempts to rise,
But in low numbers short excursions tries:
Content, if hence th'unlearn'd their wants may view,
The learn'd reflect on what before they knew.
Careless of censure, nor too fond of fame;
Still pleas'd to praise, yet not afraid to blame,
Averse alike to flatter, or offend;
Not free from faults, nor yet too vain to mend.   (TE 1:325–26)

This is an amazing hymn to an orderly generational transfer of resources. The sixteen lines run in parallel constructions marked by strong caesuras. There is strong parallelism, too, in the way the lines figure Walsh's and Pope's relation to each other: the first four describe Walsh from a perspective, as it were, below him (he has transcended the world); the last four describe Pope himself from a perspective, it seems, slightly above him (he is held in check by the world). The structure of the lines is like a Doric column, with Walsh perched atop and Pope holding up the base. The central column depicts Pope's Muse as a vehicle on which Walsh's spirit is carried down to Pope, who, self-disciplined, disciplines others in turn. This is the ideal relationship for a young man to have with an old man. The old man is dead; the young man stands between his spirit and the world, becoming the very standard of obligation. This portrait had an afterlife, however: Pope consciously echoed it a few years later in a darker, more searing meditation on male rivalry.

Addison, Politeness, and Moral Duty

Quod Te Roma legit, Rumpitur Invidia!
If meagre Gildon draws his venal quill,
I wish the man a dinner, and sit still;
If D———s rhymes, and raves in furious fret,
I'll answer D———s, when I am in debt:
Hunger, not Malice, makes such authors print,

And who'll wage war with Bedlam or the Mint?
But were there one whom better stars conspire
To bless, whom Titan touch'd with purer Fire,
Who born with talents, bred in arts to please,
Was form'd to write, converse, and live, with ease:
Should such a man, too fond to rule alone,
Bear, like the Turk, no brother near the throne,
View him with scornful, yet with jealous eyes,
And hate for Arts that caus'd himself to rise;
Damn with faint praise, assent with civil leer,
And without sneering, teach the rest to sneer;
Or pleas'd to wound, and yet afraid to strike,
Just hint a fault, and hesitate dislike;
Alike reserv'd to blame, or to commend,
A tim'rous foe, and a suspicious friend:
Fearing e'vn fools, by flatterers besieg'd;
And so obliging that he ne'er oblig'd;
Who when two Wits on rival themes contest,
Approves them both, but likes the worst the best:
Like Cato, give his little Senate laws,
And sit attentive to his own applause;
While Fops and Templars ev'ry sentence raise,
And wonder with a foolish face of praise.
What Pity, Heav'n! if such a Man there be.
Who would not weep, if A———n were he?   (TE 6:142–3)[14]

Joseph Addison preached the practical virtue of politeness to a society of spectators. Historians agree that politeness spread throughout Europe in the sixteenth and seventeenth centuries, becoming a culturally desirable standard of behavior for courtiers and aristocrats. In the early eighteenth century, Addison and Richard Steele began to disseminate the ideal of politeness to the middle classes and to recommend it for public life.[15] Addison used a careful set of distinctions when writing, as he frequently did, about this topic in *The Spectator* and elsewhere. Rather famously, he saw himself as bringing "philosophy" (by which he meant principles for the conduct of life) "out of closets and libraries, schools and colleges, to dwell in clubs and assemblies, at teatables, and coffee-houses" (*Spectator* 10, 2 March 1711; Addison and Steele 1965, 1:44). At the same time, he saw himself as a spokesman for values of refinement and gentility that, when they were practiced by courtiers, grew "troublesome" and "encumbered with show and ceremony." "At present therefore," he writes, "an unconstrained carriage, and a certain openness of behavior are the height of good breeding. The fashionable world is grown free and easie; our manners sit more loose upon us: nothing is so modish as an agreeable negligence. In a word, good breeding shows it self most, where to an ordinary eye it appears least" (*Spectator* 119, 17 July 1711; Addison and Steele 1965, 1:487).

The new middle-class ideal of politeness was especially, though problematically, connected to trade. "In theory," writes Paul Langford, "politeness comprehended, even began with, morals, but in practice it was as much a question of material acquisitions and urbane manners. It both permitted and controlled a relatively open competition for power, influence, jobs, wives and markets" (1989, 4–5). Kant might have called politeness a hypothetical imperative, something we do in order to achieve a certain end. Politeness was an ideal sought after in London, the urban center of Whiggism, mercantilism, commercialism, and fashion. It was both the hallmark of status, of having achieved gentility, and a means of achieving status. So some objects and customs were marked as polite—table manners, clothing, habitations, and so on; but politeness could also mean a quality of person in which you bind yourself with constraints, inhibitions, and displays of deference to others to pursue status more effectively. In both senses, politeness is obviously an extrinsic norm, something you do so that other people can see you doing it. Why then does Addison demand that good breeding be invisible if a person can trade more effectively by displaying his trustworthiness and gentility?

An obvious answer is that in a society in which displaying politeness can bring greater access to "power, influence, jobs, wives and markets," people should care very much whether politeness is a cover for self-interest. This was a common doubt about politeness in both its courtly and its middle-class versions. Lawrence Klein explains that Shaftesbury—who as an aristocrat and ideologue of landed gentry saw politeness as strongly *distinct* from trade— nevertheless worried that in being polite and sociable we self-servingly feed our need for high regard and esteem (1994, 76). Shaftesbury and Addison addressed the problem of self-interest differently. Shaftesbury sought to discipline the moral sense so that a person would both feel and act on the feelings that lead to politeness. Addison's answer is to bury self-interest deeper inside, an answer that is very precarious in a culture obsessed with detecting false politeness. Take, for instance, Addison's own cousin, Eustace Budgell, who in 1714 published a translation of Theophrastus's *Characters,* one of a plethora of such translations to appear in the century's early decades. As Budgell arranges the characters, the first five center around the failures of politeness and the

problem of how to detect hypocrisy. They are dissimulation, flattery, imper-
tinence in discourse, rusticity, and false complaisance. He described dissimulation as:

the art of speaking and acting in disguise, to bring about some selfish design. The dissembler makes a visit to the enemy, as if he were so far from hating him that he took
a particular pleasure in his consideration. He praises and caresses those whom he undermines, and is outwardly inconsolable for their misfortunes, whilst he rejoices at
them in his heart. If you speak ill of him, he is so meek as to forgive you. If you utter
the most bitter invectives against him, he thanks you for telling him his faults. After
having done a man an injury, he redoubles his professions of friendship, and sweetens
him out of his resentments.

The dissembler is both banal and the deeply sinister. If "we," the reader,
overlook for a moment his plan "to bring about some selfish design," we might
appreciate him for sweetening us out of our resentments. He has social gifts.
Yet somehow we suspect the cheat and begin rather unaccountably to "utter
the most bitter invectives against him." We become both paranoid and impotent. Of course, I am assuming that we identify with the "you" of the passage,
rather than with the dissembler—we are not supposed to take this passage as
a manual for succeeding at trade. However, Budgell shows how even the
appearance of politeness is not enough to satisfy us, given our suspicious
natures. Indeed, in his preface to the translation he seems to make a psycho-
aesthetic claim for suspicion, arguing that Theophrastus's characters are so
formally perfect because of their roots in intense emotion: "The very life and
soul of these characters seems to consist in their being struck at an heat, and
in a peculiar smartness and turn, which ought, if possible, to be preserved in
every sentence. If the reader is diverted in the midst of a character, and his attention called off to anything foreign to it, the lively impression it should have
made is quite broken, and it loses half its force." Budgell concludes that
"Theophrastus was the spectator of the age he lived in," as though what it
means to be a spectator is to have the capacity to detect cheaters and strike
their characters out at a heat. In turning now from "the spectator of the age
he lived in" to the author of The Spectator, we find a widespread concern with
detecting cheaters pervading Addison's milieu.

One contradiction in Addison's character has particularly fascinated his biographers (see Smithers 1968, 15ff.). This is his way of combining remarkable
reserve and generous sociability. "Of his habits, or external manners, nothing
is so often mentioned as that timorous or sullen taciturnity, which his friends
called modesty by too mild a name," wrote Samuel Johnson of a man elsewhere celebrated for his conversational ease (1967, 2:118). Pope judged Addi-

son's contrasts harshly: "Addison was perfect good company with intimates, and had something more charming in his conversation than I ever knew in any other man. But with any mixture of strangers, and sometimes with only one or with any man he was too jealous of, he seemed to preserve his dignity much, with a stiff sort of silence" (Spence 1966, 1: 62). Pope leaves us with the impression that Addison was silent less from shyness than from insecurity: charming to his close friends, he turned frostily silent when his status was challenged by an outsider. But outsiders were occasionally admitted, and they busily scrutinized each other for signs of hypocrisy.

A deliciously complicated trait in Addison is "his practice when he found any man invincibly wrong to flatter his opinions by acquiescence, and sink him yet deeper in absurdity" writes Johnson. According to Johnson, Swift found Stella adopting the same social practice, although "whether this proceeded from her easiness in general, or from her indifference to persons, or from her despair of mending them, or from the same practice which she much liked in Mr. Addison, I cannot determine; but when she saw any of the company very warm in a wrong opinion, she was more inclined to confirm them in it than oppose them. . . . 'It prevented noise,' she said, 'and saved time'" (Johnson 1967, 1:124).

What sort of trait is this? It seems to mark the height of complaisance in the sense made brilliantly vivid by Richard Wendorf writing about the life of Sir Joshua Reynolds. *Complaisance,* now an archaic form, meant "the habit or action of making oneself agreeable, obliging, courteous, polite" (OED). It is different from our familiar word *complacency,* taking "pleasure or satisfaction in one's own condition or doings, self-satisfaction" (OED). Addison was an apostle of complaisance. In the *Guardian* he described complaisance as a "social virtue" that

renders a superior amiable, an equal agreeable, and an inferior acceptable. It smooths distinction, sweetens conversation, and makes every one in the company pleased with himself. It produces good-nature and mutual benevolence, encourages the timorous, soothes the turbulent, humanises the fierce and distinguishes a society of civilised persons from a confusion of savages. In a word, complaisance is a virtue that blends all orders of men together in a friendly intercourse of words and actions, and is suited to that equality in human nature which every one ought to consider, so far as it is consistent with the order and the oeconomy of the world. (*Guardian,* 528; no.162, 1713)[16]

Addison's praise of this social virtue darkens Swift's anecdote. Addison's habit of seeming to agree with people whose opinions he finds boorish is a kind of complaisance. Certainly Stella intends complaisance by imitating it— "it prevented noise" and "saved time." But she may also, Swift hints, intend to imitate Addison while acting from her own more generous motives. And what motivated Addison to agree with those he despised? Notice that in the *Guardian* passage Addison does not argue that complaisance *diminishes* differences in status or rank—rather it "smooths distinction" and "makes every one in the company pleased with himself." The "friendly intercourse of words and actions" that results is not social space made free from status inequities. Instead it is a society in which people have simply become better adjusted to their roles. As Richard Wendorf has remarked, the goal of complaisance is social complacence—a satisfaction with one's place (1996, 15). Addison furthers this secondary goal of complaisance when he "flatters wrong opinions by acquiescence" and "sinks his opponent yet deeper in absurdity." His opponent most likely grows more pleased with himself than ever, little realizing how low he's sinking. The seeming target of complaisance—the opponent—turns out to be an occasion for complaisance directed toward other members of the group—those in the know, whose status rises on awareness of the joke. Addison's complaisance thus "makes every one in the company pleased with himself" at each other's expense, smoothing distinctions by making them both more real and less apparent.

Pope, it would seem initially, has badly misread the source of Addison's social manipulation. Far from being kind to friends and cold to strangers, Addison is kindest of all to those he hates. He grew particularly kind to Pope after Pope sent him a draft of the sketch that would later become Atticus. After this Thomas Burnet, an occasional little senator at Button's, wrote, "It has very often made me smile at the pitifull soul of the man, when I have seen Addison caressing Pope, whom at the same time he hates worse than Beelzebub & by whom he has been more than once lampooned" (quoted in Sherburn 1934, 116). Burnet is a satirist, smiling at the pitiful soul of the man; he alone can gauge the feelings that Addison is trying to conceal. His is a powerful, omniscient—and clearly socially advantageous—position. But such advantage is always temporary. Burnet's and Swift's intense search for signs of hypocrisy in others may result from their wish not to incur the very real cost in social status paid by those who fail to read Addison's affect correctly.

Pope has, of course, not misread Addison at all. Here is his story about how he came to draft and send the sketch. Sometime in the summer of 1715 or 1716,

Lord Warwick who was but a weak man himself told me one day that "it was vain of me to endeavour to be well with Mr. Addison, that his jealous temper would never admit of a settled friendship between us." To convince me of what he had said he assured me that "Addison had encouraged Gildon to publish those scandals and had given him ten guineas after they were published." The next day, while I was heated with what I heard, I wrote a letter to Mr. Addison to let him know that "I was not unacquainted with this behavior of his, that if I was to speak severely of him in return for it, it should not be in such a dirty way; that I should rather tell him himself fairly of his faults and allow his good qualities; and that it should be something in the following manner." I then adjoined the first sketch of what has been since called my satire on Addison. Mr. Addison used me very civilly ever after, and never did me any injustice that I know of from that time to his death, which was about three years after. (Spence 1966, 1:71–72)

Like Theophrastus, Pope has struck his character "out at a heat" after catching Addison at what he takes to be double-dealing. But by sending Addison the sketch in secret, Pope has (by his own account) not *cured* the vice but rather forced him to double deal more avidly and painfully. The tension lies not between the inside and outside of a group, but between the inside and outside of a person. Pope's sketch has completed Addison's social virtue of complaisance by forcing him to inhabit his social role with less show of inner difference.

Pope is only thus practicing an Addisonian norm, appropriate in some way to the new culture of politeness. In refining his notion of "good-breeding"— that quality that should be invisible to the "ordinary eye"—Addison paints a social virtue more theatrical even than complaisance. In *Spectator* 169 he writes:

There is no society of conversation to be kept up in the world without good-nature, or something which must bear its appearance, and supply its place. For this reason mankind have been forced to invent a kind of artificial humanity, which is what we express by the word *good-breeding*. For if we examine thoroughly the idea of what we call so, we shall find it to be nothing else but an imitation and mimickry of good-nature, or in other terms, affability, complaisance and easiness of temper reduced into an art. (Addison and Steele 1965, 2:165; emphasis in original)

Addison's notion here, as in the larger *Spectator* essay, is that social friction causes pain. We can alleviate that pain and encourage "compassion, benevolence, and humanity" by adopting the "artificial humanity" of good breeding. This moves us a step beyond complaisance, which does not so much relieve social pain as conceal from its object how precarious his social position really is. Complaisance allows an audience of spectators to benefit from unacknowledged social pain. But good breeding, or artificial humanity, is a social virtue in which staged interactions between audience and unwitting actor drop away. The well-bred person, whatever his inmost thoughts, imitates good nature, thus spreading the effects of good nature. Although Addison's essay briefly cautions against the wickedness of hypocrisy, hypocrisy (from the Greek *hupocrites*, 'putting on a role') that is exactly what he advocates.

In moving Addison along the track of social virtue, Pope has made him into a hypocrite—a true, complete, and practiced one—which is what the sketch diagnoses him to be. As in the Dennis portrait, there is something Longinian about a piece of art creating the very effect it describes. And yet the work of a Longinian orator is broadly public, whereas Pope initially sent the sketch privately, not publishing it until three years after Addison's death. He represents his action as fair return, tit for tat. Pope did eventually benefit from making his sketch public: the sketch has colored its moment, becoming a de facto historical record to be confronted or denied by subsequent writers, even skeptical ones.

Biographers of both Addison and Pope write as though their difficult friendship was always saturated with Pope's themes, especially the theme of double-dealing.[17] Addison once warned Lady Mary Wortley Montague to "leave [Pope] as soon as you can, he will certainly play you some devilish trick else," and diagnosed him as having an "appetite to satire" (Ault 1949, 113). Even when Addison benefited from Pope's satires, he found them uncomfortable and tasteless. John Dennis claimed that Pope approached him and asked him to write a piece of damning criticism about Addison's play *Cato* (1713). Pope then betrayed him by publishing a scurrilous pamphlet, *The Narrative of Dr. Robert Norris*, portraying Dennis as insane. Although the *Spectator* had not been especially friendly to Dennis, Addison was disgusted by Pope's tactics. Pope also published a scatological epigram about a Tory lady who pissed all over herself at a performance of *Cato* when she perceived the Whig triumph.

But if Pope was high-spirited, dirty, and aggressive, Addison was the smiler with the knife, covertly sponsoring Pope's literary rivals—Ambrose Philips's *Pastorals* and Thomas Tickell's translation of the first book of the *Iliad*. Pope also suspected Addison of paying Charles Gildon to write some satires about his body. Eventually the rivalry took on a political cast, with the Whig group at Button's coffee house opposing Pope's Tory (and later Scriblerian) friends. John Gay reported Addison's cool response to Pope's Homer:

I have just set down Sir Samuel Garth at the Opera. He bid me tell you, that every body is pleas'd with your translation, but a few at Button's; and that Sir Richard Steele told him, that Mr. Addison said Tickell's translation was the best that ever was in any language. . . . I am inform'd that at Button's your character is made very free with as to morals, &c. and Mr. A___ says, that your translation and Tickell's are both very well done, but that the latter has more of Homer. (*Corr.* 1:305; 8 July 1715)

Pope registered his annoyance about Tickell's rival translation, sponsored by the group at Button's, in a letter to James Craggs: "For they tell me, the busy part of the nation are not more divided about Whig and Tory, than these idle fellows of the feather about Mr. Tickell's and my translation. . . . [I]f our principles be well consider'd, I must appear a brave Whig, and Mr. Tickell a rank Tory; I translated Homer for the publick in general, and he to gratify the inordinate desires of one man only. We have, it seems, a great Turk in poetry, who can never bear a brother on the throne" (*Corr.* 1:306–7; 15 July 1715).

The presence of a Turkish sultan creates endless, pointless factions—pointless because they can be motivated by anything—politics, literature, jealousy. Addison, who sought to remain impartial and above the fray, has elevated faction to a formal principle, emptied of content. And yet like Hobbes, who thought that "compleasance" meant that "every man strive[s] to accommodate himselfe to the rest," Pope concludes that faction sponsored by Addison's presence can be suspended through complaisance: "But after all I have said of this great man, there is no rupture between us: We are each of us so civil and obliging, that neither thinks he is obliged. And I for my part treat with him, as we do with the Grand Monarch; who has too many great qualities not to be respected, tho' we know he watches any occasion to oppress us" (*Corr.* 1: 306–7; 15 July 1715).

Pope captures a dark aspect of the society Addison describes as based on "friendly intercourse of words and actions." In this society people watch each other suspiciously. The lower ranks, grudgingly respectful, scan for signs that their status is being lowered; the higher ranks look for their chance to oppress. In a society whose main currency is rivalry, any occasion for jealousy will serve as well as any other. Pope shows this neatly in a pun. Through the practice of civility he and Addison have avoided a rupture, he tells Craggs. In one version of the sketch Pope sent Addison, the word *rupture* is foregrounded. The tag reads, *"Quod Te Roma legit, Rumpitur Invidia!"* (That Rome chooses you, envy bursts forth! and also, That Rome reads you, envy bursts forth!) In a republic like Rome, advancement breeds an answering envy. Addison has been preferred by a Whig ruling elite, and his play has been lauded. That he is "chosen" or "read" (*legit*) can mean that people are jealous of either his political or his literary success. Or Rome can refer not to the Whig circle but to other members of the society of spectators. Their envy bursts forth not when they read Addison's play but when they discover his concealed motives.

Pope claimed to be an objective—if heated—monitor of Addison's virtues and vices: to punish Addison he "should rather tell him . . . fairly of his faults and allow his good qualities." We have seen that this mild-seeming diagnosis had a complicated effect on Addison, heightening the tension between out-ward appearance and inner feeling to an unbearable pitch. Pope knew what he had done: much later he told Spence that Addison "was very kind to me at first but my bitter enemy afterwards," revealing that he knew Addison's smiles were outward show (Spence 1966, 1:67). But presumably he didn't care in the way he had before that Addison was double-dealing, as long as he was not victimized by it.

We should, however, be as suspicious of a portrait that makes a hypocrite as Pope was of the hypocrite himself. A reading of the portrait will show that however cleverly Pope cures the vice by making it worse, he had more public (and finally more aesthetic) ambitions, and these ambitions committed him to a higher standard of moral complexity. For there is more to the sketch than a delineation of Addison's good and bad points. It also imagines a complicated interplay between its author, its audience, and its object, a complexity worthy of (indeed modeled on) Addison's practice of complaisance. And the complexity elevates the portrait above the vice it diagnoses. To see why, we should approach the structural complexity by following the lines of normativity: What obligation, exactly, is being imposed? What claim could the portrait have had on Addison? What made Addison regulate his conduct by that portrait?

If we imagine the portrait as intended for private circulation, it clearly meets one criterion of obligation: it gives Addison a reason to change his behavior. Yet in so doing, the portrait undercuts what might be called its moral force. For it makes no sense—does it?—to say that normative force comes from the portrait's recommendation of hypocrisy. We like to think that for a norm to have genuine force, it should penetrate us all the way through; yet by definition hypocrisy can not penetrate us that way. No one can be a hypocrite through and through. As Christine Korsgaard has written, "If you think that a characteristic is a vice, you might seriously dislike someone for having it: if it is bad enough, you may exclude that person from your society. Indeed your whole sense that another is for you a person, someone with whom you can interact in characteristically human ways, seems to depend on her having a certain complement of the moral virtues—or at least enough honesty and integrity so that you are neither a tool in her hands nor she in yours" (1996, 11). You would be unlikely to recommend that the person actively pursue the vice in order to arrive at virtue, she might add.

But Pope does just that, recommending a reason that most of us—including Addison—would reject as bad. The portrait forces Addison to be obli-gated by a motive the portrait itself disdains. Let's formulate Addison's thought this way: "I ought to *seem* to be good, and here is this portrait showing me *seeming* to be good, a condition that the portrait represents as bad." Pope's portrait seems to have a normative force only in an Addisonian—or Mandevillian—moral universe. And Mandevillianism is troubling precisely because we can so easily look through good motives to discover bad ones. Recall that the goal of complaisance is social harmony, but that goal can be served if you simply *look* as though you are being complaisant without actually *being* so. Kant, for one, found the pattern of submissiveness required by a benevolent society so distasteful that he based his moral system entirely within the individual consciousness. J. B. Schneewind explains: "A society built around the virtues of benevolence and kindness is for Kant a society requiring not only inequality but servility as well. If nothing is properly mine except what someone graciously gives me, I am forever dependent on how the donor feels toward me" (1992, 311).

Kant's follower Christine Korsgaard makes a point of puncturing this sort of false morality: "If the need to establish a cooperative system can obligate us to conform to the social contract, why doesn't that same need obligate us to behave ourselves in the first place?" (1996, 28). Why, in other words, doesn't Addison's complaisance lead him to be *good* rather than just *gentlemanly*? By obligating himself all the way down, he might have avoided trouble. Pope's exquisitely sensitive nervous system has detected Addison in a posture of false moral self-advertisement. Addison would have done well to conceal his motives a bit more effectively, expecting the society of avid spectators to detect the cheat as well. But the round of unmasking does not stop there: just as Pope can easily detect Addison's bad motives and hollow politeness, we readers find him recapitulating the lie by passing off an immoral motive as a moral one.

The most important fact about Addison's bad motives, in Pope's moralist view of them, is that they are visible. We might initially think that insight should cease now, when the moralist adopts his stance. A successful moralist must hide his shadow; moralism's shine must blind us. But Pope's character sketch leads us back into the territory of Wittgenstein's duck/rabbit, its normative authority deriving, in some odd sense, from its bad faith. Or so the portrait suggests. To see why, let us glance briefly at one of the most famous eighteenth-century avatars of moral perfection, Marcus Catonis Uticensis (Cato the younger), as depicted by Addison himself. In the play, Cato is holed up in Utica on the North African coast with a small band of Roman senators—his little senate. Julius Caesar, imperial dictator of Rome, is fast approaching, having conquered all of Rome's territories. Cato and his followers hold out for Republican principles. A rogue senator tries to foment rebellion, which Cato quashes by setting a stern example of virtuous behavior. Eventually Caesar defeats Cato's troops and offers him clemency, but Cato falls on his sword rather than live under a dictatorship. Addison represents Cato as having two motives for acting as he does—one early, one late. The first is a certain tendency to identify himself with what he takes to be Rome. Cato says, "My life is grafted on the fate of Rome" (21); "What a pity is it that we can die but once to serve our country"; "Thy life is not thine own when Rome demands it" (43). His confused associates repeatedly press him to fill in the emotional content of being Roman, but Cato refuses. Decius suggests rivalry, asking "What is a Roman, that is Caesar's foe?" But like Pope later in life, Cato points to the abstract: "Greater than Caesar, he's a friend to virtue" (21). Being a stoic, Cato is something of an assertive realist. He repeatedly eschews content for his motives, asserting that he is a Roman and therefore must act like a Roman. No wonder that a commentator has complained, "The trouble with [the] central character in this play is that he seems not to manifest virtue but rather to lay claim to it" (Lindsay [1974] 1988, x).

Yet by the final act of the play, we find Cato in a different mood. Now he is thinking about killing himself, and he sits alone, reading Plato's *Phaedo* on the immortality of the soul. He says:

> It must be so—Plato, thou reasonest well—
> Else whence this pleasing hope, this fond desire,
> This longing after immortality?
> Or whence this secret dread, and inward horror
> Of falling into naught? Why shrinks the soul
> Back in on herself, and startles at destruction?
> 'Tis the divinity that stirs within us;
> 'Tis heaven itself that points out an hereafter,
> And intimates eternity to man. . . .
> If there's a power above us
> (And that there is, all nature cries aloud
> Through all her works), he must delight in virtue;
> And that which he delights in, must be happy.
> But when, or where?—This world was made for Caesar:
> I'm weary of conjectures—this must end 'em.   (45–46)

Cato's identification with Rome seemed initially to be a moral action without a motive—a duty of a completely formal nature. But here we find out that Cato's moral duty has content. Why should he kill himself, he wonders? He answers: he *feels* that his soul is immortal, and therefore it must *be* immortal. This answer comes to him from looking around at his world. In nature he finds evidence of a power above him; the power above him must delight in virtue because he feels as though it does; and finally, the shoddy world is fit only for his sleazy rival Caesar, so best to take himself out of it. Putting both of Cato's reasons for acting together—one grounded in motives (I act this way because I feel I ought to), the other completely motiveless (I act this way because I act this way)—we have a realist duty arising from personal sentiment. Cato's feelings, in other words, track the truth. They correspond to the way things really are, out there.

But let us not forget that Cato is a character in a play, dramatizing his realism in front of an audience. Members of that audience were quick to fill in motives of sentiment, finding Cato's early stoicism, rather than his death scene, especially moving. Were these audience members moved to the cause of Rome, or were they moved to some analogous duty in their own lives? Pope says both. In his prologue to *Cato,* he asked: "While Cato gives his little senate laws, / What bosom beats not in his country's cause?" The *his* here is ambiguous—it suggests either patriotism directed toward England or (oddly?) directed towards Cato's Rome. But in a letter to John Caryll, Pope was more explicit about the moral function of the drama:

I have had lately the entertainment of reading Mr. Addison's tragedy of Cato. The scene is in Utica, and the time, the last night of his life. It drew tears from me in several parts of the fourth and fifth acts, where the beauty of the virtue appears so charming that I believe (if it comes upon the theatre) we shall enjoy that which Plato thought the greatest pleasure an exalted soul could be capable of, a view of virtue itself great in person, colour, and action. The emotion which the mind will feel from this character and the sentiments of humanity which the distress of such a person as Cato will stir in us, must necessarily fill an audience with so glorious a disposition, and so warm a love of virtue, that I question if any play had ever conduced so immediately to morals as this. (*Corr.* 1:173; February 1712/13?)

Even if we doubt whether all of Cato's actions are moral in any sense, we would endorse (observing how Cato's feelings stir at the thought of death, the Numidian prince Juba says, "Rome fills his eyes / with tears, that flowed not o'er his own dead son"), the "beauty of [his] virtue" "conduces" us to "morals." Cato now becomes the conduit through which our own feelings track the truth. Watching the play, we get a little realist hit. Ironically, both the Whigs and Tories in the audience felt that they were the beneficiaries of that realist hit.

We are now in a position to appreciate the normative force of Pope's Addison portrait. Like Cato, "A——n" is a stoic of sorts. Refusing to acknowledge his rivalrous feelings, he claims affective detachment, choosing life above the fray. Emotional risk is avoided through passivity; sociability is commuted into sublime indifference. But sociability is the broadest context and meaning of his behavior, especially the ranked social life of anxious men, of men not only prone to faction, loyalty, and groupishness, but also subject to jealous fractures and rivalries. Cato, looking like a stiff piece of antique furniture, is hauled out onto the stage; and suddenly London is alive with excitement— the excitement of pouring out its patriotic feelings onto a sublimely immovable figure, the excitement of having all that emotion count as virtue. "A———n" too looks wooden, yet covertly demands and solicits emotion. His little senators take his demands as regulative, subsuming themselves under their law-like character. His impersonalism allows them both to vent their feelings and to succor the illusion of objectivity. Because of the presence of their sultan, "A———n," their partial, possibly self-deceptive feelings track the truth. This is what it means to be part of a group of males tightly wound around a single dominant figure and his cause.

Pope had sat stonily by while Gildon drew his poisoned pen for money and Dennis raved and fretted. He now finds himself awash in sentiment, appealing to heaven itself to pass judgment on "such a man." The impersonal structure of the question ("Who would not weep?") allows the portrait to function imperatively, as a moral type of emotional meaning. But the impersonal address also implies a broader audience—a small coterie of polite friends, perhaps. Now the pathos of the scene resides not in "A———n"'s covert manipulations, but in the sure bonds between an invisible group of men openly weeping for the fall of one of their own, one who was "born," "bred," and "form'd" to join their club.

Traditionally on the evidence of such lines, Pope critics have found that his poetry forms part of what Thomas Woodman calls a "polite consensus" among cultivated males of the period (1989, 126). Depending on our critical commitments, we might find ourselves nostalgic for such a consensus or repelled by it. Pope's portrait, its low motives and high rhetoric both in view, makes it clear, however, that being part of such a polite consensus allows us to play the game of exposure. "A———n"'s friends think their emotions track the truth. Their claim of realism gives Pope an occasion to expose their bad motives. Exposing their realism as fantasy gives Pope the feeling that he tracks the truth. Exposing his low motives gives us that feeling too, and so on.

Writing in 1695, Abel Boyer defined politeness as the art of pleasing in public. This was an ideal that Addison refined and promoted; in fact, the culture of politeness, in all of its appeal and limitations, is still associated with his name. There are various narratives to tell, each with a different theoretical resonance, about how the Addisonian ideal caused later writers to imitate or rebel. Many of these narratives depend on the concept of *internalization*, a word with strong Nietzschian resonances deployed most recently by Foucauldians like Judith Butler (1997) to describe how power creates a subject-effect. Kantians, for example, tell a story about how the great project of Kantian moral psychology, and by extension the Enlightenment self, was born in reaction to spectator morality. And Romanticists like M. H. Abrams and Harold Bloom have long pointed to an eighteenth-century revolution in inwardness and self-consciousness during which reflective humans began to take features of the natural world to be dependant on their psychology.

In a few of these scenarios, conflict with other people plays a decisive role in how we acquire our capacity for self-reflection. In the Bloomian version, agon is the introjection of battles for status and power. The story I have been telling here involves Pope's arms race to outsmart his fellow social animals across the course of his early career. In this story, early status games are introjected, and what results is an elaborately ritualized psychology of dominance and submission. These portraits demand that we reject any clear dualism of psychology and society, inner and outer, private and public. For they show us how normative realism, delighted exposure, and the moral stance again are psychological positions that people assume because of the demands of their spectator culture. Blindness and insight are inevitably bound. The engine driving the evolution of the moral law within is other people. The rule that guides the evolution of morality could be phrased as a variant of Harold Bloom's well-known interpretive rule that the meaning of a poem is always another poem: the reason for a person is always another person.

Chapter Four

Abstraction, Reference, and the Dualism of Pope's *Dunciad*

Like most metaphors, the *Dunciad* (1728–43) is supposed to engage us on two semantic levels: first, what the poem says; and second, what it implies or subtly impresses upon us.[1] The two levels can be described according to common binaries found in recent literary theory: presence/absence, conscious/unconscious, manifest content/latent content, overt meaning/hidden power. Or they can be described as awesome and ineffable: "The *Dunciad*," muses Helen Deutsch "like a ruined building in a classical garden, mesmerizes like an 'Ornament and Curiosity on dead bodies'" (1996, 180).[2] Emrys Jones has reflected carefully on the situation, and I borrow the terminology of "two levels" from him:

> Like some other great works of its age . . . the *Dunciad* seems to engage us on more than one level. The first level one might describe as a level of deliberate artistry: the poet works in terms of play of wit, purposeful allegory, triumphantly pointed writing, in all of which we are made aware of the pressure of a highly critical and aggressive mind. But on another level the poetry works more mysteriously and obscurely: one seems to see *past* the personal names and topical allusion to a large fantasy-world, an imaginative realm which is infused with a powerful sense of gratification and indulgence. The first level is primarily stimulating to the mind, while the second works affectively in altogether more obscure ways. (1980, 616)

I have already used the vocabulary of two levels to liken the *Dunciad* to a metaphor, but we might, by a simple translation, liken the poem to language itself, to a dream, or to the human psyche. Yet what strikes us about the *Dunciad* from Emrys Jones's and almost every other substantive description of it is that the two levels do not interpenetrate: they remain separate, each untranslated by the other. Unlike most metaphors, the tenor and vehicle of the poem seem mutually indifferent if not exclusive. Sensuousness ("primarily stimulating to the mind") and abstraction (working "in altogether more obscure ways") do not flow between the two levels, but they flow instead between each level and some discrete capacity of the reader's. Whereas terms for metaphor in literary theory describe a fusion of sensuous and abstract, the vocabulary of two levels leaves us with no mechanism for explaining why the *Dunciad* is not simply two different poems inhabiting the same space.

This chapter will show that the pervasive mode of interpretation of the *Dunciad* is dualist, holding it to be two unfused poems. Such a reading is not something we impose to explain the poem's aesthetic difficulty (even failure). Earlier in this century, the poem's undigested doubleness was indeed considered an embarrassment for aesthetic criteria by formalists in Pope studies.[3] Various formalist bandages were applied to cover up the poem's holes, yet these seemed like special pleading on behalf of organic unity. The dualism results, not from our attempts to salvage sublimity within the poem's localism, but from the very impossibility of Pope's historical project. Any mode of reading, from the most formalist to the most historicist, will fail to make the poem coherent because Pope failed to make the poem coherent. This incoherence, this unknitting of a continuous authorial intention, is no trivial matter. It is not the result of slippages in language or of the independent career of the poem's words; nor is it the case that a continuous poetic intention is in some trivial sense impossible. If any general feature of language is to blame, it is that words do not "hook on" to the world. And the poem's fascination only increases when we adopt a charitable stance toward Pope's intentions, understanding his massive attempts to suture words and the world. The poem's dualism results from Pope's ambitious and increasingly strident desire to engage in reference. Why this project should fail is the question this chapter seeks to answer.

Without much reflection, we can see that Pope failed in his ambition. He meant his poem to have material effects on real people, to "rid [himself] of these insects" (TE 5:xi). Lytton Strachey wrote appreciatively, if figuratively, that our having been born after Pope means that "we run no danger of waking up one morning to find ourselves exposed, both now and forever, to the ridicule of the polite world—that we are hanging by the neck, and kicking our legs, on the elegant gibbet that has been put up for us by the little monster of Twit'nam" (1925, 1). Yet Pope never stopped revising, despite the straightforward mode of reference he practiced in the poem's early drafts. Why not? Pope never felt sure his work was done, the gibbet erected, the victim hung—if he had, the *Dunciad* would have been done, the poem spent. Instead, the little monster's poem grew into a big monster, its "universal darkness" effectively swallowing the little monster himself (for powerful reflections on this topic, see Noggle 1996). And suddenly the final draft begins confusingly to refer to events and people long past with a fresh, almost manic, energy.[4]

Pope faced two insurmountable barriers to reference—one generic, one linguistic. The *Dunciad* may have practical failure built in: it is widely acknowledged that satire bakes no bread, nor does it unseat any governments.[5] The second barrier to reference is markedly general, having little to do with the *Dunciad* itself. According to the empiricist linguistic tradition that begins with John Locke, abstraction is unavoidable when we seek to refer to objects. Following out this line, we could shape the thought this way: abstraction of language causes a complicated failure of poetic reference; this in turn causes the poem's failure to achieve material effects on real people.[6]

Abstraction and Reference

Allow me to explore this latter hypothesis at length. Proper names play the same role in Pope's *Dunciad* that they play in eighteenth-century theories of language: they anchor the poem in its particularity, just as for Locke and Berkeley, proper names anchor words to the world first and last. A corollary is that proper names play the same role with respect to generality in Pope's poem as in these philosophical systems. A special case of reference, proper names convey meaning into the system as a whole, where it (meaning) becomes locked into the figurative aspects of language. This chapter describes the resulting oblique relationship between the system and its initial "building blocks"[7]—that is, between general terms and proper names—a relationship that at its uneasiest links two different orders of language, one figuratively and one causally connected to the world. In essence, this relationship places some words, which have meaning, in tension with others, which have reference.

The conflict between meaning and reference seems most vital and most intractable in light of critique—Berkeley's critique of Locke's *Essay Concerning Human Understanding* (1690) in the opening pages of *Principles of Human Knowledge* (1710), and Pope's revisionary critique of the *Dunciad* (1728), and *Dunciad Variorum* (1729) in the *New Dunciad* (1742) and *Dunciad in Four Books* (1743). All of these critiques name the source of the tension between meaning and reference as a variant of *abstraction*, that is, the mode by which the particular becomes the general. But it is also an ambiguous and self-contradictory feature of human psychology—one whose necessity Berkeley doubts in a thought experiment about a "solitary man" who "shall never have had occasion to make use of universal signs for his ideas" (1909, introduction). Here the analogy between Pope's poetic and an empiricist philosophical interest in the relation between particular and general terms hardens. The analogy between Pope's early Dunciads and Locke's system looks surprisingly apt when we realize that both writers distinguish between abstraction and figurativeness (a special variety of abstraction), and that both are committed to naming the latter as the true cause of rupture between reference and meaning.[8]

I will return to Pope's uneasiness on this point later; Locke's uneasiness is somewhat easier to summarize. Locke's system initially accommodates both particular and general terms; he posits no essential conflict between reference and meaning.[9] He distinguished between abstraction and figure, seeking to understand the process by which proper names become general terms, while stripping words of their sophistical power to "interpose themselves so much between our understandings and the truth which it would contemplate and apprehend that, like the medium through which visible objects pass, their obscurity and disorder does not seldom cast a mist before our eyes and impose upon our understandings" (1988, 488). For Locke, abstraction is the process that moves us seamlessly from the particular to the general; while figurativeness, a "perfect cheat," is the condition that prevents us from returning back down the same road.[10]

From the earliest framing of the *Dunciad* to its final revision, Pope was vexed by how to translate figurative into causal languages, meaning into reference. That they remain untranslated is the true origin of a widespread formalist view cited earlier that the *Dunciad* is aesthetically problematic. For if a poem has two incommensurable orders of language within it, one roughly corresponding to poetry and the other to reference, it fails by definition to achieve internal consistency. The lack of internal consistency has been a surprisingly fertile source of anxiety for Pope's critics. Historically, formalist critics have been optimistic about Pope's aesthetic success, arguing that he eventually discarded all of the poem's indigestible matter, or what his nineteenth-century editor called the "inference(s) which Pope chose to found on the real actions of the various persons whom he satirizes," in favor of a higher, more sublime, aesthetic (Whitwell Elwin in Pope 1871–89, 4:21). In the poem's early versions, so the argument goes, the poetic and the merely personal rival each other for space: personal satire and invective sit uncomfortably alongside material Pope recycles from the Bible, Virgil, and Milton. Tending to prefer the Bible, Virgil, and Milton to "giant libel," most critics have discovered that in the last two versions of his poem (1742 and 1743), Pope committed an especially Virgilian maneuver (A. Williams 1955, 6). He turned away from a low pastoral focus on hacks and dunces toward an epic focus on the sublime, maturely substituting "theology for Grub-street" (J. Warton 1782, 369) and "metaphysics for mock-heroic" (Brower 1959, 343).[11] As Brower put it, "Pope, we might say, found in the *New Dunciad* the poem he had been half-consciously writing 'toward' for some ten or fifteen years" (332).

Can we really think of the "two levels" as coming together in the 1742/1743 poem? Arguments that Pope made progress toward a unified poem seem borne out by his relative lack of hostility toward actual persons in the *New Dunciad,* the wealth of names in the earlier version having faded to ghostly blanks useful only for filling out the meter: "Great Shades of **, **, **, *" (line 537). Did Pope then simply lose the desire to correct the Dunces? Did his growing friendship with the clergyman William Warburton, whom he appointed his literary executor, induce him to seek a higher moral ground?[12] Or did he find such a slyly successful method of satirizing people that their identities have simply eluded generations of editors? His Twickenham editors note, for instance, that many Dunces in later versions of the poem have never been successfully identified (TE 5:xxxii).

A case in point concerns the manifest difficulties in interpreting Paridel, "a lazy, lolling sort" whom Dullness finds "stretched on the rack of a too easy chair" (TE 5:376). Paridel seems motivated mainly by his difference from Spenser's wandering squire Paridel in Book 3 of the *Faerie Queen.* The latter's restlessness, in turn, is not the antithesis to idleness but is thematically appropriate to his Trojan lineage and connection to Brute, Aeneas's descendant and founder of Troy-novant (i.e., the City of London, seat of an increasingly mobile finance capital and of Dullness herself). A plausible interpretation would be that Pope uses the name Paridel to highlights how far we have fallen from the principle of epic motivation in Spenser. Epic motivation, on this view, is antithetical to the obscurity of the Dunce—his distance from the Aeneas figures in Books 1 and 4 and his appearance in the poem after Dullness has left the City of London and claimed her seat at the palace of St. James make him seem a figure for lack of motivation. Are we to understand instead that Pope has someone definite in mind, a person whose identity would clear up the obscurity of the allusion and render such interpretive activity moot?

Pope neither gave up his aim of satirizing particular people nor began to speak in some obscure Spenserian code. Instead, he paradoxically embraced his enemy, adopting the very abstraction that he had been battling as a feature of language in earlier versions of the poem, even divesting it of its pictorialism, its figurativeness, its concrete particulars. We know that Pope never abandoned his satirical aim: in the decade or so between the publication of the old and new Dunciads, Pope visibly sought a more intense way to achieve an effect on his targets than just referring to them by name (or personal attributes), a practice he optimistically called "hunting one or two from the herd" (*Corr.* 3:423; 2 August 1734). In the *New Dunciad*, abstraction produces the effect that a wealth of particulars had failed to deliver. To Hugh Bethel, Pope wrote the following account of the *New Dunciad*: "And to give you ease in relation to the event of my poem; which, dealing much in General, not particular satire, has stirrd up little or no resentment. Tho it be leveld much higher than the former, yet men not being singled out from the herd, bear chastisement better, (like gally slaves for being all linkd in a string, & on the same rank)" (*Corr.* 4:396; 21 May 1742).

The *New Dunciad*, being general rather than personal, has failed to stir up the usual resentment; is this because it is a less effective piece of satire? Or, as Pope implies, is the lack of response to it evidence that it is a more effective piece of satire? If the latter is true, its greater effectiveness seems to have something to do with deindividuation: the poem's persons are stripped of their individuality and subordinated like "gally slaves." By 1742 Pope embraced abstraction in order to get around language's figurative habit of not referring to things, not—as readers as different as William Warburton and Colley Cibber thought—because he finally had to admit the impossibility of corrective satire.

To understand why Pope embraced abstraction in the *New Dunciad*, we must understand how his letter to Bethel both continues some of his earlier obsessions and reverses some of his earlier poetic procedures. At each stage of the composition of the whole *Dunciad* sequence, Pope claimed to have increased the satiric pressure on his targets, who were neither fictional characters nor personified abstractions, but real people whose characteristics could be checked against Pope's representations. Pope's obsession with correction had not lessened since 1726 when he wrote *Peri Bathous,* arguably the first piece in the enlarged Dunciad sequence. Yet if in 1742 his poetic procedure can be described as obscuring essentialism, in 1726 it can only be described as enlightening specificity. In *Peri Bathous* he defines obscure authors mostly by using recognizable parts of their names: "The Eels are obscure Authors, that wrap themselves up in their own Mud, but are mighty nimble and pert. L.W. L.T. P.M. General C"—L.W. is clearly Leonard Welsted and so forth. This technique of using names to point to specific persons depends on the empiricist hypothesis that particulars refer most intensely, and that proper terms, having no general applications, are the most particular terms of all.

This empirically based technique seems to have been Pope's ruling hypothesis through at least the mid-1730s. For example, in 1734 Pope defended personal satire to John Arbuthnot, who so disapproved of the practice that he

half-seriously made its abandonment a condition of his continuing friendship
with Pope: "To attack vices in the abstract, without touching persons may be
safe fighting indeed, but it is fighting with shadows. General propositions are
obscure, misty, and uncertain, compared with plain, full and home examples:
precepts only apply to our reason which in most men is but weak: examples
are pictures, and strike the senses, nay raise the passions, and call in those (the
strongest and most general of all motives) to the aid of reformation" (*Corr.*
3:419; 26 July 1734). Pope's defense of particular satire is notable partly because
in the letter to Bethel eight years later (quoted above) he uses identical terms
to argue for an opposite point of view. In the earlier letter, clarity of reference
is a feature of particulars; correction comes about through greater clarity of
reference and therefore through greater particularism. Pope's initial hypothesis about satiric effects is that the more particular he can be about a person,
the more closely he refers to that person; the more closely he refers to him or
her, the stronger the example he or she makes; the stronger the example the
person makes, the greater his or her motive (and that of Pope's readers) for
"reformation."

Pope took a strongly particularist line in the prefatory advertisement to the
Dunciad Variorum (1729): "Of the Persons it was judged proper to give some
account: for since it is only in this monument that they must expect to survive . . . it seemed but humanity to bestow a word or two upon each, just to
tell what he was, what he writ, when he lived, or when he dy'd. If a word or
two more are added upon the chief Offenders; 'tis only as a paper pinned upon
the breast, to mark the Enormities for which they suffered; lest the Correction
only should be remembered, and the Crime forgotten" (TE 5:8–9). How then
did Pope come to reverse himself by substituting for a description of the condition of actual people a question about their condition: What is it to be a person? We sharpen this question when we realize what a great barrier abstraction erects against the kind of reference Pope intended—indeed, how closely
most theories of satiric correction entail a fantasy of being able to tack words
directly onto the world by pinning a paper to a breast. Yet however powerful
it is, this particularist fantasy contains the seeds of its own destruction.

When Pope abandons his particularist line, deciding to subtract instead of
adding attributes, he leaves us with the following puzzle. Stripping a person
of her attributes may be a hostile gesture. Yet if one strips away too many attributes, a person ceases to be recognizable; therefore, the gesture seems no
longer hostile but merely misguided. How, then, did Pope come to think that
stripping people of all of their attributes was the best way to refer to the

essence, not just of the kind or species, but of the particular persons reading his poems? How, in short, did Pope come to see abstraction as a way to achieve the very intensity of effect that particular references were formerly meant to deliver?

To answer this question we need to understand Pope's successive attempts (corresponding to successive versions of the *Dunciad* and to movements within each version of the poem) to tether satiric correction to reference. We also need to understand his Lockean level of frustration with the pull of language toward figure, which imposes itself between the word and the world, deforming reference. Finally, we must try to understand how, in the final drafts, Pope's desire to have satire connect with its target, or to have meaning coincide with a referent, ends up promoting a situation in which it looks as though the world outside the poem has been annihilated.

Reference and the Descriptive Content of Proper Names

It is a curious fact that Pope's optimism about proper name references takes the same form as his pessimism about them. "Great Shades of **, **, **, *" (1742) is visually indistinguishable from many lines in the 1728 *Dunciad*, whose blanks were filled in by later versions of (and some spurious "keys" to) the poem: "**, **, and **, the wretches caught" (TE 5:xx). Pope's Twickenham editors suggest that he was initially anxious about legal recriminations (TE 5:xx), but a well-known loophole in eighteenth-century libel law specified that "innuendo," or "any word the referent for which was not immediately obvious when the word was taken out of context," did not count as evidence of a satirist's libelous intention.[13] At first Pope thought that by naming names he could attain perfectly indexical references without producing any knowledge of those referents: "I would not have the reader too much troubled or anxious, if he cannot decipher them; since when he shall have found them out, he will probably know no more of the Persons than before" (TE 5:206). In distinguishing between catching the wretches and characterizing them, Pope distinguishes between reference and meaning. Yet I think the 1742 edition imagines the Dunces as fictional characters ("great shades") because Pope found it impossible to make his references stick. To borrow terminology from a recent account of fictionality in the eighteenth century, it is not that the Dunces are ontological nobodies, although we cannot find that out from reading the *Dunciad*. But rather, we are increasingly forced to fall back on characterizing them as social or intellectual nobodies while remaining agnostic about their real existence. A reader of all the poem's versions might find herself witnessing the birth of a fictional mode as proper names gradually become unstuck from the Dunces' real selves.[14]

As it happens, modern philosophy has sponsored at least four distinct ventures in proper-name theory, each of which has been committed to understanding how proper names stick to their referents. They are (chronologically): the no-sense theory (J. S. Mill), sense theories (Gottlob Frege, Bertrand Russell), identifying (cluster) description theories (John Searle), and rigid designation/historical explanation theories (Saul Kripke, Keith Donellan). All presume the uniqueness of proper names: unlike general names, such as "cow" and "jelly," which designate a plurality or a class, proper names designate only one object.

Does this uniqueness entail a special set of rules for reference? Locke thought of general terms as the divergent case requiring explanation and rules; proper names are straightforwardly particular terms fitted to the particularity of things (1988, bk. 3, chap. 3, esp. 409–11). Yet post-Lockean philosophers have had no such confidence, unanimously finding that meaning is an obstacle to, instead of a guarantee of, true proper-name references. Thus Mill argues that proper names are necessarily meaningless—words become proper names as soon as they shed their connotations; they stop being proper names as soon as they acquire them again (see Gardner 1940, 8). At the other end of the line, Saul A. Kripke has argued that proper names are analytically true of their bearers whether or not any related identifying description can be found to be true of them. Thus the name *Aristotle* just refers to the person whose name that was, whether or not it is true that the person was the author of the works of Aristotle or was responsible for any of the deeds commonly ascribed to him (1972, esp. 23–70).[15]

John Searle's theory is the closest of all to Pope's practice; we can see the difficulties with Searle's theory by looking also at the difficulties Pope faces in the *Dunciad Variorum*. Heir to the empiricist tradition, Searle holds an "identifying description" theory, arguing that proper name references are fixed through a set of descriptive phrases associated with a name (1958, 170–73). The name *Aristotle* means that person who fulfills any set of descriptions: the teacher of Alexander, Plato's top student. We thus have to imagine a name surrounded by a cluster of descriptions as a planet is surrounded by satellites. Any single one of these descriptions could turn out to be untrue, but if the entire set turned out to be untrue, or if under historical investigation it comes to be replaced by a different set, *Aristotle* would come to mean the person who performed the set of actions newly associated with his name. The identity of the planet is thus determined by the configuration of its satellites.

Searle's is the only theory that states that the meaning of a proper name determines its referent (Frege's states that the meaning of a proper name is identical with the object for which it stands).[16] Yet because such a determination is contingent rather than necessary, it leaves open a significant area for doubt. I single out Searle's theory because if satire corresponds to any one of these theories, it corresponds to his. Understanding this, we have a way of explaining why satire is potentially always general rather than personal. A problem with Searle's view might be put like this: even when grouped into clusters, identifying descriptions can potentially fall wide of their mark. One can multiply identifying descriptions to an infinite degree without being sure that one has picked out the correct referent. Finally, even if one nails down all the relevant identifying descriptions of Aristotle and feels confident that the person referred to has a definite extension of those properties, one could always find out that Aristotle was an obscure Venetian nobleman of the fifteenth century (Kripke 1972, 27). Extension strongly predicts but can never guarantee intension.[17]

Translated into terms of art, Searle's problem means that one can never be sure one has caught the right wretch; periphrastic descriptions are exactly that—they speak around the person in question. Boileau shrewdly observes a certain "explicitness" in Horace's practice of naming his targets: "Horace is not contented with calling people by their names; he seems so afraid they should be mistaken, that he gives us even their sir-names; nay tells us the trade they followed or the employments they exercis'd: 'We were glad to leave (says he) the town of Fundi of which one Ausidius Luscus was Praetor, but it was not without laughing heartily at the folly of this man, who having been a clerk, took upon him the airs of a senator and a person of quality.' Could a man be described more precisely?" (quoted in Harte 1730, 13–14).

Horace does indeed describe Ausidius precisely by giving us explicit directions about how to find him if we so desire. Similarly, in Pat Rogers's vision of the *Dunciad*, Pope gives us a startlingly accurate street map of London and "fastidiously precise directions" to the homes of hack writers, complete with copious descriptive detail substituting for street numbers not yet in use ([1972] 1980, 79). Yet Boileau's final question seems to ask: Has this explicitness picked out the poem's referents or only looked as if it had done so?

This question point us to the *Dunciad Variorum*, which seems designed to answer two sorts of doubt about reference. The first is the straightforward doubt about whom Pope meant to name in the 1728 version of the poem, the one with the names left blank. Pope claimed to be writing the *Dunciad Variorum* as a key to the earlier poem (*Corr.* 2:502n). Such a key was necessary because authors of spurious keys had written incorrect names into the blanks, causing Pope to aim inadvertently at the wrong targets:

> It will be sufficient to say of this Edition, that the reader has here a much more correct and compleat copy of the Dunciad, than has hitherto appeared: I cannot answer but some mistakes may have slipt into it, but a vast number of others will be prevented, by the Names being now not only set at length, but justified by the authorities and reasons given. I make no doubt, the Author's own motive to use real rather than feign'd names, was his care to preserve the Innocent from any false Applications; whereas in the former editions which had no more than the Initial letters, he was made by Keys printed here, to hurt the inoffensive; and (what was worse) to abuse his friends, by an impression at Dublin. (TE 5:8)

The case would be trivial if the 1728 version had provided no descriptive information about those to whom the blanks referred (other than, say, metrical cues), but in fact, the blanks were incorrectly filled in despite a high degree of descriptive explicitness. For example, Dullness anoints Tibbald's head "And lo! her Bird (a monster of a fowl! / Something betwixt a H*** and Owl) / Perch'd on his crown!" In the earlier edition, a note appended to this line reads: "A strange Bird from Switzerland," suggesting that H*** is John James Heidegger, a Swiss theatrical impresario described as "the most ugly man that ever was formed." Yet because a Dublin edition had Hungerford (a lawyer and MP) for H***, Pope was made to add "a word or two more": "A strange bird from Switzerland, and not (as some have supposed) the name of an eminent Person, who was a man of parts, and as was said of Petronius, Arbiter Elegantiarum" (TE 5:92).

Pope's initial note nudges his readers into picking out a name; he presumes that our stock of common connotations is sufficiently predictable that we will supply the right name; yet he can deliver no guarantees. A foreign, independent-minded (or rebelliously disrespectful) group of readers ignore the clues, settling on another referent and setting in motion a train of connotations that becomes a permanent part of the poem's textual apparatus. The poem thus canonizes its own misreadings as connotations are heaped on connotations and two equally plausible referents compete for our attention. Moreover, as Aubrey Williams writes, the *Variorum*'s notes exert a "continuous de-historicizing pressure" on any single name, which "tends to attract to itself, to pull in, any suggestive meanings the poet may place in its vicinity" (1955, 67).

Swift envisioned this escalating scenario when he read the 1728 *Dunciad*.

He warned Pope against relying on his readers' common stock of connotations precisely because they would fail to grasp the poem's denotative reference; their failure, willful or not, would open the poem to their subversive misreadings: "The notes I could wish to be very large, in what relates to the persons concerned; for I have long observed that twenty miles from London nobody understands hints, initial letters, or town-facts and passages; and in a few years not even those who live in London. I would have the names of those scribblers printed indexically at the beginning or end of the poem, with an account of their works, for the reader to refer to. . . . I insist, you must have your asterisks filled up with some real names of real Dunces" (*Corr.* 2:504–5; 16 July 1728).

The first doubt the *Dunciad Variorum* seems meant to answer is whether identifying descriptions deliver the right name; at most, they can nudge us in the direction of supplying it ourselves, and they open the poem to our misreadings. The second doubt is potentially much more serious: whether the name of any Dunce can deliver the person of the Dunce—a doubt, in short, about whether proper names refer at all. By analogy to the first doubt, we ought at most to suppose that names only point us toward the right person, not help us fasten onto him. But if we are right about the second doubt, the consequences for poetry are severe. The existence of the first doubt injures one particular poem, causing it to grow excrescences to cover its bruised spots. But the existence of the second doubt admits of the inefficacy of corrective satire, thus nullifying the poem's purpose. Pope's fantasy is to pin a paper to the breast of each miscreant. Yet figurative language is such that we may always transfer our interest from the breast to the paper pinned to it, consigning ourselves to the realm of connotation and of general satire. This doubt takes us into the territory of fiction: Does it make any difference to the poem that it satirizes real people as opposed to creating composite portraits or fictional characters?

It is important to recognize that, prior to the most recent historicist turn (of which more in a moment), most twentieth-century criticism of the *Dunciad* has answered the last question with an emphatic "No!" Some of Pope's own statements also lead us to think that he would have answered that question negatively, although for his own reasons. Pope wrote, for example, "Whoever will consider the Unity of the whole design, will be sensible, that the Poem was not made for these Authors, but these Authors for the Poem: And I should judge they were clapp'd in as they rose, fresh and fresh, and chang'd from day to day, in like manner as when the old boughs wither, we thrust new ones into a chimney" (TE 5:205–6). His comment wittily produces further satire: first, there is nothing distinctive enough in any of the Dunces to individuate them; and second, only a person as touchy and self-absorbed as Colley Cibber would be stupid enough to take personally a set of descriptions originally intended for Lewis Theobald.

This is crucially different from the defense of Pope mounted by twentieth-century formalists that the poem's connotative pressures overwhelm its denotative ones, that the poem's Dunces are representations divided from the historical persons who may have borne a striking resemblance to them.[18] Two well-known accounts of Pope's poetry have argued that proper names are rhetorical abstractions from their referents in order to defend Pope against the charge of literary libel. Both Maynard Mack and William Wimsatt identify Pope's proper names, not with real people, but with the figurative heights his poetry is capable of attaining, arguing that people enter the satire only to be whisked up into a free play of connotation. I quote from Wimsatt, who takes these *Variorum*-like lines from the "Epistle to Arbuthnot": "Yet ne'er one sprig of laurel graced these ribbalds, / From slashing Bentley down to piddling Tibbalds" (TE 4:108). His comment here is that "the words sprig and piddling play a part too in proving what it means to have a name like that" (1949, 202).[19] Wimsatt makes sense of Pope's satire by emphasizing the linguistic basis of the banishment of real people and seems confirmed by the following lines quoted by Mack to the same effect:

> Twas chatt'ring, grinning, mouthing, jabb'ring all,
> And Noise, and Norton, Brangling, and Breval,
> Dennis and Dissonance.   (TE 5:128)

Both Mack and Wimsatt strongly separate meaning (the new connotations liberated by placing proper names in a metonymic chain) from reference. Both identify poetry with the former, with the connotative rather than the strictly denotative or referential aspects of the names, a view that frees poetry from the merely personal and local.

I have been outlining a pervasive formalist reading of the poem in which satire is always general because the very nonreferentiality of proper names consigns us to the realm of emblem. That reading needs now to be broken down into different parts and assessed. Everybody on the formalist side of the equation agrees that proper names do not refer to persons outside the poem and that what is important about them is the range of connotations they evoke. (The neoempiricist theories of proper-name reference that I canvassed earlier lend tacit support for this formalist view). Yet while one school—

roughly Mack, Wimsatt, and Aubrey Williams—thinks that meaning is liberated by giving up the fantasy of reference, another thinks that meaning is constrained by giving up reference. Laura Brown, a proponent of the latter view, thinks that proper names in the poem are essentially separate from the persons they represent and that they attract connotations to themselves; but she also thinks that the poem's formalism operates at a cost to meaning itself. She writes: "When proper nouns, noises and abstract qualities are listed as if they were objects, nothing can retain its autonomy, and here not only the persons of the duncies but human actions and discourse itself are reified" (1985, 135). Not only does the poem's formalism produce meaningless noise, but it does so disastrously by imitating the very materiality from which it is abstracted: in making abstract entities look like material ones, the poem's inside comes to resemble its outside (it is reified).

If the formalist argument splits between producing and occluding meaning, what about the antiformalist reading of the poem that says that the poem's context determines its meaning? Support for this reading comes directly from the poem's revision history, especially from Pope's care about getting the names just right, as though he were fighting language's very tendency to slide around a bit. Support comes also from the *Variorum* apparatus with its cacophony of competing authorities explaining who's who (as though such explanations are just the response an interpreter of the poem is looking for). Furthermore, it comes from a longstanding critical truism about the *Dunciad,* namely, that its intense worldly engagements make it a difficult poem for readers outside Pope's literary culture to interpret. This truism still circulates in the work of historically minded critics, who nevertheless cite Swift's complaint and other contemporary comments that strongly suggest that the poem was difficult for readers inside Pope's literary culture as well. My own view is that Swift's comment is symptomatic of the way readers have responded to the *Dunciad* since its publication: the poem tempts us to think there is a further inner circle to which someone else must have privileged access; interpretation is an activity someone else out there, possessing a key, must be practicing. As Pope wrote in the advertisement of the *Dunciad Variorum,* "The reader cannot but derive one pleasure from the very Obscurity of the persons it treats of, that it partakes of the nature of a Secret, which most people love to be let into, tho' the Men or the Things be ever so inconsiderable or trivial" (TE 5:8). This last thought presumes that since this is a poem, there must be a way to interpret it. In a historicist climate, one temptation will be to think that the best way to figure out what a poem means is to research its referents.[20]

Reference and Anti-Reference

To test these hypotheses, let us examine the portrait of James More Smythe, who plays such an important, albeit passive role as the main prize awarded in the contests of authors, stationers, and booksellers in Book 2 of the *Dunciad Variorum*. I choose Book 2 because the very difficulty of differentiating fictional from literal agents is patently connected to interpretation. Reuben Brower (a polemical formalist) has contrasted Book 2 with Book 4, finding the former wanting because its very openness to the world outside the poem affects the poem's agents, who come to seem thin and underrepresented: "The main weakness of Book 2 is obvious. We find it hard to care about the objects of the satire, in part, . . . because they are so inadequately dramatized and so little 'present' in the poetry. In part, too, because Pope rarely lifts our attention to the large moral and aesthetic concerns that give dignity and meaning to the satire of Book 4 (where it is worth noting, the characters are more often fictional and symbolic)" (1959, 332, 335). Yet what exactly is the source of this porousness? One answer is that the characters in Book 2 seem inadequate by comparison to some standard of fictionality that we can all recognize, perhaps one that came into being around the time of Book IV (the early 1740s). A better answer is that the poem's characters seem inadequate by whatever standard we adopt. If we try to figure out who they are only by looking around inside the poem, we will soon happen upon glaring patches of indeterminacy; if, on the other hand, we slavishly fill in the background of each Dunce, his representedness in the poem mocks our efforts.

James More Smythe is a case in point. The dissipated James More Smythe died in 1734 at the age of thirty-two. In the late 1720s, he provoked Pope by borrowing some lines and appending them to his play, *The Rival Modes*. Pope had initially granted and then withheld permission, but More (Smythe was a name "borrowed" from his maternal grandfather on promise of a legacy) used the lines anyway and boasted about it in print. More soon becomes a rather complicated allegory of "Plagiary"—plagiarism not simply as a textual matter, but as a matter of various appropriations, including bodily ones. Pope was interested in More as a target, producing a small epigram in the early 1730s and an epitaph for him.[21] The epitaph is notable for comically expressing the very angst about satiric reference that began to afflict Pope around this period:

> Here lyes what had nor Birth, nor Shape, nor Fame;
> No Gentleman! no man! no-thing! no name!
> For Jammie ne'er grew James; and what they call

More, shrunk to Smith—and Smith's no name at all.
Yet dye thou can'st not, Phantom, oddly fated:
For how can no-thing be annihilated?   (TE 6:326–27)

Pope's fullest portrait of More is fascinating for the way it translates the question "For how can nothing be annihilated?" into a puzzle about form. In a portrait that apparently bears a striking resemblance to the person, More's "nothingness" complicates any neat distribution of figurative and literal across the inside and outside of the poem:

> A Poet's form she placed before their eyes,
> And bad the nimblest racer seize the prize;
> No meagre, muse-rid mope, adust and thin,
> In a dun night-gown of his own loose skin,
> But such a bulk as no twelve bards could raise,
> Twelve starveling bards of these degenerate days.
> All as a partridge plump, full-fed, and fair,
> She formed this image of well-bodied air,
> With pert flat eyes she windowed well its head,
> A brain of feathers, and a heart of lead,
> And empty words she gave, and sounding strain,
> But senseless, lifeless! Idol void and vain!
> Never was dashed out, at one lucky hit,
> A fool, so just a copy of a Wit;
> So like, that criticks said and courtiers swore,
> A wit it was, and called the phantom, More.   (TE 5:99–101)

More is simultaneously a textual representation (a "copy") and a grotesquely inflated body. Insubstantial and fat, his body is formed from air and a container for hollow space. Yet whether he is a fat man or a phantom depends on one's position inside or outside the poem: the starveling bards who heft him up feel not his hollowness but his weight, while to the audience of classifying "criticks," More is merely "a copy of a Wit." Notice that it is these represented readers of the poem who "call" the phantom "More," as though dubbing him with a proper name from their own (imaginary) milieu. The portrait thus represents itself as being the sort of thing that has an outside, while remaining agnostic about the relationship between such apparent references and the portrait's "actual" referents.

To complicate matters, Pope explains in a note how this representation counts as an allegory of Plagiary. He quotes from the *Aeneid* a passage in which Juno seeks to protect Aeneas's foe Turnus from harm in battle by making him believe that he has conquered Aeneas. Juno thus disguises herself as Aeneas, challenges Turnus to a fight, and allows herself to be chased off. She "made a bodiless shape of spectral mist / In likeness of Aeneas, weird and strange, / Adorned the image with Dardanian arms / And matched the godlike hero's shield and plume, / Gave unreal words, a voice without a mind, / A way of walking, modeled after his" (Virgil 1983, 10:317). On the face of it, James More Smythe is the Aeneas figure, Dullness is Juno, and the Booksellers fighting to get a piece of the phantom are Turnus. But this "key" makes interpreting the figure rather difficult—it implies a heroic distance between the real James More Smythe and his phantom equivalent to that between Aeneas and Juno's impersonation of him. In an action modeled unironically on that of her Latin predecessor, Dullness makes a fictional representation of More by straight-forwardly copying him—outside the poem, More is a wit, inside the poem he is a copy of a wit.

But if this is the reason that More counts as an allegory of Plagiary, then every Dunce must also count as an allegory of plagiary, and the phantom More is at once overly generalized and nonsensical (how do we account for the over-all theme of the portrait, which seems to be the strange cubism of his body?). It would make more sense to ignore some of the notes directing us to inter-pret him as "Plagiary," and instead to follow other notes (predictably those written by the connotation-loving Scriblerus) directing us to interpret him as "stupidity" because his name, More, is derived from the Greek *moros*. Yet this is not much help either, since such punning is little more than name-calling. Far from making sense of the phantom More in formal terms, the connota-tions of his name provide us with a short stick to beat him with. Even if our sophisticated instincts about language make us skeptical about whether the stick will find its target, we must assume a target outside the poem to be hit.

So we scrutinize the apparatus notes for clues and find the portrait de-scribed in terms of a rather elaborate chiasmus: "Our author [was] obliged to represent this gentleman as a Plagiary, or to pass for one himself. His case in-deed was like that of a man I have heard of, who as he was sitting in company, perceived his next neighbour had stollen his handkerchief. 'Sir' (said the Thief, finding himself detected) 'do not expose me, I did it for mere want: be so good but to take it privately out of my pocket again, and say nothing.' the honest man did so, but the other cry'd out, 'See Gentlemen! what a Thief we have among us! look, he is stealing my handkerchief'" (TE 5:101). As another "key" to the figure, this story leads us to understand the complicated dance of per-mission and borrowing as a chiasmus, so that More is not so much imper-sonating himself as he is impersonating Pope. Pope confirms this by saying that he could either represent More as a plagiarist or to let himself be represented as one; either More is a phantom of Pope, or Pope is a phantom of More. More seems powerfully attracted to the poetry of chiasmus: the lines of Pope's that he steals are studded with that particular rhetorical figure. In trading the lines back and forth, Pope and More become locked in a dynamic that imitates the formal technique used in the very text in dispute.

A complicated dialectic of inside and outside, materiality and immateriality, structures More's portrait, connecting the reader's position to aspects of the representation that become available according to her interpretive agenda. More changes dimension as we weave in and out of the poem: the farther inside the poem we go, the heftier More becomes, but the more he also becomes two-dimensional (a caricature). The farther outside the poem we go, the more he becomes both a literary imitation and a rich figure for Pope himself. Wherever we choose to locate ourselves (and Pope tantalizingly provides bait for us to snatch at one starting point or another), we are soon forced to confront the uncomfortable fact that our line of sight makes some of More's features clearer and others more opaque. The very difficulty of hammering out an interpretation has as a theme the interrelation of particular and general: the particular location yields a general sense of the portrait that is then frustrated by stray and insistent particulars. The phantom More is a character who is oddly meaningful with respect to certain attributes, and meaningless with respect to others.

The peculiarity of this situation is connected with the difficulty of figuring out what genre he belongs to: personifications, allegories, and character progresses are determinate with respect to some properties and indeterminate with respect to others (and demand as a minimal requirement of the genre that each of the extant attributes relates to an overall theme). Even characters marked as realistic can be so described, as in this fascinating recent contribution to the way we think about the difference between fictional characters and a real persons: "In the case of 'Sherlock Holmes' we get an incomplete, possible, non-existent object, some of whose nuclear properties are: being a detective, catching criminals, smoking a pipe, etc. Typically, fictional objects will be incomplete, for the body of literature in question will not determine all of their properties. For example, it is not true that according to the Conan Doyle novels, Holmes had a mole on his left leg, not is it true that according to those novels he didn't have a mole on his left leg . . . he is *indeterminate with respect to* that property" (Parsons 1974, 80, emphasis in original; quoted in R. Rorty 1982, 124).

By contrast to Sherlock Holmes's mole, the phantom More is tantalizingly marked as a real person, his indeterminacy a set of blanks that readers of the poem could fill in by historical investigation. But were we to take that route, we would not get very far in figuring out what the portrait means, since Pope blocks roman-à-clef questions off from questions of what the portrait means. Crucially, the portrait's meaning resists investigation: the more one tries to investigate it, the less meaningful it becomes (three "keys" and untold numbers of hypotheses later). We must rest content with our initial intuition that the portrait is a mix of meaning and nonsense, of conceptual clarity and incoherence. We must finally be chastened by the realization that what the More portrait means is relative to our shifting perspective. (Among other things, this explains why the portrait can be shown to provide limited but very real justification for each of the lines of Pope criticism canvassed above, from pure formalism to pure contextualism.)

What I am proposing is that with the figure of More, Pope starts to reorient his satiric portraits so that they become objects existing in their own space, their apparent referentiality reduced to just another attribute. This reorientation happens, ineluctably, by stripping particulars of their authoritative grip on the real. Abstraction is the force that strips particulars of authority, creating a defensive shine around its newly won territory. The portrait of More defeats the distinction between reference and meaning by making apparent reference just one more source of meaning, and not an especially privileged one. In the New Dunciad, Pope will take this development to its logical conclusion, evacuating any recognizable pictorialism from his abstract entities and thus bearing witness to the final defeat of figure by abstraction.

The New Dunciad: Private Meaning

Berkeley said of Locke's theory of how we frame universals that it is the "tacking together of numberless inconsistencies" (quoted in Aaron 1968, 31). This statement could serve as a description of character portraits, such as the phantom More, in the Dunciad Variorum. It could equally serve as a description of the scientistic ethos of the New Dunciad, where "numberless inconsistencies" do not shape themselves into recognizable portraits:

> Prompt at the call, around the Goddess roll
> Broad hats, and hoods, and caps, a sable shoal:
> Thick and more thick the black blockade extends,
> A hundred head of Aristotle's friends. (TE 5:360)

In the *New Dunciad,* particulars, the raw materials acted upon by Dullness's "force inertly strong," do not come from outside the poem; instead, they are recognizable as those rhetorical figures, such as metonymy, long associated with Pope's poetic mastery and thus constitute a retrospective of his rhetorical tools. Pope chooses metonymy to represent the particulars that get swept up into a black blockade for two other reasons. First, metonymy marks a part/ whole relation, thus suggesting that the particular only makes sense in relation to the general. Second, by orienting the part to the whole, Pope voids the power of particulars to individuate: the Dunces are individuated in *New Dunciad* less than at any other stage in the Dunciad sequence in part because their attributes (broad hats and caps) do not pick them out personally but negate their difference by pointing directly to their collective essence. The folding inward of particulars has a Newtonian-Lockean analogue. Pope and Warburton include a note explaining that the "force inertly strong" of Dullness that converts "broad hats" into a "black blockade" "alludes to the vis inertiae of matter, which, though it really be no power, is yet the foundation of all qualities and attributes of that sluggish substance" (TE 5:340). A more scientifically tendentious way of putting the same thing is to say that accidents do not signify essences but are identical with them.

The fact that attributes are no longer a means of individuation—or a sign of anything at all—helps to explain why the transition from the Dunciad of the 1720s to the Dunciad of the 1740s is a transition from a figurative mode to a nonfigurative mode. Yet abstraction is at the core of both modes. When critics used to think about such things, they argued that abstraction is the favored style of a neoclassical aesthetic, while debating back and forth about whether neoclassical abstraction was at heart figurative or nonfigurative. Their arguments presupposed massive developments in the philosophy of language: historically, they argued, a neoclassical aesthetic depended on the Lockean reorientation of the relation between particular and general terms and other similar shifts.[22]

So far my argument has tended to confirm this older style of thought about cultural change: what I have said about Pope does not distinguish his interest in linguistic abstraction from any other applied instance of Locke's insights. But abstraction has many different uses in art, even in a movement as hard to define and defend as neoclassicism. In the *New Dunciad,* Pope reorients his interest in abstraction from language to the entire material and immaterial realm. No longer is abstraction essentially a linguistic matter, leaking out onto persons from the descriptive connotations of their proper names. Now it is the ruling code of the representational field, the fate of the human and non-human physical world at the hands of Dullness. Two principle effects consistent with abstraction are achieved. First, Dullness reduces difference to sameness: "With the same Cement, ever sure to bind / We bring to one dead level ev'ry mind" (TE 5:370). Second, she unhooks words from the world: words refer only to themselves, and the process of making their meaning explicit does not involve searching out their hidden truths but rather "explaining a thing till all men doubt it." "Words are man's province, Words we teach alone," and Pope invents a striking image for expounding them: "So spins the silk-worm small its slender store, / And labours till it clouds itself all o'er" (TE 5:369).

If Dullness reorients objects and persons to a unified field, then it makes no sense to seek objects and persons outside the field. Does this mean that Pope has abandoned his extensive interest in the ways of reference? Certainly the poem's contemporary readers thought so, and they expressed what amounts to a longing for its return. The *Universal Spectator* for 3 April 1742 cites a sampling of town opinion: "The Censure they pass is, that the Satire is too allegorical, and the Characters he has drawn are too conceal'd: That real Names should have been inserted instead of fictitious ones" (TE 5:xxxi). The authors of the *Universal Spectator* are seeking the usual distribution of figurative and literal across the inside and outside of the poem; they fail to find it because Pope has collapsed them together. Attributes do not point to an essence, just as connotations do not now signal an external referent.

Yet this reduction of the poem's "two levels" to one does not by itself produce a conceptually complete New Critical masterwork, as so many of the critics writing in the 1950s and 60s thought. We have already seen in the case of the Paridel figure that the lack of a verifiable referent for many of the *New Dunciad*'s "fictitious names" does not make the names any easier to interpret. In fact, the contrary holds: the end of reference signals the beginning of new, more intensely private forms of meaning. Now that particulars have lost their status as the sign of the real, even the most public of names are reduced to objects of private obsession. A case in point occurs during one of the poem's longest set pieces, a Dunce's lament over his dead carnation, CAROLINE, killed by a zealous birder indifferent to the fate of the "rose or carnation" beneath his bird (TE 5:382). The meaning of the Dunce's grief and of his rival Dunce's murderous carelessness is the same. The first Dunce carefully husbands his flower, spreading its leaves within a paper collar and "throning it in glass" for better viewing, calling forth the praise of maids and youths. In a blazing public tribute to his queen, he names it after her; but as soon as he does so, his flower is killed. His obsessions blind him to the fact of his flower in the natural world and to alternate perspectives such as those of nectar-hunting birds. The second Dunce, a scientist who pledges his allegiance to the undisguised "naked fact," kills through absorption in his own particular.

What these Dunces murder through their private obsession is the public name. This tale, like some others scattered throughout the poem, is an allegory of the privatization of meaning. Pope, increasingly subject to many of Dullness's other effects, falls victim to this one too. Some proper names stand out boldly and clearly against the background of the "involuntary throng"—Chesterfield, Atterbury, Murray. We soon realize that Pope floats the names of friends, members of the Walpole Opposition, belatedly praising them for their opposition to the "force inertly strong" of Dullness, who blots out distinctions between "true and false in individuals." To be praised is to have failed: in order to be named, a person must already have succumbed to Dullness. Read in light of Pope's private praise for failed public names, the Dunce with his CAROLINE becomes oddly aligned with his author. It seems out of place to celebrate the completion of Pope's intentions in a poem that so profoundly thematizes the "uncreating word"; with the passing of reference, we might find ourselves mourning the passing of meaning as well. The "two levels," however frustrating to some, keep meaning in play by keeping the hope of reference alive.[23]

We nevertheless ought to doubt that Pope became cured of his fantasies of reference, however much it may have looked to his contemporaries as though he grew blindly absorbed in private meaning. Colley Cibber, upon getting wind of his hypostatization to king of the Dunces, mocked the existential futility of Pope's gesture—"You seem angry at the rain for wetting you; why then do you go out in it?" (1742, 13), nevertheless earlier in the chapter, I quoted Pope's letter to Hugh Bethel to show that while Pope thought he was being ever more subtle, his contemporaries thought he was being merely obscure. And in fact, during the 1730s, his period of intensifying political satire, Pope grew more interested in hitting targets in verse, even to the extent of fantasizing about literally and mechanically doing so. London Alderman John Barber wrote to Swift on the subject of the Lord Mayor's Day parade: "Mr. Pope and I were thinking of having a large machine carried through the city, with a printing-press, author, publishers, hawkers, devils, etc., and a satirical poem printed and thrown from the press to the mob, in public view . . . but your absence spoils that design" (Swift 1963, 4:62).

Given this fantasy of shooting his poems out into the crowd like stones, Pope might have been pleased by the historical survival of his reputation as a poet able to produce material effects on real people. De Quincey wrote: "Pope finds himself unable to resettle the equilibrium in his nervous system until he has taken out his revenge by an extra kicking administered to some old mendicant or vagrant lying in a ditch" (quoted in Colomb 1992, 67). But perhaps the pathos of his case is hit better by the poet Thom Gunn (reflecting on occasional verse): "Later I had for a while a theory of poetry as 'loot,' a prize grabbed from the outside world and taken permanently into the poet's possession. But of course it isn't taken, it continues out there in the world living its own independent existence, stepping from the tube-train at a later stop, coolly unaware of all the furore it is causing" (1985, 192).

Part II

The Spectator Morality
of the Enlightenment

Chapter Five

The Kindness of Strangers

Johnson's *Life of Savage* and the Culture of Altruism

Mother, miscall'd, farewell . . .
All I was wretched by, to you I ow'd
Alone from strangers ev'ry comfort flow'd!

—RICHARD SAVAGE, *The Bastard*

Among the many peculiar, overdetermined moments in Samuel Johnson's *Account of the Life of Mr. Richard Savage* (1744) is the scene in which Savage encounters a prostitute who had given evidence against him at his trial for murdering James Sinclair:

Some time after he had obtained his liberty, he met in the street the woman that had sworn with so much malignity against him. She informed him that she was in distress, and, with a degree of confidence not easily attainable, desired him to relieve her. He, instead of insulting her misery, and taking pleasure in the calamitie of one who had brought his life into danger, reproved her gently for her perjury, and changing the only guinea that he had, divided it equally between her and himself. (1971, 40)

Johnson ostentatiously calls this an act of "compassion," a virtue that, he tells us, was "indeed the distinguishing quality of Savage." If compassion is Savage's distinctive quality, prudence—the quality Johnson repeatedly tells us he lacks—must be its opposite.[1]

Both prudence and compassion are virtues, yet Johnson structures Savage's moral psychology by opposing them. In fact, Johnson is drawing on a strong tradition of defining prudence as self-interest (though with a positive valence): "a due concern about our own interest . . . and a reasonable endeavour to secure and promote it" and "that constant habitual sense of private interest and good which we always carry about with us" (the definitions were supplied by Bishop Butler in 1736) (Selby-Bigge 1897, 1:250). Compassion, on the other hand, meant "the feeling or emotion, when a person is moved by the suffering or distress of another, and by the desire to relieve it" (OED). In this light, the opposition makes more sense. It neatly encapsulates two of the more prominent moral philosophical antitheses of the eighteenth century: passions against reason, and selfishness against concern for others.

Something is still odd. We might expect these two oppositions to line up neatly with each other: our passions make us selfish, while our reason helps us to think beyond first-order desires to include other people in our circle of concern. But Johnson frustrates this expectation by making prudence stand for both reason and selfishness. Here too he is drawing on contemporary meanings of the word: "foreseeing by natural instinct" and "wisdom applied to practice" are definitions Johnson supplies in his *Dictionary*. Prudence may be closer to what we call practical reason or foresight than it is to full-blown Enlightenment reason; we might think of it, provisionally, as acting in such a way as to procure future benefit or avoid future harm to the self.[2] Still prudence owes more to reason than it does to passion: in the final paragraph of the *Life of Savage,* Johnson compares it to other intellectual faculties like knowledge, wit, and genius; and he contrasts it with negligence and irregularity.

The circumstances in which Johnson composed the *Life of Savage* have become part of the text's mythology. Having reached the age of thirty-five despite illness and grinding poverty, Johnson was working as a Grub Street hack employed in writing political pamphlets, imagining parliamentary debates, and translating poems. His old friend and fellow distressed poet, Richard Savage, died in Newgate prison. Soon thereafter, Edward Cave's *Gentleman's Magazine* printed a letter promising that "Savage's life will speedily be published by a person who was favoured with his confidence" (other people might promise to write his life, but they "will publish only a novel, filled with romantick adventures, and imaginary amours" [quoted in Boswell 1934, 1:165). Johnson fulfilled his promise of speed in an uncomfortably literal way: having procrastinated, he wrote the whole thing (140 pages) in a few days by sitting up every night.

To find Johnson weaving Savage's character on the warp of prudence and the woof of compassion, then, is to find him weaving moralist's cloth: concern for self is the antithesis of concern for others. Savage is most imprudent when it comes to money, and most compassionate at a moment when he has so little of it. He contemns material things and spreads liberally his small bounty.

This gesture provokes Johnson's awe: "an action which in some ages would have made a saint, and perhaps in others a hero," "an instance of uncommon generosity," and so on (41). That Johnson should celebrate the virtue of compassion seems to suit the text's moral project exactly.

But Johnson's moral project founders on a surprising shoal: compassion itself. The deeper he delves into the meaning of Savage's compassion, the more self-interested that compassion begins to seem. Savage's act is shot through with various motives and aims, only some of which could be called compassionate. The scene involves a female prostitute, a male night walker, an approach, a solicitation, an exchange of money. Yet it is rather unexpectedly the man who has become the object of the woman's strongly instrumental desire: she "desired him to relieve her." Paying her off, as if in exchange for a service, is the one course of action Savage can take to restore his instrumentality—to become, as it were, the man again. (How far Johnson associates using people as a means to an end with a gendered division of the psyche is a topic to which we will return later). This Savage does, dividing his guinea "equally between her and himself."

In dividing a guinea, Savage has accomplished a slew of other things too. The narrator explains: Savage has performed "an act of complicated virtue, by which he at once relieved the poor, corrected the vicious, and forgave an enemy, by which he at once remitted the strongest provocations, and exercised the most ardent charity" (40). The narrator's repetition of "by which" suggests how strongly instrumental Savage's action is; it suggests too that instrumentality must play some part in what it means for Savage's virtue to be complicated. Savage has benefited as much as—indeed, more than—the prostitute: by dividing his guinea equally, he receives half a guinea, balm for his anxious, satirical spirit, a restored masculinity, and a starring part in an *imitatio Christi*.

An investment of a mere half-guinea has paid off handsomely. By a series of substitutions, what begins as a story about a man picking up a prostitute becomes a saint's life: rather than her relieving him, he relieves the poor. Soon, however, the investment goes sour: the saint's life is at the same time a story of growing spiritual depravity. A story about sex becomes a story about money—we might almost say that the narrative exchanges money for sex. But then, by the same logic, it exchanges charity for money; and suddenly we find ourselves reading a story, not just about prostitution, but about simony—the selling of spiritual benefit for money. Our central character is no flawed saint but a corrupting preacher. This narrative transformation further complicates the relationship between compassion and selfishness, for the corrupt preacher

has not exactly made the prostitute pay him for dispensing spiritual beneficence to her. Instead, he has paid himself; and as he does, both money and
spiritual aid have leaked out onto her.

Had Savage been able to foresee this outcome, it is doubtful that he would
have given half a guinea. But this makes foresight—prudence—look just as
bad as self-interested compassion, and we can understand why Johnson
equates it with selfishness. Reason is a cynic, turning a stirring example of altruism into something demonic, exposing Saint Savage as Chaucer's Pardoner.
Of course it is the narrator's own censorious voice that has pushed us in this
direction. Here a distinction is required. The narrator's voice is that of a
moralist, but this character is not identical to Johnson, although Johnson
fitfully identifies with him (to his own detriment, as we will see).

As the text progresses, the moralist grows ever more critical of Savage's imprudence in money matters. His thunderous final judgment that "those, who
in confidence of superior capacities or attainments disregard the common
maxims of life, shall be reminded that nothing will supply the want of prudence" (140) seems designed to be taken as a literal warning about compen-
sations: "nothing" will be the fitting return for "want of prudence." The moralist's initial tone of awe during the prostitute scene only means Savage has
farther to fall. The moralist begins to demand that we expose Savage's lack of
real altruism, making his motives clearer to us than they are to him, who lacks
foresight, or to the prostitute, who, after all, has gotten half a guinea. Were he
in the position to respond, Savage might say, "So what if in reason's hot glare
I look like the Pardoner? The prostitute has ended up with half a guinea, and
that is all that matters."

Is the *Life of Savage* a moralist's text? Written a few years before the start of
what W. J. Bate (1977, 297–317) has influentially described as Johnson's great
moral period (1748 to 1760), it bristles with moral energy. Its stated intention
is fostering altruism, energy directed toward others. It is perhaps the most direct appeal for sympathy in all of English literature: "To these mournful narratives, I am about to add the life of Richard Savage, a man whose writings en-
title him to an eminent rank in the classes of learning, and whose misfortunes
claim a degree of compassion, not always due to the unhappy, as they were often the consequences of the crimes of others, rather than his own" (4). The
moralist, on the other hand, is controlling, punitive, judgmental, seeking to
make people aware of their obligations. Yet even here, in the text's moral
frame, a conflict arises that puts Johnson's moral project in serious jeopardy.
In this chapter I will argue that Johnson's singular achievement was to recognize the extent and power of this conflict and not to shirk its implications.

The conflict comes into play because Johnson chooses Richard Savage as the focus of both the text's demand for sympathy and its moralizing. Savage is at once the person to be sympathized with and the one who most stands in need of punitive correction. He is the object of compassion and the subject of obligation. In what follows, I will develop this opposition into two substantive positions and show why they conflict. There are two ways of imagining the obligations humans have to one another, one based in sympathy, the other in the moral command. The conflict is rhetorical, psychological, thematic, social. Perhaps the most interesting version of it pits Savage himself against the narrator of his life. For Savage, as we shall see, has his own ideas about obligation, ideas that he uses to mount a wholesale critique of the moralist's point of view.

The conflict between Savage and the moralist, the purveyor of the official view, becomes nothing less than a conflict between sympathy and reason. This dichotomy—to us a cliché of the taxonomical impulse that dominated an earlier era of eighteenth-century studies—was the untilled ground of psychological speculation in Johnson's intellectual culture. Eventually it nurtured two thoroughgoing philosophical positions that survive even today as utilitarianism and rationalism. But when Johnson was writing, Hume's *Treatise of Human Nature*—the first self-conscious secular polemic about the distinction—had only recently fallen dead-born from the press. Johnson's achievement consists in grasping the powerful appeal of both sympathy and reason for those concerned to promote altruism. He did so somewhat against his own prejudices, which ran in favor of the moralist's hierarchical authoritarianism.[3] He also grasped their limitations. Sympathy and reason are incompatible with each other, but separately they are insufficient instruments of morality. Johnson develops two positions nascent in his intellectual culture into a thoroughgoing conflict, making it meaningful, compelling, and hard. It would be tempting simply to celebrate the aesthetic complexity (or, in what amounts to much the same thing, to parade the rhetorical failure) of Johnson's opening his text to a point of view that undermines it. But this would be to contain the conflict and thereby to underestimate Johnson's achievement.

I want to step back from the prostitute scene for a moment to consider some of the broader questions about altruism, reciprocity, and society that it raises. The discipline of moral philosophy has long been centered on the problem of altruism. Behind its many guises, the problem looks like this: What motivates people to act in the interests of other people when by so doing they harm their own? While few people would recognize such a clean split between altruism and egoism, this formulation has some advantages.

First, it helps us see that if we are concerned to promote altruism, as most moral philosophers are, we have to acknowledge some high hurdles. The real problem of altruism is selfishness: concern for others is less common than concern for self; the interests of others can interfere with self-interest; preserving other people's interests can be costly; concern for others is therefore rare and hard to induce. These propositions are hard to dispute, at least in broad outline: eighteenth-century writers pioneered this line of discussion by attending to the closely related problem of sympathy.

Second, this way of putting the problem of altruism feeds our dualist intuitions. Whether the moral command is external (shame-based) or internal (guilt-based), morality seems to take us out of our immediate desires, giving us a set of more distant, second-order motives. Thomas Nagel defines one pole of this opposition, pure egoism: "Egoism holds that each individual's reasons for acting and possible motivations for acting, must arise from his own interests and desires, however those interests may be defined. The interests of one person can on this view motivate another or provide him with a reason only if they are connected with his interests or are objects of some sentiment of his, like sympathy, pity, or benevolence" (1970, 84).[4]

These tropes of desire and interest are compelling, if imprecise. They oppose feeling (immediate and sensory) to reason (distant and effortful). Common tropes for the moral command are punitive, suggesting an external force. They hint at compulsion, or being led away from what we really want. (Think of Eve at the lake in Book 4 of *Paradise Lost* falling in love with her own image. A voice "warns" her that her purpose is elsewhere with Adam, and she yields to the command: "What could I do, / but follow straight, invisibly thus led?" [ll. 475–76]) Selfishness, it would seem, is rooted in the body, in our immediate needs; while altruism flowers in reason, in community, in recognizing the needs of other people, in a general standard.[5] Many moral rationalists have claimed that there is a special relationship between reason and reciprocity (Nagel 1970).

Perhaps the most enduring set of associations is a dichotomy between pleasure and pain. Nurturing our interests is pleasurable, like feeding our bodies. Obligation is painful, and the pain it brings is a direct measure of how much it impedes our desires. This is a point that many moral writers have made— from Hobbes, who thought that only the sovereign can command people's allegiances, to Kant, whose categorical imperative is an inner Hobbesian sovereign. Christine Korsgaard has her own version of it: "In ethics, the question can become urgent, for the day will come, for most of us, when what morality commands is *hard:* that we share decisions with people whose intelligence or integrity don't inspire our confidence; that we assume grave responsibilities to which we feel inadequate; that we sacrifice our lives, or voluntarily relinquish what makes them sweet. And then the question—*why?*—will press, and rightly so. Why should I be moral?" (1996, 9).

Recently some evolutionary moral philosophers have begun to situate the problem of altruism at the very center of human sociability. They reject as false the traditional dichotomy between altruism and egoism, proposing that morality, even when painful or puzzling, complies with our self-interest rather than thwarting it. Our capacity for genuine, serious altruism is as much a part of our evolutionary heritage as selfishness. Altruism usually conveys long-term benefit to the giver, even if, in the short term, its costs are high. This is called *reciprocal altruism,* and its effects are thought to be so important and so widespread that all of human social life and morality—even the division of labor—follow from it.

What is reciprocal altruism, and why is it so crucial to human social life? Reciprocal altruism bears some similarity to trade and barter, though with crucial differences: it is indirect and noncontractual; its narrative is not linear but spatial and three-dimensional. Suppose you are in desperate need of something that I have, something worth four units of value to me. Moved by your pleas, I give you half, reducing my share to two units. But your great need—a need I find so compelling—makes what I give you worth much more than two units when it comes time to pay me back. You pay back the whole four units. In fact, my profit may be higher: I might come to you needy and despairing, so the four units you return might be worth six to me. If I had refused to be generous in the first place, I'd have kept my four units; but now I have eight. Nothing can force you to pay me back, but here a key element of reciprocal altruism comes into play: spectator morality. Your need and my response to it are duly noted by our circle of friends: I become known as a "good person," and I am extended a strong line of social credit. My social credit means that in the future I might only have to pay out one unit of value, rather than two, in order to get back eight. Thoughts of my future reputation might induce me to overcome the risk that you won't reciprocate. If you fail to pay me back, I have lost ground in the short term, but I have banked my line of social credit.

Meanwhile, if you decide to cheat, what are the consequences? In the short run you have made off with a large profit, something for nothing. But the second time you find yourself in need, you will certainly find me less sympathetic. If you are lucky enough to live in a society where you do not encounter the same person twice, and where people don't gossip, you can exploit others without consequence. But if you live in a small world, then spectator moral-ity is in force. If spectator morality is in force and you exploit others on a reg-ular basis, you will soon find yourself expelled from the round of reciprocal altruism and the social benefits it brings.

Of course, people do not always calculate the costs and benefits of their generosity as I have done in this example. Emotion and identification are equally important means of binding people to the system. Moral rules can come to seem instinctive; the moral sense means that these rules have been in-ternalized. But these are realms of psychological complexity only hinted at in my example. Before we broach these topics, we need to look at some basic ways that reciprocal altruism can organize the psyche.

The most important fact about reciprocal altruism is that it is a non-zero-sum enterprise: one person's gain is not another person's loss; both parties gain by engaging in it, and the benefits are spread across society. An immedi-ate effect of this feature is increased psychological complexity. To see how these two go together, imagine three worlds, each populated by self-interested creatures. For the creatures in the first of these worlds, exchange is a zero-sum proposition: each creature's gain is another creature's loss. The second world is inhabited by creatures for whom exchange is non-zero-sum, yet occurs in-stantaneously. The members of this society give one unit of value in exchange for one unit of value; they have no concept that repayment can be delayed or asymmetrical. We can see immediately that creatures in the second world would have to be more psychologically complex than those in the first, who, after all, would destroy their society after a few rounds of exchange—after the first round, half the creatures would win, half would lose; after the second round, half of the winners would lose, and so on until there was one clear win-ner. In the second world, some concept of society comes into play, for the in-habitants must cooperate at a rudimentary level. This society must have some rules, and its inhabitants need to know what those rules are and how to fol-low them. They need to recognize cheating and dole out punishment. They need to have a sense of others and of potential conflicts of interest. But their psychological strategy is still relatively simple and mechanistic: call it one round of "tit for tat" (Axelrod 1984).

What about the creatures living in the third of our imagined worlds? How much more complex do their psyches have to be to negotiate their system? In-finitely. Reciprocal altruists need foresight, planning, self-awareness, self-reflectiveness, conscience, intention, purpose, desire—in a word, conscious-ness. They also need to be socialized. They should be able to credit (within limits) other creatures with the same deep mental space they experience, partly so that they can use the most effective pressures to get what they want. They need to be able to adopt perspectives other than their own, sometimes those of other participants in the system, sometimes that of the system itself.

All of my hypothetical examples have made sense of reciprocal altruism in vaguely economic terms. The psyches of reciprocal altruists seem particularly attuned to economic exchanges. If we want to find detailed information about the psychic organization of reciprocal altruists, we should look in the written records of a culture in which economic and psychological speculation coincide. English society in the early part of the eighteenth century is such a culture: eighteenth-century English men and women brought to the fore two discourses, more or less self-consciously navigating their world by them. The first is a discourse about economic life, the second of human motivation. The two are certainly connected: the material conditions that gave rise to public discussions of trade, finance, and public credit in late-seventeenth- and early-eighteenth-century England also created a practical need for increased psychological awareness. This psychological awareness might include tests for sincerity, trustworthiness, predictability, and lying. Indeed, the very concepts of sympathy, altruism, and selfishness that preoccupy moral philosophers today originated in the moral philosophy of eighteenth-century Britain. So too did the abstract idea of mind against which these concepts make sense. I suspect that moral philosophy arose in the first place to answer the needs of people living in a rapidly changing economic system.

Eighteenth-century England was awash in financial anxiety. Take the example of trade: at its most abstract, trade seems to be like the case of our second world. It involves a non-zero-sum exchange in which I hand over a unit of value in exchange for an equivalent unit of value. Trade ought to be rule-based, governed by the kind of "general maxims" that John Locke thought could be apprehended by "reasonable gentleman," if not by "children, idiots, or the greater part of mankind" (quoted in Nicholson 1994, 8). And indeed, many political and economic writers of the late seventeenth century in England sought to formulate the rules of trade along scientific lines. John Cary, a Bristol merchant, argued that "in order to discover whether a nation gets or loses by its trade, 'tis necessary first to enquire into the principles whereupon it is built; for trade hath its principles as other sciences have, and as difficult to understand" (1717, 2). Yet the discourse of trade rapidly became incontinent. Instead of rules and rational maxims, talk about trade produced figures for every kind of social anxiety. By a series of powerful metonymies, trade became a way of talking about the "characters of men" (to use one of the age's favorite phrases), and about luxury, gender relations, families and inheritance, private and public, nations and states, goods and services, war and peace.

Trade, unsurprisingly, also became an occasion for moralizing, for talk about justice and injustice. A widely despised figure in satires and caricatures of the period is the free-rider, someone who enriches him- or herself at the expense of society as a whole. On a wide range of political and social topics, and from many points of view, satirists found that labeling someone as greedy brought its own rewards. Consider an anonymous print from 1721 reflecting on the South Sea Company stock speculation crisis. "Lucifer's New Row Barge" (fig. 4) depicts a knight, cashier of the South Sea Company, standing on a barge called the "S.S. Inquisition." He is an outsized figure, surrounded by diminutives: some devils, some humans (one man flogging another, a man standing in a pillory), a horse, a snake, a hanging jack of diamonds, and a sea-monster whose open mouth is the gate to hell. Two devils row the barge on which he stands, atop a pile of gold labeled "the Glory of the wicked." Among other details, he holds in his left hand a cup "full of indignation," in which a burning heart declares itself to be " zealous for my countries ruin." From his left hand dangles a placard with verses from Ezekiel 22 and 23: "Thou has greedily gained of thy Neighbours by Extortion: Behold therefore I have smit-ten my Hand at thy dishonest Gain. They shall take away thy Nose, and thine Ears, and strip thee out of thy Cloaths and take away thy fair Jewels." [6] As a caption, some verses imagine that justice for this free-rider will be meted out either in this world or in the next:

> Go on vile Traytors! glory in your Sins,
> And grow profusely Rich, by wicked Means,
> Ruine your Country for your own By-ends,
> Cozen your Neighbours, and delude your Friends,
> Despise Religion, ridicule her Rules,
> And laugh at Conscience, as the Guide of Fools;
> Impov'rish Thousands by some Publick Fraud,
> And worship Int'rest as your only God:
> Thus you may gain, in time, a South-Sea Coach,
> And ride thro London, loaded with Reproach;
> Become a proud Director, and at last,
> Be bound to render what you got so fast;
> Perhaps be punish'd when your All is lost,
> With Gallows, Pillory, or Whipping-Post;
> Or, if you save your Gold, be doom'd to float,
> To H—ll, in this infernal Ferry-Boat,
> Built at the Devil's Cost, now Stock is low,
> To waft Directors downwards, downwards, ho.

The point of the satire seems uncomplicated. Yet the danger of any allegory is that details can escape the overall message, frustrating the neatness of the scheme. And moral allegory is especially dangerous, because it is designed to get people to overcome their private interests in favor of the public good. Moralists therefore posit that there are objective, agent-neutral values; yet moral allegorists have to assign agent-neutral values to agents. In this print, the most straightforward moralizing comes from the devils, who jauntily announce, "Helm a Lee for H-ll." Unlike the writer of the verses, the devils are not confused about the jurisdiction of moral punishment. Confusion creeps in with human psychology, with the perspectives of satirist, audience, and the Knight himself. Why is the Knight's cup full of indignation? He seems to be taking on some of the satirist's *saeva indignatio,* or perhaps the satirist empathizes with the Knight's burning heart. The Knight seems also to have a past: a sun peeps out from his hat, under which the banner reads "How Glorious was (the) Beginning." The Knight, in short, is a rounded character, incapable of being reduced to the allegorical flatness of the devils. What saves him from reduction is human psychology.

Johnson's *Life of Savage* is the period's most sophisticated example of economic satire. In Savage, Johnson created a memorable portrait of a free-rider trapped in a world of reciprocal altruists who eventually hound him to his death over his unpaid debts. To summarize the *Life of Savage* this way makes it sound unrecognizably allegorical. As someone investigating human moral psychology from an evolutionary viewpoint, I am inclined to agree with Boswell that it is among the most interesting narratives in the English language. For Johnson, no less than empiricist moral philosophers today, places the problem of altruism at the very center of human sociability, using it to explore the fundamental issue in moral psychology: the relationship between society and an individual saturated by its values. But even if our interest is not moral psychology but simply allegory itself, Boswell's judgment holds. For in Savage, Johnson created an intense psychological portrait of a person for whom the literary notions of roundness and flatness express the complexity of living in the social world.

The *Life of Savage* brings a complete world into being. The world is highly divided into spaces, roles, local cultures, and individual psyches; yet it is neither fragmented nor atomistic. It is compressed, like a Dutch interior, and layered into groups of people with similar status and rank. Its inhabitants regularly interact. They contract debts and remember what they owe. They are keenly aware of each other's histories and interests. They have sex, marry, fight, eat, and talk politics. The strict lines of class contain their desires. Many of them are known by specific roles or professions, by high status or low: the

Figure 4. Anonymous, Lucifer's New Row Barge. Photo courtesy of the Newberry Library, Chicago.

king, the queen, a shoemaker in Holborn, a maid, a bawd, some soldiers. The list of characters whom Johnson introduces early on is impressive: Richard Savage; Ann Countess of Macclesfield; her husband, the Earl of Macclesfield; the Earl Rivers; the parliament; ecclesiastical judges; a poor woman; the Lady Mason; Mrs. Lloyd, his godmother; the executors to Mrs. Lloyd's will; his nurse; his master; all the literary world, whose attention was engrossed by the Bangorian controversy; some players; Sir Richard Steele; Steele's coachman; Steele's creditors; a great number of persons of the first quality; Steele's natural daughter on whom he intended to bestow a thousand pounds; an officious informant or malicious tale-bearer; the czarina; Mrs. Oldfield; the Duke of Dorset; the nobility; all of Savage's relatives; parents who murder their infants; Sir Thomas Overbury; Mr. Cibber; Mr. Hill, another critic of a very different class; many persons eminent for their rank, their virtue, and their wit; the pastoral Alexis, friendless and alone. A casual glance at this list will reveal perhaps the most crucial aspect of this society: identity is relational. It is based on place, name, family, claims of kinship, profession, action.

In this world, dominance hierarchies are an accepted part of social life; and since life is better for those at the top, competition for place is intense. Although mobility is limited, hierarchies can become unstable within a small sphere. The spheres of high and low classes are marked by male conflict over the control of resources. Each sphere values different resources. For the upper classes, rewards are mediated and representational; in the lower classes, men fight each other for access to women and to public spaces. Consider what happens when the king dies and the male-dominated hierarchy becomes briefly unstable: "Soon afterwards the Death of the King furnished a general subject for a poetical Contest, in which Mr. Savage engaged, and is allowed to have carried the Prize of Honour from his Competitors; but I know not whether he gained by his Performance any other Advantage than the Increase of his Reputation" (30).

This is a theme to which we will return: Savage signals his interest in moving up the social scale by foregoing material rewards in favor of the intangible "increase of his reputation." But Savage is uniquely a cross-over figure, participating too in the low world. In the low world, justice is rougher and the rewards are more visceral. Its public spaces are inhabited by drunk and bawdy men buying the services of prostitutes. Violence can break out with little warning or premeditation. Trivial altercations, such as over the use of a room in a brothel, can lead to death by stabbing. Coffeehouses, although sponsors of the new middle-class male ideal of politeness, still seem to be places of breathtakingly casual violence. The law regulates status competitions in both worlds, but it regulates them differently. Among the upper classes, the law smooths the path of inherited wealth—women and children, especially sons, are among the prime resources requiring control. In the low world, the law mostly punishes violence.

Let us call this whole system—the high and the low, the powerful and the powerless, the dominant and the submissive—the *patriarchy*. This word may be slightly misleading, suggesting the conscious dominion of powerful males who compete for the control of resources and exchange women like goods. In fact, the most desirable resources are the immaterial ones associated with the upper classes—resources that come under the heading of *psychic capital*.[7] Nobody seems to know this better than the dispossessed: the propertyless, the poor, the females, the children, the sexually immature junior males. Johnson, Savage, and Lady Macclesfield are three such dispossessed persons (I am referring to their representatives in the text, and therefore ultimately to Johnson's imagination). Felicity Nussbaum has convincingly argued that the system impedes the interests of many people—not only women but powerless males, economically exploited colonial subjects, and so on: "What remains unrecognized in the *Life of Savage* are the oppressive conditions that Savage, his mother, and the 'savage' share—the mother because of the sexual difference that renders her voiceless and associates her with whore and adulteress, Savage because of illegitimacy, Johnson and Savage because of impoverishment, the 'savage' of both sexes oppressed because of enslavement and colonization. All are unable to see their association, their alignment within domination. Instead, the emphasis on difference yields psychic and cultural misery, as well as mutual desire alternating with antagonism and violence" (1995, 65).

Dispossession and the desire for status lead Savage, Lady Macclesfield, and Johnson all to develop identifiable social strategies. Savage's and Lady Macclesfield's are almost identical, while Johnson's opposes theirs. All three strategies have a common impetus: they seek to redraw the ratio of freedom to obligation in their society so that it favors their own interests. Freedom means the pursuit of individual interest; obligation means subsuming individual interests into the collective. Johnson (and through him his characters) perceives that freedom and obligation are inversely proportional: the more freedom there is, the less obligation; the more obligation, the less freedom (again, all within the boundaries of a closed but dynamic system).

Savage and Lady Macclesfield seek freedom. The words *liberty* and *freedom* appear with stunning frequency in their vicinity. Their quest for freedom has all sorts of consequences—psychological, economic, structural. Both characters find dominant institutions, and the obligations they impose, oppressive. Their strategy is to undo these dominant institutions by fomenting chaos. They act as a solvent on the social order. Institutions become unstable. The mightiest members of the society become unable to "complete their intentions" with respect to their own property. The most prominent of these dominant institutions is the family. At first glance this may seem counterintuitive, for what Savage seems most to desire is a restoration of the family ties from which his mother severs him. Yet as we will see in the last section of this chapter when we consider his point of view, this desire is symbolic and diffuse. It is driven by the fantasy that making strangers his family, indeed creating a new culture of altruism based not on property but on sympathy, can free him from local obligation. Particular families are most often the target of Savage's antisocial probing:

> He was sometimes so far compassionated by those who knew both his merit and his distresses that they received him into their families, but they soon discovered him to be a very incommodious inmate; for being always accustomed to an irregular manner of life, he could not confine himself to any stated hours, or pay any regard to the rules of a family, but would prolong his conversation till midnight, without considering that business might require his friend's application in the morning; nor, when he had persuaded himself to retire to bed, was he, without equal difficulty, called up to dinner; it was therefore impossible to pay him any distinction without the entire subversion of all economy, a kind of establishment which, wherever he went, he always appeared ambitious to overthrow. (98)

The play of metaphors in this passage is stunning. The family is a prison, a source of obligation, a system of rules that "confine." Savage is restless, difficult, aimless. He runs his own shadow economy, a travesty of the official regulatory "establishment." He is a carnivalesque figure, "ambitious to overthrow" the system.

Of course, Savage's and Lady Macclesfield's interests diverge more than they overlap. Savage perceives that women have caused his dispossession. Two months after he was born, he was "illegitimated" by an act of Parliament. When his mother remarries, Savage is left without meaningful bonds in a society whose main currency is paternalism: "Thus, while legally the son of one Earl, and naturally of another, I am, nominally, nobody's son at all" (27). He is left in the care of women, none of whom possess the economic power to settle their meager financial resources on him: "Though [Mrs. Lloyd, his godmother] kindly endeavoured to alleviate his loss by a legacy of three hundred pounds, yet, as he had none to prosecute his claim, or call in law to the assistance of justice, her will was eluded by the executors, and no part of the money was ever paid" (7).

Savage becomes adept at indirection as a result. Toni Bowers astutely notes that he repeatedly seeks to get money from his mother by couching his desires in the language of sentiment: "All Savage's efforts 'to awaken her tenderness and attract her regard' have as their final goal not merely Anne Brett's recognition, but also the opening of her pocketbook" (1992, 125). Female power consists in deflecting material power through immaterial means. So too, Savage desires to create an economy of unmeasurable things. Certainly male desire takes immaterial resources as its object, but male power is more instrumental, less deflected, than female power. (This may explain why Johnson tethers Savage's masculinity to his capacity to pay the prostitute.)

Savage's and Lady Macclesfield's pursuit of freedom has deep psychological consequences. I have said that identity is relational and that the divisions of social space make people who they are. This is because of a startling psychological fact: people are deeply susceptible to the pressures of other people—with two notable exceptions. Savage and Lady Macclesfield refuse even the most conventional of obligations, namely letting the speech of other people influence them. But resisting other people's pressure is difficult; doing so requires an elaborate set of filters. The surest means of filtering out the pressures of other people seems to be, for both Savage and Lady Macclesfield, to give up having an inner life with its usual complement of reason and explicable motives. Savage is slave to his passions—prideful, obstinate, childish, motiveless—as is his cosmic maternal foil who "with an implacable and restless cruelty" continues "her persecution from the first hour of his life to the last." Both of them resist having their mental lives exposed. They are public about their passions and private about their reasons. As Savage so memorably puts it, "I have my private reasons; which I am not obliged to explain to any one" (131).

The moralist circles compulsively around these two, seeking some emission of light, his impatience growing ever more palpable: "It cannot be said that he made use of his abilities for the direction of his own conduct; an irregular and dissipated manner of life had made him the slave of every passion that happened to be excited by the presence of its object, and that slavery to his passions reciprocally produced a life irregular and dissipated. He was not master of his own motions, nor could promise any thing for the next day" (137).

With this psychological turn, we begin to approach the heart of the conflict between freedom and obligation. Johnson's first moral imperative is to obligate Savage and Lady Macclesfield. In a book on moral philosophy called *Taking Darwin Seriously,* Michael Ruse writes: "Suppose I help you, because I feel morally obliged to do so, but that you do not reciprocate, either by help- ing me or by throwing your help into the general pool. In the name of moral- ity, I can demand help from you because *it is right for you to help me.* My be- ing a moral individual does not entail my being a sucker. You should help me and others because it is the moral thing to do, and I can demand this of you" (1986, 243; emphasis in the original).

Ruse correctly identifies one response to the nonreciprocator, but begs a further question about where my sense that "it is right for you to help me" comes from. One source might be the moral impulse itself. Since an argument from reciprocity will have no force for someone who does not abide by a sys- tem of reciprocal altruism, a kind of arms race should develop between the free-rider and the reciprocal altruist. As Ruse notes, if you (a free-rider) do not reciprocate, I (a reciprocal altruist) am in danger of being made a sucker. But being made a sucker lowers my inclusive fitness, so I develop a normative response, insisting that you reciprocate because "it is right." Norms can thus arise out of the sublimation of anger and the need to invent rules that serve the moralist. Here is one plausible origin of the moral impulse.

A system of reciprocal altruism requires an all-seeing eye, a prophet of ob- jectivity to police everyone's honesty. The moralist is born to fill this need and flourishes by exposing exploiters of the system. The narrator ostentatiously assumes this role, becoming increasingly vocal about Savage's ruptured con- tracts. Variants on the word *obligation* appear with greater and greater fre- quency. The last part of the story—when Savage travels to Bristol—becomes a contest between Savage and the moralist over Savage's failing moral ac- counts. The moralist is dominant and watchful, not missing an opportunity to undercut any claim of honesty that Savage makes. He becomes intense and censorious. Savage, in turn, becomes secretive, frantic, and yet somehow valiant in his continued self-regard. They look like Victor Frankenstein and his monster flying across the frozen tundra on their dogsleds. In one scene, after landing in prison for his debts, Savage has just written a harsh satire on Bristol's inhabitants. The moralist responds:

Such was his imprudence, and such his obstinate adherence to his own resolutions, however absurd. A prisoner! supported by charity! and, whatever insults he might have received during the latter part of his stay at Bristol, once caressed, esteemed, and presented with a liberal collection, he could forget on a sudden his danger and his obligations, to gratify the petulance of his wit, or the eagerness of his resentment, and publish a satire by which he might reasonably expect that he should alienate those who then supported him, and provoke those whom he could neither resist nor escape. (132)

Against being damned to such an eternity of moral blackness, Savage has his defenses. These defenses are all psychologically fascinating. He manipulates information he takes in about the world in favor of himself. Savage has a strong capacity for self-deception: "He contented himself with the applause of men of judgment; and he was somewhat disposed to exclude all those from the character of men of judgment, who did not applaud him. . . . By arts like these, arts which every man practices in some degree, and to which to much of the little tranquillity of life is to be ascribed, Savage was always able to live at peace with himself " (73).

The moralist is quick to correct us if we find this comic or benign. If Savage only deceives himself to "alleviate the loss or want of fortune," his gift might be mentioned as an instance of the "philosophical mind" that Johnson will pursue through "The Vanity of Human Wishes" and *Rasselas*. Instead, the moralist, observing dryly that "it were doubtless to be wished that truth and reason were universally prevalent," labels Savage's attitude a "pleasing intoxication" that makes him turn "his eyes from the light of reason, when it would have discovered the illusion and shown him what he never wished to see, his real state" (73).

There are two ways of describing what the moralist is doing here. Either he is a classical rationalist digging for the truth, or he is simply another character with interests playing the game of moral objectivity to settle conflicts in his favor. Paradoxically, both descriptions are true. A thoroughgoing rationalist must hold either that someone is self-deceived or that she is morally culpable: after all, if someone is self-deceived, she is no more culpable than if she is being deceived by someone else. Amelie Oksenberg Rorty describes the rationalist picture of the self that would require this distinction: "If the self is essentially unified or at least strongly integrated, capable of critical, truth-oriented reflection, with its various functions in principle accessible to, and corrigible by, one another, it cannot deceive itself. According to the classical picture, the self is oriented to truth, or at least directed by principles of corrigibility that do not intentionally preserve error" (1988, 13). The moralist would seem to hold this picture of the self, because he objects to Savage's self-deception in the name of other people, the society, the collective good: Savage indecently "forgot that he gave others pain to avoid it himself." The moralist becomes increasingly obsessed with Savage's interiority. Is he even capable of experiencing obligation in a normal sense? From this rationalist perspective, Savage is less self-deceived than he is deceptive.

We should, perhaps, be skeptical of the moralist's motives. A key evolutionary insight is that in any conflict of interest "each party may be expected to use whatever means are available to manipulate the other's behavior in the direction of one's own optimum, whether by deceit, coercion, or sheer nagging" (Daly and Wilson 1988, 97). Our skepticism might lead us to suspect that Savage's self-deception threatens the moralist's top-down perspective because it is such an effective tool in the battle to avoid obligation. Why is it such an effective tool? Self-deception can penetrate us all the way through, becoming a way for us to deceive other people without having to regard ourselves as immoral. We can just be committed to our causes. Or, as the moralist cannily, sympathetically, and somewhat self-reflexively puts it after Savage exercises one of his little "arts of tranquility": "But this is only an instance of that partiality which almost every man indulges with regard to himself" (49).

Let us explore further this hypothesis about the origins of self-deception. Richard Alexander writes:

A measure of the effects of the new precision in evolutionary theory on biology can be taken by considering that until a few years ago biologists had interpreted "communication" as little more than the honest, accurate transfer of information between and among individuals. Similarly, linguists have tended to regard the function of human language as to serve as a vehicle for transmitting accurate information. Now biologists realize that the conflicts of interests that exist because of histories of genetic difference imply instead that nearly all communicative signals, human or otherwise, should be expected to involve significant deceit. (1987, 73)

If most communication is deceptive, especially between individuals whose interests diverge, then individuals should develop reliable ways of exposing instances of self-interested lying. The liar should then evolve greater and greater capacities for deception. Soon the arms race is on. To disseminate her propaganda more effectively, the liar should eventually develop the capacity to deceive even herself about her motives and intentions. She might relegate information harmful to her interests to her subconscious—indeed the exposing moralist might have a hard task in getting her to see her "real state."

Evidence suggests that Savage opts for an arms race of just this sort. Consider a peculiar observation that Johnson throws in at the end of the biography, almost as an afterthought: "A kinder name than that of vanity ought to be given to the delicacy with which he was always careful to separate his own merit from every other man's; and to reject that praise to which he had no claim. He did not forget, in mentioning his performances, to mark every line that had been suggested or amended, and was so accurate as to relate that he owed *three words* in *The Wanderer,* to the Advice of his Friends" (138; emphasis in original). This observation comes in the last pages, when Johnson is summing up Savage's character. By now we have come to experience Savage as a universal debtor, somebody who borrows from everyone he meets and brazenly refuses to pay back what he owes. Savage has long since exhausted his line of social credit. He has been banished to Wales and sent to prison "for a debt of about eight pounds, which he owed at a coffee-house" (121), and he is about to die in confinement in Newgate prison. Why, then, at the very end of the narrative, do we find Savage willingly obligating himself, scrupulously insisting that he owes a debt of three small words, in a poem that contains over two thousand lines?

Imagine Savage puffed up with rectitude, enormously gratified by his own honesty. The point of the gesture is to communicate it: his little act of "moral economics" (a phrase coined by Helen Deutsch [1995]) seems designed to show his friends that he is capable of being obligated. And what better way to communicate an essential, deep inner honesty than to really feel that honesty? Yet the moralist has already harshly discounted Savage's honesty by piling it with skepticism and scorn. Here is the moralist opining on the "value" of Savage's friendship (a passage that, as it happens, appears right before the passage about three small words in *The Wanderer*):

His friendship was therefore of little value; for though he was zealous in the support or vindication of those whom he loved, yet it was always dangerous to trust him, because he considered himself discharged by the first quarrel, from all ties of honour or gratitude; and would betray those secrets which in the warmth of confidence had been imparted to him. This practice drew upon him an universal accusation of ingratitude; nor can it be denied that he was very ready to set himself free from the load of obligation; for he could not bear to conceive himself in a state of dependence, his pride being equally powerful with his other passions, and appearing in the form of insolence at one time and of vanity at another. (138)

The moralist shades all information in his own favor. After such a passage, who would believe that Savage will pay back his debts? Savage's overly scrupulous honesty is exposed for what it is: a callow and hypocritical self-advertisement designed to distract the spectator moralists.

Knowing that the moralist has his interests does not entirely settle the moral question in Savage's favor. For Savage tailors his strategies to the moralist's overwhelming rationalism, leaving open the possibility that he too is a secret rationalist, just as the moralist supposes. Savage is canny enough about the system and its demands on him to have intuited that, as Richard Alexander has written, the realms in which secretiveness in behavior are required . . . expand as one tends to operate contrarily in respect to rules generally accepted by others. Since it is in everyone's interests to identify anyone not committed to the rules that are generally accepted and followed, it becomes increasingly difficult, risky, and self-consuming to add to the list of generally accepted rules one is going to avoid following. More and more of conscious time is used up in the effort to deceive successfully, and discovery becomes an increasingly expensive threat because of the significance of deliberateness in the effort, if it is discovered. Hence, also, at least part of the virtues of moralizing. (1987, 122)

Savage is a brazen cheater with a markedly secretive air. His habit of withdrawing "to his darling privacy" (96) when he is flush with a little cash is symptomatic of his resistance to a more general demand that he convert to *homo economicus.* Until he is forcibly imprisoned in Newgate, he is certainly "master of his own motions." Thoroughly disgusted by his freeloading, Savage's friends raise a subscription for him to retire to Wales. Savage agrees, briefly becoming a man of maxims, adopting their general perspective and "being now determined to commence a rigid economist" (114). But soon his friends receive a letter saying that he is still on the road, and like some mechanical entertainment, "could not proceed without a remittance." They send him "the money that was in their hands," and he travels on to Bristol. Yet once there he complains about them loudly enough so that they stop his supply of money. He retires to Wales for a year, a man "very much dissatisfied with the diminution of his salary" but obsessed, still, with status: he "contracted, as in other places acquaintance with those who were most distinguished in that country" (116).

In Wales Savage completes a tragedy and makes known his plan to travel back to London to put it on the stage. His chief benefactor, Pope, strongly advises him to turn it over to some other writers to fit it for the stage. After its success, his friends will hold the profits and pay Savage a pension. Savage rejects this proposal "with the utmost contempt. He was by no means convinced that the judgment of those to whom he was required to submit, was superior to his own. He was now determined, as he expressed it, to be *no longer kept in leading-strings,* and had no elevated idea of *his bounty,* who proposed to *pension him out of the profits of his own labours*" (116; emphasis in original).

Keeping the profits of his own labor are, for Savage, integral to the moral project of freedom. But what is freedom exactly? Why does Savage prefer to be a mechanical entertainment to being in leading strings? Why does he accept the remittance and refuse the pension? Why is it better to be a machine than a baby? Or perhaps the more appropriate image is an adult child: if his friends withhold his money, they "abandon" him like bad parents; and if they pension him, they keep him in a "state of infancy." (I will explore these odd metaphors at greater length in the final section of this chapter when I try to reconstruct Savage's sense of obligation from a nonrationalist point of view.)

Savage's strategy of avoiding payment extends and complicates some traditional ways of conceiving the relationship between freedom, reason, and privacy in discussions of eighteenth-century thought. Having an inner life is usually equated with a zone of freedom, however enforced by, and shot through with, social values (and even if that freedom is, according to one powerful tradition, an illusion [Habermas 1989, 111 passim]). Yet Savage perceives that having an inner life is tantamount to having the capacity to be obligated. Interiority is the conduit to society's normative demands. Savage's willful ignorance of other people's claims and his lack of conscience help to explain why social pressure has been totally ineffectual in forcing him to conform to its demands. "Whoever was acquainted with him was certain to be solicited for small sums," writes Johnson. But "it was observed that he always asked favours of this kind without the least submission or apparent consciousness of dependence, and that he did to look upon a compliance with his request as an obligation that deserved any extraordinary acknowledgments, but a refusal was resented by him as an affront, or complained of as an injury; nor did he readily reconcile himself to those who either denied to lend, or gave him afterwards any intimation that they expected to be repaid" (98).

The society's normative demands glance off Savage's glassy surface, which proves especially resistant to its demand for interiority, for depth. Johnson's tone here, as throughout the *Life of Savage,* is quite complex. On the one hand, his irony seems to cut hardest against Savage, pinning him in the gaze of the society whose shaming, spectatorial authority he invokes in his passives and nominalizations. "A refusal" is the action of one of Savage's unnamed interlocutors, and it stands like a stern watchman over Savage's foaming chaos of resentment and complaint. All the other agents in this passage are authoritative, disembodied, and invisible, inhabiting the objective perspective of the view from nowhere: "it was observed" and so on. But even as he invokes community standards, Johnson defends Savage against the pressure they collectively exert. Why do Savage's interlocutors require "extraordinary acknowledgments" of their "compliance" (a word that suggests a certain grudging attitude)? Shouldn't ordinary acknowledgments suffice? Interiority, then, seems in some measure inseparable from an "apparent consciousness of dependence." In resisting consciousness, in resisting having an inner life, Savage seems almost heroic. He is able to resist the very charge of "dependence" thrown at him by his enemies.

In the moral economy of reciprocal altruism, being reasonable means having reasons you can share, which in turn means opening yourself up to the will of others. For Savage, as we shall see, opening yourself up to the will of others means losing resources to people higher up the social ladder, and thus reverse strategies can develop to acquire resources from those higher-ups. To acknowledge the claims of reason is to open yourself to the instrumentality of the will of a society that demands that people's motives be "exposed." In Savage's resistance to depth psychology, exposure is a figure for the civilizing impulse itself. Exposure is also fatal. The final scene of Savage's life deserves to be quoted at length:

When he had been six months in prison he received from one of his friends, in whose kindness he had the greatest confidence, and on whose assistance he chiefly depended, a letter that contained a charge of very atrocious ingratitude, drawn up in such terms as sudden resentment dictated. Henley, in one of his advertisements had mentioned 'Pope's treatment of Savage'. This was supposed by Pope to be the consequence of a complaint made by Savage to Henley, and was therefore mentioned by him with much resentment. Mr. Savage returned a very solemn protestation of his innocence, but however he appeared much disturbed at the accusation. Some days afterwards he was seized with a pain in his back and side, which, as it was not violent, was not suspected to be dangerous; but growing daily more languid and dejected on the 25th of July he confined himself to his room, and a fever seized his spirits. The symptoms grew every day more formidable, but his condition did not enable him to procure any assistance. The last time that the keeper saw him was on July the 31st, 1743; when Savage, seeing him at his bed-side, said, with an uncommon earnestness, 'I have something to say to you, Sir'; but after a pause, moved his hand in a melancholy manner, and finding himself unable to recollect what he was going to communicate, said, ' 'Tis gone!' The keeper soon after left him, and the next morning he died. He was buried in the churchyard of St. Peter, at the expense of the keeper. (134–35)

This scene seems to confirm our rationalist intuitions. Up until now, Savage has avoided obligation by turning himself into a flat character. What eventually seems to kill him is having to confront his inner (rationalist) knowledge of his roundness. The details of his death scene—a parody of the deathbed confessional—help us gauge the depths of Savage's battle. Abandoned by his last friend and forced to see his "real state," he develops a pain in his side. For those of us searching for signs of inner life, the pain is ambiguous. It seems at once to be both psychosomatic (a pain in the heart) and evidence that there is no inner life beyond the raw play of sensation across his body. The confession on the tip of his tongue is more hopeful. It suggests that he struggles until his final breath to suppress his interiority, warding off his spirit with a gesture rather than confiding in his keeper (because to confide is to be dependent and thus obligated). And this small arms race he wins, obligating his keeper to pay his funeral expenses. Of course, this reading is based on a rationalist intuition so hermeneutically tight as to be self-confirming. The rationalist mind (ours, the moralist's) expects a self hierarchically oriented through deep inner space. Only from a rationalist's perspective could flatness be a countervailing strategy.

If the pursuit of freedom in a culture of reciprocal altruism can lead to death, the defense of obligation also has debilitating psychological consequences. Morality is costly for the moralist. Having something to lose if free-riders dominate the system, the moralist seeks to advance his own interests under the cover of objectivity. He may feel guilty, like an anxious fraud who himself will be exposed. He may face resistance from other members of the system who reject his moral demand even as they benefit from his keeping other people honest. Johnson's moralist is open to analysis of just this kind. He is powerful enough to bring a world into being, but he brings rebellion and resistance into being at the same time. Johnson becomes both a familiar figure from post-Freudian biography (the tormented and ambivalent moralist maturing into his great middle period) and a Shelleyan version of Milton's God (the vision of Bate's great biography of Johnson [1977]). He betrays ambivalence about reason itself.

The *Life of Savage* has long fascinated its readers. Boswell describes how Joshua Reynolds "upon his return from Italy . . . met with it in Devonshire, knowing nothing of its author, and began to read it while he was standing with his arm leaning against a chimney-piece. It seized his attention so strongly, that, not being able to lay down the book till he had finished it, when he attempted to move, he found his arm totally benumbed" (1934, 1:165). We never learn what seized Reynolds's attention so strongly, but judging by other readers' responses there are some likely candidates. All of them turn, in one way or another, on what makes moral psychology so fascinating to (us) reciprocal altruists.

Both of Johnson's eighteenth-century biographers were mystified by the force that Savage—"marked by profligacy, insolence, and ingratitude"— could exert over Johnson's otherwise skeptical mind (Boswell 1934, 1:161). Boswell thrills to the forensic mystery of Savage's parentage, trooping off to Holborn to investigate the parish records where Lady Macclesfield's son was baptized. So too do Clarence Tracy and Richard Holmes, Savage's twentieth-century biographers. No solution has been forthcoming, and as Boswell wrote, "The world must vibrate in a state of uncertainty on the question" (1934, 1:174).

Richard Holmes vibrates in a state of uncertainty about other mysteries too. He suggests that Savage's unaccountable sway over Johnson and others may have been erotic: "[Savage's sexual ambiguity] may stretch at times to the male patrons. Numerous contemporaries refer to Savage as strangely 'fascinating'; and without some subliminal psychological attraction such as this, it is genuinely difficult to account for Savage's extraordinary (if temporary) influence over so many different kinds and classes of people: aristocrats, intellectuals, players, tavern cronies and (at the last) a simple jail-keeper" (1993, 67). All of these reasons—the detective mystery, the mystery of influence, even the pull of the erotic—are shared by eighteenth- and twentieth-century readers. (We know eighteenth-century readers share the last one because we first hear the moralist gathering himself to oppose their hunt for "romantick adventures and imaginary amours.")

There is one point, however, on which eighteenth- and twentieth-century readers seem to part company: eighteenth-century readers are apparently more tolerant of the moralist and his authoritarian maxims than twentieth-century readers are. Twentieth-century readers engage in some rhetorical eye-rolling, recognizing that Johnson has a moral project but finding it irrelevant, if not downright antithetical, to what makes the text compelling for them. (At the very least, twentieth-century readers have to gear up to scale the wall of that machine of maxims, the periodic sentence).[8] For twentieth-century readers, Johnson's moral project misfires for many reasons. The most general one is that the moralist is only one among the text's many characters, and not an especially appealing or reliable one. Eighteenth-century readers are far more willing to allow that the moralist might have some meliorative effects. Sir John Hawkins writes:

Interspersed in the course of the narrative are a great variety of moral sentiments, prudential maxims, and miscellaneous observations on men and things; but the sentiment that seems to pervade the whole is, that idleness, whether voluntary or necessitated, is productive of the greatest evils that human nature is exposed to; and this the author exemplifies in an enumeration of the calamities that a man is subject to by the want of a profession, and by shewing how far less happy such an one must be than he who has only a mere manual occupation to depend on for his support. (1787, 155)

In fact, this apparent difference masks some important similarities. From Boswell on, critical work on Johnson's text has been devoted to resisting it: eighteenth-century readers are no more willing to be obligated than twentieth-century ones. Obligation is hard, as Johnson well knew. About *Paradise Lost*, he famously wrote that "its perusal is a duty rather than a pleasure. We read Milton for instruction, retire harassed and overburdened, and look else-where for recreation; we desert our master, and seek for companions" (1967, 1:184). His own moralist persona met with more particular local resistance as well for, among other things, his cruelty toward Lady Brett, former Countess of Macclesfield, who was by then a "rich, sad and reclusive widow in her late seventies, living alone in a small house in Old Bond Street" (Holmes 1993, 59). Boswell chided Johnson: "As you expelled Lady Macclesfield from society, why not so bury Wilkes, Kenrick, Campbell & c.?" And Johnson seemed chastened: "Sir, I don't know but I've been wrong" (Boswell 1956, 168; quoted in Nuss-baum 1995, 223 n. 20).[9]

Nor have eighteenth-century readers enjoyed the particular advantage of twentieth-century readers, that of being able to turn some of its aggression back around by deploying broadly psychoanalytic reading techniques. Twen-tieth-century readers are openly skeptical, turning their gaze on Johnson him-self. For example, Louise Barnett writes: "What is more intriguing than John-son's failure to penetrate Savage's murky history is his elaboration upon his primary source . . . in order to make the putative mother appear truly mon-strous. How Johnson regarded his own mother and motherhood in general seems germane to this line of inquiry" (1992, 857).

But the difference between the two positions, rather than being evidence of greater eighteenth-century tolerance of authority or twentieth-century skepticism, may be largely semantic and technical. Eighteenth-century read-ers conflate under the category of moral all kinds of things that we would call psychological; our reading practices and tactics of explanation differ accord-ingly. Hawkins, for instance, seems repeatedly drawn to what he calls the "moral" component of Johnson's text, but this term masks the fact that "moral" can refer both to the things he admires about Johnson and the stance from which he criticizes him. After commending Johnson for choosing to write about his friend, whose life gives the world "many admirable lessons of morality," Hawkins turns the same biographer's scrutiny on Johnson himself. First he writes: "His moral character displayed itself in the sincerity of his friendships, his love of justice and of truth, and his placability" (1787, 164). A few pages later he writes:

In the lesser duties of morality he was remiss: he slept when he should have studied, and watched when he should have been at rest: his habits were slovenly and the ne-glect of his person and garb so great as to render his appearance disgusting. He was an ill husband of his time, and so regardless of the hours of refection, that at two he might be found at breakfast, and at dinner at eight. In his studies, and I may add, in his de-votional exercises, he was both intense and remiss, and in the prosecution of his literary employments, dilatory and hasty, unwilling, as himself confessed, to work, and working with vigour and haste. (165)

The term *moral*, whether referring to a set of practices or to a personal ethos, can be as much a tool of critique as the term *psychological* is for twentieth-century critics.

Indeed, the eighteenth-century term *moral* and the twentieth-century term *psychological* refer to the same dynamic process of resistance, failure, lapse. In his famous twentieth-century psychobiography of Johnson, W. J. Bate sees Johnson's attempts to police his own perceived failings as evidence of a punishing superego:

> [Johnson was] left completely naked and vulnerable to the cruelest of psychological burdens that he was to face throughout his life (though it was naturally to prove an indispensable source of his greatness when kept in healthful interplay with other qualities). This was the fierce and exacting sense of self-demand—for which Freud gave the now-common term 'superego'—with its remorseless capacity, in some natures, to punish the self through a crippling sense of guilt and through the resulting anxieties, paralysis, and psychosomatic illness that guilt, grown habitual and strongly enough felt, begins to sprout. (1977, 121)

Bate's reading brings the resistance to the moralist into some focus. It is self-resistance. Just as reason exposes the motives of other people, it exposes its own motives too. Even when a moralist identifies with reason, there is no escaping the ambivalent knowledge that reason can be a cover for selfishness. Reason seems no closer than any other strategy to solving the problem of altruism. Hume jauntily explained that it is not "contrary to reason to prefer the destruction of the whole world to the scratching of my finger" (T 416). But for the moralist who manipulates evidence in the name of objectivity, reason can induce moral sickness. Paradoxically, the moralist is the one most likely to succumb to a pressure he applies in the name of other people.

Sympathy, Violence, and Obligation: Savage's Family Thinking

> [T]o marvel at the "triviality" of the circumstances precipitating
> such altercations is patronizing and ultimately unenlightening. . . .
> An implicit contrast is drawn between the foolishness of violent
> men and the more rational motives that move sensible people like
> ourselves. The combatants are in effect denigrated as creatures of
> some lower order of mental functioning, evidently governed by
> immediate stimuli rather than by foresightful contemplation.
> —MARTIN DALY AND MARGO WILSON, *Homicide*

Thus far we have described Savage's world as though it existed on a vertical plane, with obligation imposed from the top and resisted from the bottom. In these dimensions, Savage appears flat, while the moralist is cursed with a hideous, self-consuming complexity. Yet there is another plane on which the terms of the modern and postmodern critique of Enlightenment rationalism seem already to have been inscribed: sympathy, anticolonialism, violence, gender, and oedipalism. How different is this picture of the world? Is it Savage's picture? What does the view from the "ashes of a glass-house" (where Savage spends the night) look like?

As the prostitute example shows, Johnson wants to paint Savage as a person whose morals are spontaneous rather than reasoned. He depicts Savage's consciousness as extending along a horizontal axis of sympathy. He praises his poems for their wide views and expansive images. The stylistic hallmarks of that poetry—metonymy, the fleeting touch, the pleasing and bewildering speculation—become the vehicle on which Savage's imagination rides to "the settlement of colonies in uninhabited countries . . . the acquisition of property without injury to any . . . and the enjoyment of those gifts which heaven has scattered upon regions uncultivated and unoccupied" (92). These habits of thought should recall some of the abstract mechanisms of sympathy identified by the sentimental philosophers: resemblance, contiguity, associationism, and the conversion of the idea of another's emotion into our own vividly felt impression.[10]

Savage, too, sponsors this view of his moral life. In the occasional moments when he speaks for himself, he resists any rational accounting of his motives.[11] The most dramatic event of his life is his murdering James Sinclair in a brothel late at night. Afterward, he proffers a defense to Judge Page: "No doubt you distinguish between offences, which arise out of premeditation, and a disposition habituated to vice or immorality, and transgressions, which are the unhappy and unforeseen effects of a casual absence of reason, and sudden impulse of passion: We therefore hope you will contribute all you can to an extension of that mercy, which the Gentlemen of the Jury have been pleased to shew Mr. Merchant, who (allowing facts as sworn against us by the evidence) has led us into this our calamity" (36). This is a comic moment, staged for us moralists who can so easily point out that lacking reason is strategically useful and that Savage's two mitigating claims contradict each other: in a fit of passion, a person is impelled by an unstoppable force from within; in the heat of a violent group, he is led by forces from without. But we are here considering Savage's point of view, not trying to expose it (at least not too hastily).

Whatever the source of the compulsion, Savage claims to be passive before his action, caught frozen with his sword raised and James Sinclair mysteriously impaled on the other end.

Impelled by passion or compelled by Merchant, Savage seems, at the moment when the system grasps him most firmly, to have achieved his dream of becoming a machine. Passive before the forces acting on him, he is free from the first demand of reciprocal altruism: having to consider other people's perspectives. But while Savage's stance dovetails perfectly with a sentimental picture of the mind, it is sponsored less by theory than by a terrible dilemma facing the male inhabitant of the low public space, a dilemma to which becoming a machine is a fitting response. What rational motive could justify killing another human being? How can someone represent that action to himself? To be a man in this world is to be impelled by violence but then to have to live within a system that—because it is centered on intersubjectivity—describes you as having motives, the sort of thing you can only have in relation to something or someone else. Under the circumstances, the best thing to be is an instrument, acting without consequence. Male violence rips open a hole in the system of reciprocal altruism. To admit to having motives is to admit that there is some kind of conflict of interest, which is then to admit that the person you killed had interests of his own, which is then to admit that he had a phenomenology, which is then to face up to the fact that you extinguished that phenomenology. Obligation, in short, can grip at you even when you are most blind to its claims.

In sifting the trial evidence, Richard Holmes offers an intriguing hypothesis about Savage's motives that squares with this account. One of the eyewitnesses to testify against the three men was a maid at the brothel. Her evidence, according to Holmes, concentrated on the attitudes of Savage and his friends as they pushed their way into the parlor, emphasizing "the whole party's insistence on having absolute and immediate deference paid to their wishes." "What emerges," he writes, "is a clash of social hierarchies and class assumptions. This points towards the heart of the trial, and the underlying cause of the affray. Savage and his friends had assumed social precedence, the privilege of moneyed gentlemen to command and bully, which the habitues of Robinson's Coffee-house were not prepared to grant them. In this sense, the events of that drunken night were not mere chance. They were a logical outcome of all Savage's obsessively pursued claims to social distinction and recognition" (1993, 106). A nobleman is the sort of person who can impose his will without consequence. Savage's little stolen moments of freedom, strung together, represent a larger nostalgia for that original moment of freedom, now lost, when he was a nobleman and before he was forced out into the system of reciprocal altruism.

We have not yet fully confronted the question of what forces Savage into the system of reciprocal altruism. Evolutionary psychologists have posited that reciprocal altruism is an extension of kin selection combined with nepotism. And what forces Savage to become a failed reciprocal altruist is, of course, the failures of the previous systems. Kin selection has failed Savage, and so have the bonds of nepotism. To understand Savage's response to these failures, we need to approach his mental life from a different angle; we need to understand his habit of turning kin relations into symbolic or psychic capital.

In David Hume's view, sympathy's most powerful mechanism is consanguinity. Hume's straightforward assessment is that "the relation of blood produces the strongest tie the mind is capable of in the love of parents to their children, and a lesser degree of the same affection, as the relation lessens" (T 352). Our love for others tends to weaken as our relation to them grows more distant and to strengthen as it grows closer.[12] As many critics have pointed out, Lady Macclesfield is an obvious counterexample to the presumed naturalism of parental love; yet Johnson's scandalized attitude toward her makes clear that he shares Hume's presumption. Savage, by contrast, realizes how important consanguinity is to producing sympathy, but he has no illusion that it needs to be natural. Rather, by symbolically attaching himself to nonrelatives as kin, he tempts them to look after their interests. To Johnson's great amusement, Savage organizes his world on the principle that "the inhumanity of his mother had given him a right to find every good man his father" (13). This mode of attachment I will call *family thinking*.

Family thinking is the representation of relations between strangers as relations between kin, and the use of kin metaphors to explain other kinds of relations. It is a principle tool of psychoanalytic thought; indeed, Savage's family thinking has more in common with Freudianism than it does with Humeanism. For family thinking by definition is never descriptive; it is almost always normative and manipulative. Its goal, like that of the moralists, is to tempt people into making reciprocal altruism mistakes—to pay out a little more in the interests of others than they get back. This critique of Freudian family thinking has been made most trenchantly by the Canadian sociologists Martin Daly and Margo Wilson in their study of the causes of violent conflict:

Psychoanalytic writers have thoroughly misapprehended the manipulative uses of taboo and symbolism by which individuals promote their own interests at others' expense. Freud, for example, interpreted the fact that incest prohibitions are extended to distant relatives and affines as a nonadaptive vestige of "group marriage," never realizing that manipulative elaborations of primary incest avoidance serve the interests of the rule-makers. A young man's natural sexual interest in his father's junior wife, for example, is proclaimed the equivalent of that unnatural abomination "incest with the mother," in a transparent attempt to exploit the repugnance of real mother-son incest in the father's reproductive interest.

Similarly, Freud turned the metaphor of king as "father" on its head. Instead of perceiving that powerful people exploit metaphors of familial relatedness in order to claim entitlement to respect, obedience, and affection, Freud imagined that the subjects create a symbolic father to satisfy their own (guilty) psychological needs. In 1609, King James I of England proclaimed himself "parens patriae, the political father of his people"; the title was not thrust upon him by his "children." The following analysis by sociologist Pierre van den Berghe (1985) is much more insightful than Freud's: "If power is to be justified (so as to be more readily exercised), the aim of power must be hidden or denied. The best denial of the effect of power is that oppression is in the best interest of the oppressed. . . . Paternalism mimics the genuine *concern* of the parent for the child, which is founded on the real overlap of interest inherent in genetically based nepotism, and thus hides the overwhelmingly conflictual basis of the ruler-subject relationship. Paternalism models itself on a relationship of genuine *dependence* and incapacity, in which the helpless child's survival and well-being is contingent on adult care, and extends it to a situation in which the dependence is *reversed*. The ruler who parasitizes the subject disguises parasitism as altruism." (1988, 113)

According to this critique, a typical piece of family thinking consists in defusing resistance or revolution by describing it as "oedipal," thus "implicitly assert[ing] the rebel's irrationality and deny[ing] the legitimacy of his grievances." "Oedipal theory," Daly and Wilson write, "has thus become a weapon of authoritarianism" (1988, 113–14).[13]

Savage's family thinking, although no less manipulative, does not so much impose obligation as respond to deprivation. The strategy is the same: to turn conflicts of interest to one's own advantage by representing them symbolically as confluences of interest. The lines from Savage's poem *The Bastard* quoted as the epigraph to this chapter announce his intention of sowing the seeds of obligation far from his mother's rocky bed. If he could have his way, strangers would be as kind to him as though he were their son. The culture would mother him. He transfers his affections to a sublime unnamable queen:

> Lost to the life you gave, your son no more,
> And now adopted, who was doom'd before,
> New-born I may a nobler mother claim;
> But dare not whisper her immortal name;

Supreamly lovely, and serenely great!
Majestic mother of a kneeling state!
Queen of a people's hearts, who ne'er before
Agreed—yet now with one consent adore!
One contest yet remains in this desire,
Who most shall give applause, where all admire.   (1962, 92)

Family thinking seems designed to reduce mental agitation by overcoming conflict: in the last lines, a potentially vicious sibling rivalry becomes a contest to outshine by praising; family thinking discharges uncivil energy, binding people together in protonationalist unity. (In the *Dunciad,* Pope slyly critiques this mode of normative manipulation when he imagines that boy poets would compete rather than unite for the affection of their mother/queen.) An especially interesting case of family thinking occurs in Savage's relationship with the actress Ann Oldfield, who bestows on him a pension without seeming to attach any demands of reciprocity. Although Mrs. Oldfield's shady reputation might lead the spectator moralists to wonder whether she expected sexual favors in return, Savage makes a show of mourning her loss "as for a mother."

Family thinking is designed to discharge the anxiety of social conflict, but in this economy something is never got for nothing. Family thinking breeds its own dark fantasies, especially fantasies of infanticide: Savage repeatedly imagines that he was exposed and abandoned as a baby, a fear he projects onto the culture at large. Family thinking personalizes vast impersonal economic relations, but this is a two-edged sword. On the one hand, Savage uses it to manipulate those economic forces to his own advantage; but on the other, he imagines himself as personally victimized by those same forces. Consider his infanticide fantasies. The vast literature on infanticide—a practice recorded in every known human culture—posits that men and women who kill their children are driven by economic factors. Far from being insane, people who commit infanticide may be acting from a position of economically suspended agency. Young mothers who are poor and unwed are many times more likely to kill their babies than are mature, financially secure women. The sociologist Maria Piers has written that in many communities throughout history in times of economic hardship "people took it for granted that infants had to die so that the bigger children and grown-ups could survive" (1978, 44).

By this logic, Savage was an especially unlikely candidate for infanticide. His mother was already thirty when she had her first child, and even though he was the product of an adulterous relationship, she had a second child with the same man. That man had other children out of wedlock, making generous provisions for them in his will. Savage's mother too had financial means: when her husband demanded a divorce, he repaid her marriage settlement. All this suggests that she was not facing the typical dilemma of the infanticidal parent: whether to sacrifice her child for the sake of future healthy offspring. Johnson, too, perceived that Lady Macclesfield's economic circumstances were not conducive to infanticide (though he mistakes those particular circumstances), and he therefore supposes that she is innately wicked, if not insane: "It is not indeed easy to discover what motives could be found to overbalance that natural affection of a parent, or what interest could be promoted by neglect or cruelty" (6).

Savage fantasizes that his mother attempts infanticide against him throughout his life. A widely accepted definition of infanticide is "the willful destruction of newborn babies through exposure, starvation, strangulation, smothering, poisoning, or through the use of some lethal weapon" (quoted in Hrdy 1997, 404). Savage's fantasies are a bit peculiar, for while they suppose willful intent on the part of the mother, they also suppose cowardly displacement—having him shipped off to the colonies—and the unintentional collusion of people like the queen. One part of Savage's fantasy may have some validity, and it relates directly to reciprocal altruism. Wet-nursing, it is thought, was practically a legalized form of infanticide. Maria Piers writes: "It must have been common knowledge among her customers that the [wet-nurse] was a professional feeder and a professional killer. . . . The phenomenon is reflected in the vernacular of at least two languages. In English, the wet nurse was referred to as 'angel maker,' in German as 'Engelmacherin'" (1978, 52). Piers also notes that while the penalty for infanticide in most European countries was death, wet nurses were punished if at all by a fine and whipping (1978, 51). What explains this peculiar set of circumstances? Class stratification, a division of labor, reciprocal altruism, and, indeed, a degree of class warfare are all presupposed by wet-nursing—"when the mother or both parents contract with another woman to suckle their infant, an arrangement which encumbers the wet-nurse but frees the mother both for status or labor-related pursuits and simultaneously also renders the mother fertile for subsequent pregnancies" (Hrdy 1997, 405).

Wet nurses were typically poor women who were themselves postpartum and lactating. Hired by rich women, they were in effect being paid to deprive their own babies. Sarah Blaffer Hrdy writes: "Given that any shift away from breastmilk would have introduced new opportunities for infection and lowered survivorship for infants thus deprived of milk their mothers provided to the children of others, wet-nurses were directly contributing to the death of their own offspring. Maternal decision-making in these instances must however be examined in social context. . . . The price paid by these mothers for remaining within the system at all (perceived by them with some accuracy as synonymous with survival?) was to redirect their own milk to non-relatives" (1997, 410).

Here in a nutshell is Savage's dilemma: to survive within the system means transferring his scant resources up the social ladder. Yet Savage is not only a figurative wet nurse, a forced and resisting altruist; he is also, by his own reckoning, one of the wet nurse's noble "angels," a high-class child sacrificed down the system to his mother's interests. The evidence that Piers and others bring forward suggests that no part of this system operated in the interests of babies, poor or rich. Why did rich mothers buy into a system that was almost as bad for their own babies as for the babies of the wet-nursing class? How did this division of reproductive labor serve their interests? Given the high rates of infant mortality in eighteenth-century Europe, wet-nursing may have allowed some women to be marginally more reproductively successful, thus helping them raise more healthy children. However unknowable the reasons, intentional malice certainly played no part; yet intentional malice is precisely the cause Johnson chooses to attribute to Lady Macclesfield: "Whatever were her motives, no sooner was her son born than she discovered a resolution of disowning him; and in a very short time removed him from her sight, by committing him to the care of a poor woman" (6).

Wet-nursing is Savage's induction into the harsh and depersonalizing world of reciprocal altruism. In response, he seeks to make the culture parent him. Johnson neatly captures Savage's impulse toward family thinking in an epigram, the first of Johnson's published comments on Savage: "Humani studium generis cui pectore fervet, / O! colat humanum Te foveatque genus!" (Devotion to mankind burns in your breast! / O! may mankind in turn cherish and protect you!)[14] William Epstein points out that the verb *foveo* can mean "to patronize, as well as to make warm, give comfort to, soothe, relieve, fondle, caress, nurse, foster, nurture, minister to, favor, support, encourage, befriend, promote, cherish, and cultivate" (1986, 149). Wet-nursing is the first stop on the royal road to authorship, Savage's most personal symbol for an emotional lack that the culture as a whole has to be made to fill.

Savage uses family thinking to alter the direction of power in the patriarchal system. He is a junior male without resources, who imputes his lack of power to a primal fitness tradeoff made by his mother to favor her interests over his. This fitness tradeoff has (in his mind) kept him from controlling any resources of his own; he fights back by seeking to build an alliance with the patriarchs, whom he imagines as a collective source of power against massed female interests:

[Savage] was once told by the Duke of Dorset, that it was just to consider him as an injured Nobleman, and that in his opinion the nobility ought to think themselves obliged without solicitation to take every opportunity of supporting him by their countenance and patronage. But he had generally the mortification to hear that the whole interest of his mother was employed to frustrate his applications, and that she never left any expedient untried, by which he might be cut off from the possibility of supporting life. (20)

The Duke of Dorset holds out the promise that Savage's primal injury will be repaired, a hope once again dashed by his mother. This passage can be read as a compressed version of Savage's story. From an original unity in which there was no gap between him and his role, Savage is forced into obligation by the perception of his mother's interests. Indeed, the very concept of interest forces such a gap because it is relative: it leads to difference and indirection, to choice and obligation. Family thinking is the closest he can come to reestablishing an undifferentiated personal identity. And his message might be taken to heart by anyone: to seek to get out of the culture of reciprocal altruism is to yearn for that original unity before we perceived that our mothers had "interests" and that they might be different from ours.

In the introduction to this book, I proposed that Johnson's text raises certain questions about the moral life: What can we do to be more moral? Is there such a thing as opting out of the system of morality altogether? Is it possible to be an amoralist? We are now in a position to offer an answer of sorts. Morality comes from having to take other people's interests into account, which means that we are already moral. Johnson's exploration of the limits of sympathy and the moral command delivers good news and bad news. The bad news is that there is nothing special we can do to be moral; the good news is that as reciprocal altruists we already *are* moral.

Chapter Six

Pride's Reasons

Hume's Spectator Morality

Earlier, men had sought to decipher the concealed or partially revealed will of God; now they sought to understand the concealed
or partially exposed wills of human beings. That, in a nutshell, was
what being enlightened was all about.

—GORDON S. WOOD, "Conspiracy and the Paranoid Style"

Naturalism, like the empiricism of which it is a branch, raises certain philosophical questions. Chief among them is the question of how facts and values
are related. The contemporary empiricist, an evolutionary naturalist, might
focus on sex. If human nature evolved according to an algorithm in which
adaptations enhance reproductive fitness, what claims can we make about
how anatomical or sexual facts relate to cultural values? (This question has, of
course, been at the center of feminist-inflected poststructuralist theory to
which evolutionary psychology, staring across the two-cultures divide, has
been unremittingly and pointlessly hostile).

Like their late-twentieth-century counterparts, eighteenth-century empiricists worried about the fact/value distinction, but they tended to place at
the center of human nature features other than sexuality: cognition and perception, the passions, sympathy, the sense of justice. Certainly some eighteenth-century intellectuals were asking how sexual facts relate to social values, but they tended to be artists—social novelists, satirists, and painters, like
Richardson, Fielding, Lady Mary Wortley Montague, and Hogarth. While
eighteenth-century precursors to today's naturalists can be found among both
philosophers and artists, each group brings a distinct inflection to the fact/
value question. The philosophers ask, in a high and serious tone, how simple
impressions become subjectivity, how "atom" becomes "structure" (Deleuze

1991, 92); the artists revel in the absurdities of that sexually awkward, obsessive, pride-smitten creature navigating his way through the thrones, dominions, princedoms, powers of court, law, family, army.

One such philosophical precursor is David Hume, and it is to his singular and visionary picture of human psychology that this chapter turns. At the end of chapter 5, we left Samuel Johnson, the moralist, trying to peer into the human soul. Hume, his great humanist rival, was also an anatomist, but he prided himself on his calm, detached attitude toward other people. Except for a few notorious incidents like his friendship with Rousseau, Hume skillfully avoided conflict in most of his relationships. His picture of the human mind is intense and detailed but far less personal that of Johnson, whose drive to know what people are like (and to expose and occasionally punish them) runs passionately up against the facts of his own world.

The subject of this chapter, therefore, is not an extended character sketch like Johnson's *Life of Savage,* but a short philosophical text, a few pages from the beginning of Book 2 of Hume's *Treatise* on the topic of pride. This chapter considers the psychological, aesthetic, moral, and political questions these pages raise. The chapter falls roughly into three parts. The first part offers a technical exposition of the fact/value distinction in Hume's theory of pride in relation to questions of inwardness and personal identity. The second part situates Hume's theory of pride within eighteenth-century writing about acting. The third part attempts briefly to broaden outward from the inner life to the social system, to ask why Hume represents the human psyche in such an admittedly odd and baroque way. The answer to this last question will be that he seeks to reflect on the connection between self-interest and property ownership, thus offering his own answer to the question of what it means to be *homo economicus.*

Let me begin with a significant recent interpretation of Hume's theory of the passions. In *A Progress of Sentiments* Annette Baier has glossed the basic issue she finds in Hume's writings on the passions as the question of the individuality or typicality of the self, specifically the question of how attributes and essence are related. She writes:

Me and my character traits, me and my abilities, disabilities, virtues and vices, me and my brain, heart, nerves, skin, pores, muscles, me and my life, me and my heap of perceptions, me and my reputation, me and my family, me and my loves, me and my ambitions, me and my country, me and my preferred vacation place and its climate, me and my evaluation of the importance or unimportance of whether the beautiful fish in the ocean is or isn't in any sense mine rather than yours, ours or no one's. What is this "I" who claims this manifold as her own? (1991, 135)

There is a well-worn track in Hume criticism leading away from the question of "What is this 'I' who claims this manifold as her own?" but Baier refuses to take it. This track has been taken by critics describing, worrying about, and celebrating Hume's seeming dissolution of the "self" at the end of Book 1 of the *Treatise* ("Of Personal Identity"). Some critics find that the dissolution of the self leads to increased possibilities for a "literary" style; others worry that Hume's supplementation of the "I" by an abstracted and institutional "humanism" leads to a politically prejudicial "I-effect." As Jerome Christensen has written, echoing Theodor Adorno, "If we consider the *Treatise* as a text defecated of any substantial 'I,' we can understand it as a residue—nuanced, articulated, inconsistent, full of opportunities for sympathy—all the easier to dominate" (1987, 80).

Rather than worrying about whether or not Hume "defecates his text of any substantial 'I,'" expresses "metaphysical agony" (Noxon 1973, 22), literary irony, or a suspicious desire to transfer human agency up the folds of greater Enlightenment institutions, Baier thinks that worries about the disappearing "I" in Hume's *Treatise* should lead us to reflect on how we credit other people with an internal life and consequently how we understand what is most "personal" about them. She interprets Hume as saying that we credit people with internal mental states, not by any method of psychological projection (for instance, by projecting pictures into their minds or by putting ourselves in a position to imagine what they are seeing), but by inferring their inner life from their contingent features and the particulars of their surroundings. Thus Baier does not believe that we can know or assume directly the answer to "What is this 'I' who claims this manifold as her own?" Rather, we scrutinize people's attributes—"skin, hair, character-traits, virtues and vices"—and reason that some unity, some "person," must bind them all together.

But this process is somewhat more complicated than just looking at a person and trying to ascertain how her hair goes together with her skin (or more practically, for a society anxious about contracts, how her expression of intention goes together with her prior mental state). There is a form of indirection, even opacity, built in to the process, since we come to make inferences of this sort only by first crediting ourselves with an internal life, and then by drawing an analogy to another person. Thus for Baier, the answer to the question "What is this 'I' who claims this manifold as her own?" turns on how "you" and "I" mutually credit ourselves with internal lives and how we mutually infer the internal life of the other person: "The answer is that I must be to what is mine whatever I take you to be to what it yours, and what you take me to be to what is mine" (1991, 136).

Baier thinks we are trained to become experts in this mutual crediting and mutual inference by our own experience of what Hume calls the "indirect" passions—passions that arise on account of some belief of ours, rather than from direct pleasure and pain stimuli. She calls this process of making inferences "a matter of the relationship between a person and what is hers, in all the 'hundred' senses of the personal possessive pronoun":

> The indirectness of the indirect passions, which later becomes simply the complication of their objects, is a matter of the relationship between a person and what is hers, in all the "hundred" senses of the possessive personal pronoun. So this indirectness and complication should shed light on Hume's reflective views about person, their perceptions and whatever objects of their perceptions they see as their own, as either part of themselves or some sort of possession of theirs. (1991, 136)

Following Baier, I take the "matter of the relationship between a person and what is hers, in all the 'hundred' senses of the personal possessive pronoun" to be the definition of the "personal" in Hume. Through an analysis of Hume's theory of pride, his paradigmatic example of an indirect passion, I will try to flesh out Baier's view that the "indirectness of the indirect passions" trains us to become aware of the personal in this sense.

Yet the point of this exposition is not simply to echo Baier, but rather to explore the authority that Hume gives to the aesthetic in his map of the human mind. After describing Hume's theory of pride at some length, I bring out an analogue to Hume's writings on the indirect passions: the acting theory of the mid-eighteenth century, particularly the branch of it seeking to explain how an actor's external expressions are formed from internal feelings. Tellingly, in the acting theory that emerges from the Garrick theater, the question of how a person and her attributes go together is not strictly an affair of personal psychology. Rather the personal, in this sense, comes to seem an aesthetic, or even literary affair in the sense described by Alvin Kernan: "Discussions of literature . . . seem . . . to assume that literary texts, old or new, differ from other types of texts in being self-consciously aware that they are not trying to be faithful to some prior literal truth" (1993, 25).

Kernan's observation about the "literary" resonates in a number of ways with Hume's writings on pride. First, we can easily recognize (as many of his harshest critics have done) that Hume's theory of the indirect passions is so far from being an "ordinary" account of emotions as to seem a literary one (his critics would call it "fictional" rather than literary). Second, Kernan's definition of literature echoes the acting theory of mid-eighteenth century, which asks how certain acting styles convey the effects of psychological verisimilitude and depth without actually referring to some prior mental state held by an actor.

But here we can introduce a complication into Kernan's definition, which neatly skirts the fact that fictional texts almost always seem to refer to "prior literal truths" ("rocks and stones and trees") without actually doing so. That is, many fictional texts can be shown to refer to objects that do have a prior literal truth—often a truth that the literary tourist can go and see for herself—while simultaneously raising the question of how an artist's consciousness transforms such objects.[1] Similarly, eighteenth-century acting theory seeks to establish a relationship between an actor's expression and his previous mental states, while doubting any actual connection between his expressions and "prior literal truth"—indeed making the opacity of such a relation the real art of the actor. The argument of the first part of this chapter is that the indirect passions, like much eighteenth-century acting theory, share this "literary" feature in common: they seek to determine the relationship between an expression and a previous mental state, while leaving open to question (indeed, at points explicitly thematizing a lack of connection between) the expressions and any actual prior representation.

Hume's Formalist Theory of Pride

By *pride*, I mean Hume's theory of pride as it stands, unsupplemented by any interpretation. Hume says about pride, which he calls a "system": "That cause, which excites the passion, is related to the object, which nature has attributed to the passion; the sensation, which the cause separately produces, is related to the sensation of the passion: From this double relation of ideas and impressions, the passion is deriv'd" (T 286).

I will go into more detail later about the different parts of this "system." In general, most readings of Hume's theory of pride have interpreted Hume as trying and failing to mean something intelligible, or at least something ordinary, by pride. As Donald Davidson memorably put it, Hume's use of the word *pride* seems not to "correspond to any use the word has in English" (1980, 278); and Jerome Neu has argued specifically about pride that "this picture of the passions is untrue to our experience" (1977, 33). According to many of Hume's readers, pride bears an unusually complex—if not frankly antithetical—relationship to ordinary emotion; yet this distance can be overcome by interpreting Hume as meaning one or another thing by pride. In Hume's theory, pride is not an ordinary emotion; rather it is a highly stylized neoclassical literary and theatrical intervention. We can read Hume as establishing pride's distance from ordinary emotion, indeed its peculiar irreducibility to an ordinary emotion, as one of its key features.

From its position at the beginning of Book 2 of Hume's *Treatise of Human Nature*, we should initially see pride as Hume's first major constructive answer to his long bout of melancholy skepticism at the end of Book 1. A reader of the first two hundred and fifty pages of the *Treatise* has gradually become familiar with that book's dialectical structure, which oscillates between constructive and destructive claims, between Hume's scientist of man persona and his hollow-eyed melancholic persona, between his naturalism and his skepticism. This oscillation takes place both within discrete sections of text (indeed Hume's turns in and out of skepticism in the last section of Book 1 seem impossible to map),[2] and within the overall shape of Book 1, which lunges finally into skepticism, massively undercutting everything that has come before. As a reader opens Book 2, she perhaps expects a loud salvo in reply, a large-scale constructive—naturalist—answer to the skepticism that overwhelmed her at the end of Book 1.

The topic of Book 2 is the passions; the first of the passions that Hume takes up is pride. What kind of naturalist answer (if any) does pride represent to Hume's previous skepticism? Pride is a very special answer to Hume's skepticism, an answer best put by Kant, who spent so much energy answering Hume's overall text. The sort of answer pride represents can be found in the following passage from Kant's *Critique of Judgment:* "Cognitions and judgments must, along with the conviction that accompanies them, admit of universal communicability; for otherwise there would be no harmony between them and the object, and they would be collectively a mere subjective play of the representative powers, exactly as skepticism desires" (1952, 75). If we settle for a notion of limited, rather than universal communicability, we find that Kant's description of the faculty of taste matches Hume's "system" of pride. We also find that pride answers Hume's previous skepticism by rendering objective judgments that up until this point in the *Treatise* remain vague, "collectively a mere subjective play of the representative powers, exactly as skepticism desires."

What are these judgments that pride renders objective? Most broadly they are the "personal" judgments I was discussing above: judgments about how aspects of my identity fit together with other aspects of my identity, and about the relationship I am capable of forming with (often very intimate) aspects of myself. For example, one such judgment might be the judgment of how I "go together" with my skin or with my character traits—with my ethnicity, my gender, my sexual orientation, my love or hatred of my family, and so forth. Yet to the extent that Hume's theory of pride delivers a way of thinking about these questions, it also places a major restriction on them. The restriction is that in feeling proud, I am able to estimate my relationship to aspects of my identity only insofar as I judge these aspects of my identity as praiseworthy or humiliating, as good or bad. Thus my judgments are not straightforward estimations of my qualities, or even of my relationship to my qualities. Rather, they are judgments of my relationship to my qualities admitted as valuable.

Once she realizes this about Hume's theory of pride, the reader of the *Treatise* may wonder why—if her previous intuitions about the structure of the book are correct—Hume provides only a limited, restricted answer to the giant Rabelaisian skepticism of Book 1. Pride allows Hume to reconstruct a "self," whose grounds he had vigorously destroyed in the "personal identity" section of his melancholy bout. In fact, so aggressively does Hume demand the return of this "self" that a reader might be forgiven for thinking that Hume reserves all of his dialectical energies for this topic alone. And yet these claims about the "self" turn out to be only the cornerstone of a doctrine that, in Annette Baier's view, "does introduce considerable complication into the simple empiricist program of Book One" (1978, 28)—a complication that seems to imply a necessary connection between emotional responses and the self.

Hume's System of Pride

Hume's theory of pride seems meant to answer the question of why we have one emotional response rather than another to a particular object, and why one particular object rather than another produces an emotional response in us. Hume will argue that some of our emotional states are knitted so closely together with their objects that features of our psychology seem to have "preselected" these objects.[3] Since Hume telegraphs his interest in pride—and its opposite humility—as the archetypes of such emotional states, his surprising focus on our psychology as a source of the "fit" between the object and our feeling is indeed, as Baier suggests, a complication of the simple empiricist program of Book 1. Hume straightforwardly asserts in Book 1 that our sense impressions cause our thoughts and beliefs, not the other way around. It is a lively question whether Hume goes fully in a Kantian direction in Book 2, suggesting that aspects of our psychology are responsible for any of the object's actual features, or whether he asserts only more modestly that our psychology is responsible for the *appropriateness* of the object to our feelings about it. (This would be only as though he had asserted in Book 1 that our psychology is responsible for the "fit" between sense impressions and their related ideas).[4]

In Book 2, part 1, sections ii and iii of the *Treatise,* Hume writes that pride consists of three distinct parts: a cause, a passion, and an object. Hume's technical terminology may be somewhat misleading: by "cause" he means what I called "object" in the previous paragraph—some person, event, or thing to which we respond emotionally. (Hume's vocabulary happily avoids the implication that the source of pride must be external to us, as the term *object* perhaps does not). By "object" Hume only ever means one thing: the "self," or that "succession of related ideas and impressions, of which we have an intimate memory and consciousness" (T 278)—and we will have occasion to see much more fully what Hume means by this startling assertion. The "cause" and the "object" are "ideas" in Hume's vocabulary, and the passion itself is a "simple and uniform impression" (T 277). He summarizes the system so far:

The first idea, that is presented to the mind, is that of the cause or productive principle. This excites the passion, connected with it; and that passion, when excited, turns our view to another idea, which is that of self. Here then is a passion plac'd betwixt two ideas, of which the one produces it, and the other is produc'd by it. (T 278)

This description of the system might lead us to wonder whether we are to identify pride with the entire system or just with that part of it that he calls the "passion": how can pride at once stand alone as a "simple and uniform impression" and still owe so much to an elaborate causal plan? Some time will pass before Hume directly takes up the relationship between the simple sensation and the overall emotion of pride; rather he spends much of these sections elaborating what he means by the terms "cause" and "object" within the system of pride. To avoid confusion, let me denominate the *sensation* of pride (e.g., "the passion plac'd betwixt two ideas") with a lowercase *p*, and the general *emotion* of Pride (the overall system) with an uppercase P.

The cause within Pride consists of two parts, a "quality" and a "subject." The subject is always related to the person who feels Proud, and the quality "inheres" in the subject. Thus—Hume's example—a man is "vain of a beautiful house, which belongs to him, or which he has built or contrived." The two limiting conditions on the cause are that the Proud man must experience the house as beautiful, and he must perceive it as connected in some way to himself. Taken together, these experiences have a general application: a cause "adapts itself" to the passions by "partaking of some general quality that naturally operates on the mind" (T 281). Hume thus stresses that Pride is a general operation, though tailored to the particular things of worth that make people Proud.

Hume says less about the object within Pride, relying on a bald assertion that Pride invariably "takes the self" as its object, or that Pride "looks to" the self. But while he takes it that the object requires little further elucidation, he is at pains to stress that there is "an original property" in the mind that activates this object of Pride: a "primary impulse" causes the mind to "exert itself" (T 280). Thus, Hume says, we need only refer to fixed principles of our psychology to explain the origin of Pride's tendency to take the self as its object. As we will see, Hume's entire system of Pride (including its "cause") is anchored firmly into our psychologies by this turn in the argument.

Having made these distinctions, Hume again discreetly forebears to talk about the sensation of pride itself (section iv). Rather, searching for some "common" source for the principles that govern Pride and Humility, he introduces a new "property of human nature." Reminding us of his earlier doctrine of the association of ideas, in which ideas succeed one another according to the rules of resemblance, contiguity, and cause, he introduces an analogous doctrine: the association of impressions. This association operates only by the rule of resemblance, the passions rapidly succeeding one another—"no sooner one arises, than the rest immediately follow"—to form a circle: "Grief and disappointment give rise to anger, anger to envy, envy to malice, and malice to grief again, till the whole circle be compleated. In like manner our temper, when elevated with joy, naturally throws itself into love, generosity, pity, courage, pride, and the other resembling affections" (T 283).

Although Hume doesn't say so directly here, the association of impressions will turn out to be the main genetic source of the impression of pride, which will in turn appear to be a parasite, sucking off the pleasure we take in the "quality" of the "cause." The sequence looks something like this:[5]

Quality (inhering in "cause") ⇒ pleasure ⇒ impression of pride ⇒ Idea of Self
(pleasant sensation)

Since pride's severely limited role in Pride secures the psychological foundation of the whole system (as we will see toward the end of this section), we should be sensitive to the fact that the association of ideas exists to connect the pleasure we take in the quality of the cause with the impression of pride itself, and to bind the fate of the latter to the emergence of the former into the circle of passions.

The doctrine of the association of ideas proves to be a focal point for complaints about the "absurdity" of Hume's system. How can Hume argue that an impression is related only by resemblance to another impression?[6] More to the point, how can he argue that this "circle of passions" is an adequate description of our emotional lives? The absurdity lies in Hume's reticence (or confusion) about the role that thoughts and beliefs play in producing each new passion. Pall S. Ardal explains Hume's obscurity with respect to the role of thoughts and beliefs: "Noticing a resemblance is no part of the operation of the association. . . . That the association does not depend on a prior conscious comparison is clearly shown by the fact that an impression is on its first occurrence supposed capable of giving rise to an associated impression which has not been previously experienced" (1966, 25). Ardal's muted exasperation at Hume's suggestion is echoed much more angrily by Jerome Neu, who calls Hume's theory "so unrealistic" as to be "seriously defective" (1977, 33). Neu's objection is that anger does not immediately turn to disappointment without the intervention of some related belief, but that "such a spectrum depends on the characteristic thought involved. (Thus regret, as involving a thought of loss, might be similar to remorse, as involving a thought of loss plus culpability. But the whole matter is enormously complex, and involves other factors in addition to thought)" (1977, 14).

The whole matter is much more complex indeed, because it involves more than just thinking about or noticing the way the passions succeed each other. In the next section, I will propose that Hume's theory of Pride requires a fully realized internal spectator, surrounded by a rather elaborate dramatic apparatus. I pause here only to point out that both Neu and Ardal fail to notice the genre of Hume's "circle of passions," which is written from the perspective of someone beholding a play of expressions and then attempting to infer the inner life of another person experiencing a tumble of emotions. Hume's "circle of passions" thus belongs to the genre of popular reports of masterful actors produced throughout the eighteenth century, reports whose authors were obsessed with the very questions of thought-dependence that Hume's commentators accuse him of evading. One of the most famous of these reports, Diderot's description in *The Paradox of Acting* (1774) of a party trick of David Garrick's, asks whether the expression of a passion necessarily implies the experience of the passion. He famously argues that acting is a technique in which the feeling of a passion is no part of its expression:

Now I will tell you a thing I have actually seen. Garrick will put his head between two folding-doors, and in the course of five or six seconds his expression will change successively from wild delight to temperate pleasure, from this to tranquillity, from tranquillity to surprise, from surprise to blank astonishment, from that to sorrow, from sorrow to the air of one overwhelmed, from that to fright, from fright to horror, from horror to despair, and thence he will go up again to the point from which he started. Can his soul have experienced all these feelings, and played this kind of scale in concert with his face? I don't believe it; nor do you. If you ask this famous man, who in himself is as well worth a visit to England as the ruins of Rome are worth a visit to Italy; if you ask him, I say, for the scene of the Pastrycook's Boy he will play it for you; if you asked him directly afterwards for the great scene in *Hamlet* he would play it for you. He was as ready to cry over the tarts in the gutter as to follow the course of [Macbeth's] air-drawn dagger. Can one laugh or cry at will? One shall make a show of doing so as well or ill as one can, and the completeness of the illusion varies as one is or is not Garrick. ([1774]1957, 38–39)

Diderot imagines that Garrick takes approximately the same kind of interest in his own expressions as Diderot himself takes in them—like Diderot or any spectator, Garrick apprehends the play of expressions as a whole phenomenon and does not have thoughts like "the source of my wild delight is not nearly as delightful as I had thought" before lapsing into temperate pleasure and thence to tranquility. Like any two spectators, Diderot and Garrick are detached from the play of Garrick's expressions (indeed, Diderot may in fact be less detached than Garrick is, if he is inclined to sympathize with Garrick's affect). But of the two, only Garrick is the ironist, since he alone lays claim to an internal spectator to his emotions as well as to an external one. Indeed, some remarks by Diderot's exasperated persona to his thick-witted interlocutor highlight the existence of this internal spectator (here imagined as an internal auditor): "Look you, before he cried 'Zaire vous pleurez,' or 'Vous y serez ma fille,' the actor has listened over and over again to his own voice. At the very moment when he touches your heart he is listening to his own voice; his talent depends not, as you think, upon feeling, but upon rendering so exactly the outward signs of feeling, that you fall into the trap" ([1774] 1957, 16).

Diderot's resolution of "the paradox of acting" was only the most prestigious answer to a historically vexing question about the transfer of aesthetic pleasure from the author to the spectator, captured here in the phrase "at the very moment when he touches your heart he is listening to his own voice." Like many aesthetic questions, the "paradox of acting" is a vehicle for large and vexing issues in eighteenth-century psychology. Diderot gives a concrete example of how eighteenth-century thinkers broadened this paradox by relating it to types of people: just as bad actors are subject to their feelings and great actors control them, so the "man of sensibility" feels all of his feelings, while "the man of genius" "observes" and distinguishes them ([1774] 1957, 40).

As Joseph Roach has spelled out the implications of Diderot's fascination with Garrick, actors are capable of detaching themselves from their expressions and feelings to a superhuman degree; nevertheless, such detachment represents in ordinary proportions a psychological tendency available to all of us. Roach writes: "The great actor's extreme rarity stemmed from his highly unusual, even freakish capacity to detach himself from his bodily machine, to divide himself into two personalities in performance, and so to direct the outward motion of his passions by an inward mental force, itself unmoved, undistorted by the physiological effects it oversees" (1985, 146).

I will return to this point—that the genre of Hume's example leads us to suspect a hidden spectator witnessing her own play of emotions—in the next section. It will become significant when we consider attempts to "defend" Hume's theory—to render it a useful description of an ordinary emotion—by stripping it of either its rational or its sensuous component. Despite his vexation about the sensuous component of Pride (that is, the impression of pride), and despite empiricism's vexation about the reasonableness of an emotional judgment, Hume insists that the two components are inseparable.

This insistence comes out most clearly in section v, which strikes at the "very being and essence" of Pride (T 286) and at the same time most forcefully complicates the empiricist program. Hume first announces his intention to "proceed to examine the passions themselves, in order to find something in them, correspondent to the suppos'd properties of their cause" (T 286). That is, Hume wants to show, in good empiricist fashion, that these "impressions of reflexion" are copied from two ideas, which themselves are copied from two impressions—the impression of pleasure we take from the quality of the cause, and our impression of our relationship to the cause.

Hume begins by making two distinctions. The first concerns the "quality" of the cause: the quality of the cause of Pride (or Humility) must produce pleasure (or pain), "*independent of those affections, which I here endeavour to explain*" (T 285; emphasis added). The second concerns the "subjects" themselves, independent of their pleasure-producing qualities. The subjects of Pride "are either parts of ourselves, or something nearly related to us" (T 285). This second condition seems to demand straightforwardly that the subject be closely related to us, though in certain rather peculiar circumstances, this restriction accounts for an estrangement of parts of ourselves from other parts of ourselves. As Annette Baier glosses these circumstances: "Even when what one takes pride [i.e., Pride] in is one's character, rather than 'cloaths, equipage or fortune' (T 288), that character is still in the relevant sense 'foreign,' since it is not oneself, but 'in' oneself. The indirectness of the indirect passions lies in non-coincidence of cause and object and in the consequent need for 'correlativity' as a substitute for, or approximation of, the perfect symmetry of identity" (1991, 38). According to Baier, Pride's estrangement effect (the "non-co-incidence of cause and object") operates most forcefully in those cases when the cause (e.g., one's capacity for kindness) is internal.

On further inspection, of course, these circumstances turn out not to be singular but typical, highlighting a key feature of the impression of pride, which is—to put it bluntly—its tendency to pick apart elements of the cause itself and to feed off some of those elements rather than others. The impression of pride, like other impressions of reflection, flourishes by substituting proximity for identity. This is an abstract way of saying that both the quality of the cause and its relation to me are separable from the subject of the cause (that is, both the beauty and its relationship to me are separable from the house itself), and these separable impressions cause the ideas that further cause the impressions of reflection. So when we feel an impression of reflection (say pride), we are feeling an impression related to qualities separate from the subject of the cause itself, which must remain unknown, unfelt. And this fact about impressions of reflection has specific consequences for those cases where we take pride in some quality of ours: presumably this feeling draws a distinction between pleasure-producing or praiseworthy qualities and those brute facts about ourselves to which we are attending.

Since Hume uses the case of our own attributes to demonstrate his great thesis of section v, namely, that "relation" (T 288) is the key to Pride, the more closely a thing is related to us, the more likely we are to be proud of it. Thus, according to Hume, we feel most proud of "the good and bad qualities of our actions and manners" and of "our personal character." In a probabilistic sense, we are as likely to be gripped by a sense of estrangement (about our internal attributes) as we are to feel the impression of pride. And in the less typical case of our being proud of external objects, this feeling of estrangement spreads it-self on to these objects as a feeling of uncanniness: Hume credits "the beauty or deformity of our person, house, equipage, or furniture" with the power to "render" us "either vain or humble" (T 285).

In distinguishing the principle of relation and its attendant sense of es-trangement, Hume speaks only of the causes of Pride and the attitude we might have about them. He has not yet defined the impression of pride itself, though he has expended a good deal of rhetorical energy promising to do so. However, when he does, the definition whooshes by, followed by a rich flood of assertion that he, at least, is convinced by the totality of the "system" he has just discovered: "I immediately find, that taking these suppositions to be just, the true system breaks in upon me with an irresistible evidence" (T 286); and,

"No wonder the whole cause, consisting of a quality and of a subject, does so unavoidably give rise to the passion" (T 289).

What is this impression of pride, whose attainment seems like a belated admission of having crossed the Alps? It seems to vanish into the zero-point of the whole "system," whose other elements Hume has so carefully detailed. Hume writes, laconically: "Pride is a pleasant sensation, and humility a painful; and upon the removal of the pleasure and pain, there is in reality no pride nor humility. Of this our very feeling convinces us; and beyond our feeling, 'tis here in vain to reason or dispute" (T 286). He can really find nothing to say about this impression of reflection, save that it is separate from the pleasure or pain produced by the "quality" of the cause. Without this pleasure and the mechanism of association of impressions, pride would not come into being. In resembling the pleasure we take in the quality of the subject, the impression of pride is only its pale after-effect.

Our intuition at this moment is that pride is an emotion nobody ever actually feels, or at least one whose distinctness from just taking pleasure in a beautiful object related to oneself is minimal. Has Hume merely asserted a distinction without defining a difference between pride and ordinary pleasure, or between humility and ordinary pain? Of course he insists repeatedly that pride is distinct, an insistence bolstered by warnings about how fragile pride is, and how rare, and how unlikely we are ever really to feel it. We can feel many other kinds of pressures and urges, Hume thinks, but until these pressures and urges meet five separate conditions, we are unjustified in calling them Pride (or Humility):

This reflection is, that the persons, who are proudest, and who in the eye of the world have most reason for their pride, are not always the happiest; nor the most humble always the most miserable, as may at first sight be imagin'd from this system. An evil may be real, tho' *its cause has no relation to us:* It may be real, without being *peculiar:* It may be real, without *shewing itself to others:* It may be real, without being *constant:* And it may be real, without *falling under the general rules.* Such evils as these will not fail to render us miserable, tho' they have little tendency to diminish pride: And perhaps the most real and the most solid evils of life will be found of this nature. (T 294; emphasis added)

We can walk around feeling miserable most of the time, while our fellows think, "She has all the reasons in the world to feel Proud." In their rush to judgment about our feeling, they have failed to notice that some key part of the system isn't firing, and consequently that the feeling of pride hasn't struck at us. The system, were it to fire on demand, would regularize a rather melancholy dissonance between our objective and subjective conditions. Paradoxically, however, to get the feeling of pride, our relationship to objects must submit to a complex government by rules.

Hume's complication of the "simple empiricist program in Book 1" is that a number of conventions must first come into play in order for us to get even a simple impression. The range of conventions selects features of objects, relates these features to us, produces pleasure, and makes our fellows sit up and take notice. We only nonreflectively "feel" after the system has fired, and then only in extremely rare cases. As Jerome Christensen has aptly stated this paradox: "The success of the systematization of pride is in the capacity of a set of representations justly to take the place of whatever we might feel," although there is no evidence that any "representations" actually come into the system (1987, 69).

All that is warranted at present is a general observation about Hume's formalism, which preserves in a different register the force of an observation of Paul H. Fry's about what he calls "method" in literary interpretation: "The commonplace objection to formalism in literature may be directed at least as appropriately against method in interpretation: as it becomes more consistent and thus more sophisticated in the use of operative terms, method finally becomes internally rather than referentially consistent. It becomes self-reflexive, that is, and has less and less to do with experience" (1983, 10).

The Internal Audience to Pride

Pride's formalist elements include its estrangement effect and its swerve away from feeling.[7] To capture the sense in which Hume's system grows independent of experience, writers have discovered comparisons to an array of figures and rhetorical strategies from which they deduce that Hume's system is rhetorical, "literary," and "representationalist." For instance, in the course of comparing Hume's system of Pride to a miser, a solitary, Aaron Hill's acting theory, Horkheimer and Adorno's characterization of the Enlightenment, a machine, "composition," and language itself, Jerome Christensen clearly states this representationalist view: "Representation alone, without any reference to a reality but referring only to 'itself' in the 'double relation of impressions and ideas' has the capacity to 'produce' all the satisfaction anyone could want" (1987, 73).

Yet this comparison is more metaphorical than it needs to be: Christensen's "representation" only resembles Hume's system in that both are self-reflexive; unlike "representation," however, Pride is precisely not capable of producing "all the satisfaction anyone could want." What does Christensen mean by "representation" here? What would constitute a wholly self-reflexive "representation" (e.g., one that refers only to itself rather than, as would seem to be more typical, referring to something else)? What kind of "representation," in the course of referring only to itself, could also be a source of boundless pleasure? So committed is Christensen to making Hume's philosophy rhetorical, aesthetic, "accommodating," conventional, "adjusted to circumstances," "general," and socially "inductive," that he fails to admit that "representations" nowhere feature in Hume's system.[8]

Still there is much to preserve in Christensen's vision of Hume as characterizing our psychologies by a variety of social/economic and aesthetic figures, particularly since Hume's writing contributes significantly to the mid-eighteenth-century obsession with troping psychology as an aesthetic phenomenon, and aesthetics as a psychological one. Like Christensen, I take the view that Hume's theory of Pride is "literary," but literary in the sense of being "internally rather than referentially consistent," of being a "theory" in Fry's sense, rather than a picture of an ordinary emotion. And there are concrete aesthetic features to Hume's system as well: the aestheticization of psychology turns out to depend on an elaborate and surprising theatrical analogy. Christensen correctly points out that Hume's system is self-reflexive and productive; we will soon discover that it accommodates an extensive spectatorial vocabulary as well. Hume connects these three elements of his system together neither by reminding us of rhetorical figures elsewhere in his text, nor by relying on a technically inaccurate concept of "representation," but by half-realizing the figure of a spectator or audience internal to the system itself. Hume's strategy is partially to personify the internal workings of the passion of Pride, imagining that its key mechanism resembles two agents looking at each other, just as an actor, on the Diderotian view, is supposed to audit the very emotions he expresses.

To capture the importance of the theatrical analogy for Hume's system, in this section I will point out the similarities between two interpretations of Hume's theory and two eighteenth-century accounts of an actor's agency. While all of these interpretations (of Hume's theory of pride; of acting techniques) seek to establish the ordinariness of their subject matter, Hume seeks to establish the heightened artificiality of his—an artificiality that depends on the very theatricality these interpretations deny. Indeed, Hume's theory of Pride is the longest sustained description of an aesthetically determined emotion in the neoclassical literary tradition.

Both Davidson and Neu desire to interpret Hume's theory of Pride so that it becomes an ordinary emotion. Both writers seek to regularize Pride by expanding Hume's account of the relationship between emotions and thoughts or beliefs. For both writers, Hume's theory of pride is inadequate as it stands. To save Hume's theory of pride, Davidson wants to add rationality to it, turning it into a rationalist account of emotions; whereas Neu wants to subtract rationality from it, turning it into a nonrationalist account of the emotions. Neither solution is without its difficulties. The difficulties are that if we add rationality, or thought-dependence, then Hume's theory of pride seems to contradict his earlier hypotheses about cause and effect in Book 1 of the *Treatise* by presenting a realist doctrine of cause (see A. Baier 1978). Rationalizing pride also seems to violate Hume's famous doctrine that "reason is, and ought only to be the slave of the passions, and can never pretend to any other office than to serve and obey them" (T 415), which then turns out to be just a slogan.

Meanwhile, subtracting rationality from pride has the advantage of squaring it with Hume's account of other passions and also with Hume's overall insistence that "a passion is an original existence, or, if you will, modification of existence, and contains not any representative quality, which renders it a copy of any other existence or modification. When I am angry, I am actually possest with the passion, and in that emotion have no more reference to any other object, than when I am thirsty, or sick, or more than five foot high" (T 415). However, this option has the disadvantage of requiring the excision of huge chunks of Hume's complex machinery of "double association of impressions and ideas," much of which, Hume insists, is necessary to produce pride in the first place. In an extended attack on Hume's theory as insufficiently thought-dependent, Neu realizes he must explain away many elements of thought-dependence that Hume built into his system (for example, by stressing the formulation "[pride] is a passion plac'd betwixt two ideas, of which the one produces it, and the other is produc'd by it" [T 278]).

Let us call these two views the thought-add and thought-subtract views. The thought-subtract view denies the existence of an internal audience, seeing Hume's gestures in that direction as evidence of the incoherence of his account. For the thought-add view, the existence of an internal audience is the point of Hume's theory of pride (however badly Hume expressed this point; Davidson: "I do not pretend that this is what Hume really meant; it is what he *should* have meant" [1980, 277]). Davidson's rationalist solution is to "attend to the role" of thoughts and beliefs, and to "let the atomism go." The role of thoughts and beliefs seems partially personified as an internal audience, or what Davidson refers to as an internal attitude of self-awareness. He describes it as a judgment or attitude of approval directed toward ourselves and separate from the impression of pride itself. Thus the proposition "I am proud that

I own a beautiful house" entails my valuing myself insofar as I am the owner of a house judged to be beautiful; I am a witness to the beauty of my own house and of its connection to me. It is to the existence of this internal attitude that Pride owes its genesis and its special characteristics as a passion— its complexity, its indirectness, its belief-dependence, and its difference from immediate impressions like hunger, which "arises internally" and, as it were, blindly (T 287). For although the source of a judgment can be social (e.g., an audience of our peers), the internal audience places a set of restrictions on pride that distinguishes it from the more general pleasure we take in things around us.

Neu, by contrast, denies that Hume gives an adequate account of the genesis of Pride, arguing that he confined himself wrongly to an analysis of incomparable simple impressions. He ultimately agrees with Davidson that emotions have a large rationalist component, but he argues that Hume is barred by his own extravagant epistemology from helping himself to any rationalist escape from the difficulties such an epistemology entails. The bare facts of Hume's "simple and uniform impressions" do not allow for "subtlety in our distinctions and discriminations of feelings"; nor does Hume's associationist mechanism explain why one emotion comes into being rather than another (1997, 19). Neu's objection is that each simple and uniform impression is as irreducible as some color, such as blue or green; therefore, it is only possible to compare these simples in virtue of their being emotions, not in virtue of the kinds of feelings they are. The incomparability of simple impressions leads Hume to hold an untenable general theory about emotions: "One ends up with (an impossible) association by resemblance of simples as simples, which is in any case (even were it possible) inadequate to produce emotions which do not vary with their objects. So pride would have many meanings, as many as it has possible causes and objects, instead of the single meaning Hume undertook to explain" (1977, 28).

The deepest objection mounted by Neu and other thought-subtractors is that Hume's epistemology prohibits us from thinking of impressions as the sorts of things that could be complex and take objects; and yet this seems precisely what Hume commits himself to when he describes Pride as taking the self for its object. Hume's desire to give a role to thoughts and beliefs in his explanations of Pride's genesis is therefore incommensurable with his epistemology as a whole.[9] Not only is it not an ordinary emotion, but it is also incoherent: a feeling is a brute fact that can, according to Hume, admit of no complexity.

The thought-add and thought-subtract views closely parallel two influential poles of debate in eighteenth-century acting theory. Both hypotheses about acting are meant to explain how certain parts of an actor fit together with other parts of him; the "fit" requiring explanation is most generally the "fit" between what we might call his "subjective" and "objective" parts. Like most other hypotheses of their kind in the history of acting theory, both rely on motivational or "instrumental" language to explain this fit, the instrumentality being of two kinds. A narrower kind of instrumentality describes how an actor's mental states contribute to his physical expressions; a broader kind of instrumentality conveys what Richard Wollheim calls "the actor's essential task": "The proper relationship of the actor's mental states to the mental states of the character whom he represents . . . should be that which best enables the actor to represent the character to the greatest benefit of his audience" (1984, 66). The broader kind of instrumentality can be distinguished into two further kinds (Wollheim here states the relationship between them as normative): a distinction between how an actor becomes (in the words of a seventeenth-century writer) "the person personated" and how an audience responds to the person, whether successfully personated or not (Heywood 1612; quoted in Stone and Kahrl 1979, 28).

These three kinds of instrumentality—how an actor's emotions motivate his physical expressions, how his own mental and physical states motivate the mental and physical states of the character he is representing, and how his character motivates the mental or physical states of his audience—are firmly linked, indeed inseparable, in the minds of eighteenth-century writers. The strand most analogous to Hume's theory of Pride is the first, the "narrower" kind of instrumentality, where what is at issue is explaining how a thought becomes an expression, or a feeling becomes a state of mind. Yet the three are so close that it is often practically impossible to distinguish between them: Hume's definition of sympathy, "the conversion of an idea into an impression by the force of imagination" (T 317), has seemed to many people to cover the operations of all three.[10]

From the Garrick theatre of about 1750, two basic positions emerge, both indebted to neoclassical aesthetic theory.[11] The Garrick theater is historically well known as a moment when individualism and naturalism replaced types and conventionalism on the stage. There have been many different ways of describing Garrick's naturalistic achievement, as against the older acting styles of Thomas Betterton and James Quin. These descriptions include the following accounts: Garrick replaced a confining declamatory style by free gesture; Quin, by contrast, was noted for repeating "a sawing kind of action" as he declaimed from the stage. Garrick presided over the moment when the notion that actors represent universal passions embedded in human beings ceded to the plasticity of individual feelings. His theater replaced logocentric, text-based productions by those favoring visual, and auditory cues.[12] Most widely commented upon was Garrick's development of naturalistic characters, each with its own individual style. As one man wrote, "Richard, Chamont, Bayes, and Lear—I never saw four actors more different from one another than you are from yourself" (Garrick 1831–32, 1:7; quoted in Duerr 1962, 225). Where Garrick rendered each part differently, a previous generation of actors had been noted for their rendering of types and distinctive passions: Charles Gildon's *The Life of Mr. Thomas Betterton* (1710), little more than an up-to-date French neoclassical acting handbook purporting to be an account of Betterton's acting style, advised that "A Patriot, a Prince, a Beggar, a Clown, &c. must each have their propriety, and Distinction in action as well as words and language" (1710, 32).[13]

Yet Garrick's conventionalism and proximity to the older styles of acting were also subject to comment: as Garrick replaced the old declamatory styles of Betterton and Quin, so he was himself criticized by the end of his career for his "clap-trap."[14] Such commentary suggests that Garrick made only small adjustments to older styles and that these styles nevertheless remained visible to his contemporaries.[15] Both the older style of Betterton and the newer style of Garrick forged a relationship between external signs and internal meanings, between parts of the body and the whole feeling they signified, between expression and emotion. In his 1741 redaction of Betterton's papers (largely composed by Charles Gildon in 1710), William Oldys quotes the following Bettertonian observation: "Every passion or emotion of the Mind . . . has from nature its peculiar and proper countenance, sound and gesture; and the whole body of man, all his looks, and every tone of his voice, like strings on an instrument, receive their sounds from the various impulse [*sic*] of the passions" (Betterton 1741, 64).

For Betterton, and for the neoclassical theorists of expression from whom this observation is drawn, a passion is represented by its contingent features. Minor adjustments to the contingent features—facial expressions, position of the head, hands, and feet—produce major shifts in the represented passions: "A lifting or tossing of the head is the gesture of pride and arrogance. Carrying the head aloft is a sign of joy. . . . A hard and bold front or forehead is looked upon as a mark of obstinacy, contumacy, perfidiousness and impudence" (Betterton 1741, 65). There is little to suggest in this theory of expression that one passion could rapidly turn into another; rather the motivational interest seems to be unidirectional—from one cock of the head we infer a state of mind, from a tilt of the eyebrow we infer a different state of mind.[16]

Theater-goers in the early eighteenth century seem to have been familiar with a determinate lexical vocabulary of cocks, tilts, and gestures.[17] Their familiarity was shaped by visual, indeed painterly, expectations: later in the century, Lessing likened acting to "transitory painting" (quoted in Roach 1985, 73). Charles Lebrun's famous *Conférence sur l'expression générale et particulier* (1698), translated in 1701 and again in 1734 as *A Method to Learn to Design the Passions,* was so familiar to eighteenth-century painting students that Hogarth could refer to it as their "common drawing-book" (quoted in Rogerson 1953, 75).[18] Lebrun's theory of how to draw the passions was explicitly instrumental, relying on a tiny number of well-publicized techniques drawn from the principle that "if man be truly said to be the epitome of the whole world, the head may well be said to be the epitome of the whole man" (1734, 55). His method relied on the eyebrow, which he took to be the epitome of the face: each of his descriptions of passions, ranging from tranquility to extreme pain, begins with an explanation of the position of the eyebrow, from which the whole passion sorts itself out. Edmund Burke can be seen as offering a late neoclassical expression theory built on Lebrunian principles when he records the following observation about himself: "I have often observed, that on mimicking the looks and gestures of angry, or placid, or frighted, or daring men, I have involuntarily found my mind turned to that passion whose appearance I endeavoured to imitate; nay, I am convinced it is hard to avoid it; though one strove to separate the passion from its correspondent gestures" (1958, 133).[19]

Garrick's main adjustments to this neoclassical schema were of two kinds: first, he reversed the direction of interest in particulars, or concrete symbols, and their signified universals; and second, he internalized the whole process of signification, allowing it to look as though it had been motivated from within. Garrick's biographers note that the Hogarth engraving of Garrick as Richard III, hand outstretched in "a fending-off gesture," catches Garrick using the postures and techniques commended by Bettertonian rhetorical manuals and ultimately by Lebrun himself (Stone and Kahrl 1979, 28). Nevertheless, the "Garrick fever" that swept London after his 1741 debut in the part seemed a response to audience's awareness that Richard III now seemed to motivate the fending-off gesture, rather than the fending-off gesture seeming to represent the feeling of wariness. The sense that Garrick had backlit his emotions can be seen quite clearly in the large number of accounts of his portrayal of Hamlet between 1742 and 1776, many of which focused on the way he "held open" the passions to sympathetic responses from his audience (see Downer 1943). One of the most famous of these accounts, a letter by the German visitor Georg Christoph Lichtenberg, describes Hamlet's carefully cooked astonishment upon seeing his father's ghost:

Hamlet appears in a black dress, the only one in the whole court, alas! still worn for his poor father, who has been dead scarce a couple of months. Horatio and Marcellus, in uniform, are with him, and they are awaiting the ghost; Hamlet has folded his arms under his cloak and pulled his hat down over his eyes; it is a cold night and just twelve o'clock; the theatre is darkened, and the whole audience of some thousands are as quiet, and their faces as motionless, as though they were painted on the walls of the theatre; even from the farthest end of the playhouse one could hear a pin drop. Suddenly, as Hamlet moves towards the back of the stage slightly to the left and turns his back on the audience, Horatio starts, and saying: 'Look, my lord, it comes,' points to the right, where the ghost has already appeared and stands motionless, before anyone is aware of him. At these words Garrick turns sharply and at the same moment staggers back two or three paces with his knees giving way under him; his hat falls to the ground and both his arms, especially the left, are stretched out nearly to their full length, with the hands as high as his head, the right arm more bent and the hand lower, and the fingers apart; his mouth is open: thus he stands rooted to the spot, with legs apart, but no loss of dignity, supported by his friends who are better acquainted with the apparition and fear lest he should collapse. His whole demeanour is so expressive of terror that it made my flesh creep even before he began to speak. The almost terror-struck silence of the audience, which preceded this appearance and filled one with a sense of insecurity, probably did much to enhance this effect. . . . What an amazing triumph it is. One might think that such applause in one of the first playhouses in the world and from an audience of the greatest sensibility would fan into flame every spark of dramatic genius in a spectator. (1938, 10–11)

Lichtenberg tacitly casts Garrick's performance as a competition with his audience over who has the new and who the traditional theory of expression (Garrick's mastery over slightly hidebound audiences recurs in descriptions of his performances). The centerpiece of Garrick's response to the ghost is a prolonged backward stagger culminating in a sculpturesque freezing. During the stagger itself, Garrick's techniques are sufficiently visible that Lichtenberg is able to give a detailed account of them ("both his arms, especially the left, are stretched out nearly to their full length, with the hands as high as his head, the right arm more bent and the hand lower, and the fingers apart").[20] Yet by staggering backward and making his astonishment legible, Garrick does not thereby lose any advantage over his audience: the audience's awareness of his tricks does not prevent them from being struck motionless with terror. Lichtenberg lets drop the detail that "their faces (were) as motionless, as though they were painted on the walls of the theatre," contrasting their motionless painted faces to Garrick's illuminated painterly movements.

Garrick's advantage seems to lie in his ability to mobilize his variety against the unity of his audience, to play off his discord against their concord. But really his advantage is deeper than that, since he displays an internal formalism—a capacity to sustain his astonishment—that produces an estrangement effect of the kind celebrated by formalist art critics: "The technique of art is to make objects 'unfamiliar,' to make forms difficult, to increase the difficulty and length of perception because the process of perception is an aesthetic end in itself and must be prolonged" (Shklovsky 1965, 12).[21] In short, Garrick made the "personal" ("the connection between the person and what is hers") more naturalistic by opening its internal artifices to view, rather than by trying to conceal or deny them.

Garrick's internalization of form and simultaneous rerouting of interest, so that his style seems motivated by a passion rather than the reverse, leads us to consider two principle ways of interpreting his art—one a treatise written in 1750/55 by John Hill, the other a response to it by Denis Diderot ([1774] 1957).[22] These theories of acting closely correspond to the thought-add/ thought-subtract interpretations of Hume's "formalist" theory of pride. Both consider the issue of whether an actor feels his passions or not. Diderot argues that passions can only be motivated by thoughts; Hill argues that they can only be motivated by internal impressions, or "sensibility": "If he is defective in this essential quality . . . he will never make others feel what he does not feel himself, and will always be as different from the thing he is to represent, as a mask from a face" (J. Hill 1750, 16).

Yet despite their opposed views on this point, they concur on two prior points: first, they both see the task of the actor as instrumentally representing the relationship between an expression and a mental state; and second, they agree that there must be some relationship between an actor's expression and that prior mental state, even if (in Diderot's view) it is only a negative relationship. Aaron Hill, a contemporary of John Hill's, phrased these two conditions in the form of a "general rule": "The first dramatick principle . . . [is] To act a passion well, the actor never must attempt its imitation, 'till his fancy has conceived so strong an image, or idea, of it, as to move the same impressive springs within his mind, which form that passion, when 'tis undesigned, and natural. This is an absolute necessary, and the only general rule" (A. Hill 1753, 4:356).

Neither John Hill nor Diderot would disagree with Aaron Hill's formulation. They would, however, disagree about whether an actor, in conceiving a strong image, leaves behind his own prior mental state (Diderot) or cultivates and modifies it so that it too comes to resemble the prior mental state that the character's expression represents (John Hill). John Hill's book contains such minatory chapter headings as "No Man Who Has Not Naturally an Elevated Soul, Will Ever Perform Well the Part of a Heroe Upon the Stage." And he advises: "We have before observed, that the actress who wishes to succeed, should always keep her mind in a state of ease, and be ready to take up every passion her part for the night requires her to shine by the feeling of; and particularly not to suffer the good or ill accidents of her private life to influence her to any peculiar settled turn of mind" (J. Hill 1750, 91).

In response, Diderot famously recreates a scene played between a feuding actress and her husband—"a scene in which both players surpassed themselves—in which they excited continual bursts of applause from pit and boxes" (Diderot 1957, 28). Nevertheless, they each maintain a full double-consciousness in the scene, speaking their loving words aloud while contradicting them sotto voce with harsh ones. Diderot's point is that a great actor seeks to disrupt his absorption in his role by experiencing a double-consciousness; the actor confirms as a matter of art that the instrumental relation between a state of mind and an expression is opaque.

Theatricality and the Return of the Self

Like Diderot's acting theory, Hume's theory of pride assumes that the (instrumental) relation between one emotion and the next is opaque; thus Pride cannot be called a true picture of an emotion any more than Garrick's shifting expressions summon his real feelings (on Diderot's view). Yet the concept of the internal spectator that Hume partially develops in his theory of the indirect passions explains how the emotion's instrumentality could seem naturally motivated. In his theory of Pride, he assumes that no mental state necessarily gives rise to any other mental state; yet we come to expect the "personal" relationship to be a settled, customary one: we expect that any two of our attributes will customarily go together. By developing a concept of an internal spectator to represent our evaluation of attributes of ourselves, Hume creates in essence a formalized, internalized version of the "personal" relation—a version that, like Garrick's astonishment, is internally, rather than referentially, consistent.

To get at this formalized, internalized version of the "personal" relationship, we have to return to the "self" that emerges in Book 2 of Hume's *Treatise*. I said earlier that Annette Baier has characterized Pride as a "person-directed" passion that both thematizes self-reflexiveness (by redirecting energy away from the causes of Pride to the self), and socializes it. Pride socializes self-reflexiveness by inducing us to draw the same inferences about another person's relationship to her attributes (or, in a Humean expansion of the notion of "what is hers," to the objects with which she surrounds herself) as we draw about our own such relationships. I quoted the striking passage in which Baier suggests how Hume's emphasis on such indirect or belief-induced passions trains us this way:

> The indirectness of the indirect passions, which later becomes simply the complication of their objects, is a matter of the relationship between a person and what is hers, in all the "hundred" senses of the possessive personal pronoun. So this indirectness and complication should shed light on Hume's reflective views about person, their perceptions and whatever objects of their perceptions they see as their own, as either part of themselves or some sort of possession of theirs. Me and my character traits, me and my abilities, disabilities, virtues and vices, me and my brain, heart, nerves, skin, pores, muscles, me and my life, me and my heap of perceptions, me and my reputation, me and my family, me and my loves, me and my ambitions, me and my country, me and my preferred vacation place and its climate, me and my evaluation of the importance or unimportance of whether the beautiful fish in the ocean is or isn't in any sense mine rather than yours, ours or no one's. What is this 'I' who claims this manifold as her own? . . . The answer is that I must be to what is mine whatever I take you to be to what it yours, and what you take me to be to what is mine. (1991, 136)

Baier's virtuosity reveals itself in the almost casual way her prose exemplifies the Humean principle that our imaginations run (according to a criterion of vivacity) from "a beautiful fish in the ocean" to, as Hume puts it, "the idea of our own person" (T 318) and back again. At the same time, Baier suggests, the representations about which we make evaluative judgments (a fish in the ocean) might have a qualitatively different feel (for us) from the representations attached to us by our circumstances: "my character traits," "my skin," or even "my preferred vacation place and its climate." What we evaluate in the case of the fish is not the fish itself but the relative importance of deciding who has a (property) interest in the beautiful fish; whereas in the case of these attributes of ours, what we evaluate is our own connection to them.

I said also that Baier avoids traditional worries amongst Hume's readers about the disappearing "self." This is because, in making this suggestion, Baier merges two questions that Hume scholars have traditionally separated but that Hume himself almost cryptically suggested should be conjoined: In virtue of what do all of my impressions belong to me? (a question usually thought to be about the unity of the self);[23] and How do I estimate the objects that I take to belong to me? Scholars have usually thought that Hume addresses the former topic in his remarks on personal identity in Book 1 of the *Treatise*, while reserving the latter (perhaps morally more, but philosophically less interesting) topic for his discussion of the passions, especially Pride. Yet as Baier has seen, Hume never seriously tries to separate these topics, allowing the (partly social) question of how I estimate the objects that I take to belong to me to depend causally on the epistemological question of how I estimate myself. As she puts it, "Hume begins Book Two with pride, because his main concern is with what can, and what cannot, bear its own survey" (1991, 135). One of the things, on this view, that must bear its own survey is not just my virtues, vices, and brain, but the manner in which I form connections to these things.

Hume most strongly voices his suggestion that we should conjoin the topics of the unity of personhood and our estimation of our personal qualities in his discussion of the "self," which he repeatedly calls the "object" of Pride (T 277). Some readers of Book 2 have confessed to a quickening sense of doubt when they encounter this formulation: how can Hume—suddenly—begin to refer to the "self" after he has so vigorously denied, at the end of Book 1, that we have any epistemological grounds for positing such an entity? These readers have various suggestions for what Hume might have meant.[24] By far the most popular and promising of these is the suggestion that Hume presses the Book 2 "self" into quite a different service from the service he demands of it in Book 1. By assembling a second self that is "always intimately present to us" (T 320), he fulfills a promise at the end of the very section of Book 1 of the *Treatise* ("Of Personal Identity") where he denies the first self.

This promise, broadly speaking, is to offer a cogent hypothesis about how personal identity can serve a system of social relationships. After describing the mind as "a kind of theatre," a theater sustaining the illusion of a self that turns out to be nothing but "several perceptions successively mak[ing] their appearance; pass[ing], re-pass[ing], glid[ing] away, and mingl[ing] in an infinite variety of postures and situations" (T 253), Hume asks why, if this is true, do we tend to ascribe identity to ourselves? He answers this question by allowing that there are two different senses in which we conceive of personal identity: "We much distinguish between personal identity, as it regards our thought or imagination, and as it regards our passions or the concern we take in ourselves" (T 253). In Book 1, "the first is our present subject" and comprises such epistemological questions of identity as Why do I assume that all of my representations are mine?

Hume never returns in Book 1 to the topic of personal identity "as it regards our passions or the concern we take in ourselves." Rather, he begins Book 2 by referring to a concept of "the self" that is intimately connected with the passion of Pride—a self, surprisingly, of which our habitual consciousness forms the basis of uniting successive perceptions. Hume is no more specific than that about what this "self" consists of, although he insists on its importance to his system as a whole. This habitual "self" is important because it is the invariable object of Pride and Humility: "Here the view always fixes when we are actuated by either of these passions. According as our idea of our self is more or less advantageous, we feel either of those opposite affections, and are elated by pride, or dejected with humility. Whatever other objects may be comprehended by the mind, they are always consider'd with a view to excite these passions, or produce the smallest encrease or diminution of them. When self enters not into the consideration, there is no room either for pride or humility" (T 277). More importantly, perhaps, Pride not only always takes the self as its object but also produces the self: "To this emotion (nature) has assign'd a certain idea, viz. that of self, which it never fails to produce" (T 287).

In elaborating upon this concept of the "self" that, in Book 2 at least, is the subject of "the concern we take in ourselves," Hume gravitates toward metaphors that seem frankly visual, even theatrical: "here the view always fixes," "when self enters not," Pride can never "look beyond self," and so forth. How seriously are we meant to take this spectatorial vocabulary? (Or, as Passmore puts it, " 'here the view' [whatever this is] 'always fixes' " [1952, 127; quoted in Neu 1977, 27]). Are we meant to sense the presence of a hidden personification? After all, these images somewhat peculiarly describe Pride as looking at the self, fixing the self in a beam of consciousness that both highlights this self and creates it. Who is the spectator? And since Hume has used the theatrical analogy so far only to express a quality of illusoriness rather than as a proscenium with a red curtain, how do we account for the fact that these images now have a constructive rather than a destructive force?

On one level, this spectatorial vocabulary is supposed to capture a causal relationship in which the idea of the self "regularly occurs later than pride" (Neu 1977, 27). But this language is not simply a substitute for a causal vocabulary, as Neu wants to think, since it takes a sharply self-reflexive turn that is somewhat difficult to explain if all Hume is doing is describing, in uncharacteristically flowery language, a constant conjunction between Pride and the self. In fact, the spectatorial model contains a double or even triple self-reflection that seems prima facie to complicate any straightforward constant-conjunction account.

The theatrical language seems to have two special provenances. Most generally, on the authority of the "mind as a kind of theatre" analogy, the spectatorship asserts itself in the vocabulary with which Hume describes the essential perceptual unit of the passions, the "secondary, or reflective impressions" (T 275). (Recall that he first divides the passions into primary and secondary, the former arising immediately from sensation; the latter—which he calls "impressions of reflexion"—arising from previous impressions and ideas, especially those of pleasure and pain).[25] Here is the origin, in Hume, of an observation that Anthony Kenny has made: "The relation between a passion and the person, or perhaps rather the mind, to which it belongs is conceived by Hume as the relation of perceived to perceiver" (1964, 21). That is, as Kenny explains, the object of perception is the passion itself, not the cause of that passion; what we properly perceive is the pleasure or the pain rather than the cause of the pleasure or the pain.

But if the very act of perceiving simple impressions already commits us to a self-reflexiveness, that self-reflexiveness in turn guarantees that we are witnesses (sometimes surprised witnesses) to our own perceptions (exhibiting surprise at his own discoveries, Hume writes: "I immediately find, that taking these suppositions to be just, the true system breaks in upon me with an irresistible evidence" [T 286]). This structure of perception, in which people spectate the contents of their consciousness, in its turn founds a further form of self-reflexiveness, specifically that special self-reflexiveness entailed by Pride, in which "the view" of a person feeling Pride "always fixes" (T 277) on the self: "'Tis absolutely impossible . . . that these passions shou'd ever look beyond self" (T 286).

Hume's theatrical metaphors cluster most intensely around this final form of self-reflexiveness, namely, when I spectate my connection to my own attributes. Thus Hume explains the difference between the emotions experienced by a guest at a dinner party and the host of that party: "We may feel joy upon being present at a feast, where our senses are regal'd with delicacies of every kind: But 'tis only the master of the feast, who, besides the same joy, has the additional passion of self-applause and vanity" (T 290). The passion of self-applause is Hume's theatrical way of imagining a host proudly spectating his connection to his feast.

Given the things people ordinarily mean by theatricality, Hume's drift here seems initially somewhat counterintuitive: why is he more interested in the (secondary? parasitic?) theatricality of our awareness of our relationship to our chosen vacation spots than in the seemingly more plausible—to an empiricist—theatricality of our spectatorial appraisal of a beautiful fish in the ocean? We can give this question a different emphasis: why does Hume begin Book 2 with Pride, an emotion whose very structure is inseparable from such parasitic theatricality (because dependent on impressions of reflection)?

After all, Pride's appeal is not immediately clear—despite its being the first of the seven deadly sins—and thus a candidate on which only Hume could have loved to found his system of morals.

But especially on theatrical grounds does Pride seem an implausible choice: after all, in moments of self-applause the audience is so tiny as to seem restrictively antitheatrical rather than expansively spectatorial. What kinds of claims does Hume make about this second kind of theatricality, the theatricality specific to Pride (as opposed to the relatively straightforward theatricality of empiricist psychology in which we are aware in general of our impressions)? Hume imagines that when someone is in the grip of a passion of self-applause, she plays not to one audience but to two : an external audience and an internal audience. The external audience secures pride as a social emotion, confirming our judgment that the object of which we feel proud is praiseworthy; the existence of this audience helps to explain why pride is a passion that attaches particularly to property owners, like Hume's "vain man" (T 310), for whom pride is practically a perpetual emotion. The division between the two audiences also explains the paradox that self-applause is more theatrical than mere applause: we depend on social judgments to validate our "personal" ones, and to the extent that we deem our "personal" attributes praiseworthy, we put our whole relationship to them on display. By contrast, we display nothing about ourselves by simply noticing a beautiful, free-swimming fish, unless we display hunger, acquisitiveness, or a crack ability to calculate the property values of the lagoon in which the fish is swimming.

What kind of creature are we? A property owner, able and willing to make a set of internal distinctions that Hume describes as theater. Hume is obsessed with building up the social world from a few impressions and ideas; he builds systems always from the inside out, traveling obsessively from the mind to culture. The British utilitarian moral philosophers, beginning with Adam Smith, will develop the notion that we behave ourselves because of spectator morality—a concept that will achieve its fullest articulation in the work of Jeremy Bentham. Hume's version of it, like his philosophy generally, is only indirectly influential. Rather than condemning the proud man as disrupting the party of humanity, Hume imagines that he is its epitome. The proud man epitomizes the party of humanity because he regulates himself in relation to the objects around him. Thus spectator morality, internalized, is the passport to social harmony. Here is Hume's visionariness: to other secular moralists, pride and self-interest are scandalous. To Hume they are the crucial emotional architecture of the self in relation to the social system.

Chapter Seven

Jovial Fanatics

Hume, Warton, Cowper

> But what greater temptation than to appear a missionary, a
> prophet, an ambassador from heaven? Who would not encounter
> many dangers and difficulties, in order to attain so sublime a char-
> acter? Or if, by the help of vanity and a heated imagination, a man
> has first made a convert of himself, and entered seriously into the
> delusion; who ever scruples to make use of pious frauds, in sup-
> port of so holy and meritorious a cause?
>
> —DAVID HUME, "Of Miracles"

This chapter explores a Humean paradox—that ordinary beliefs can go on
holiday, but they are immune to translation—and relates it to eighteenth-century literary modes. Skepticism, imagination, melancholia, and religious fanaticism are all modes in which one's beliefs go on holiday. Yet when an ordinary believer comes face to face with another person whose beliefs are in a
state of suspension, he asserts the immunity of true belief from translation.
Or so Hume tells us. My examples, drawn from Hume, Thomas Warton,
William Cowper, and William Hayley, characterize agents and their beliefs in
philosophical rather than historical terms, because that is how Hume mapped
the terrain.[1] Yet these examples may show that some eighteenth-century
British persons conceived of their beliefs—holding them, revising them, experiencing the way they change and endure, and, strangely, marking them as
impermeable—in literary terms, and that any historical theory of this area of
human life must be explored as a theory of the literary itself.

I begin with a familiar picture of Hume. Coleridge notoriously attacks
Hume's attitudes toward religion by reminding his readers that in Hume's *History of Great Britain,* "The founders and martyrs of our church and constitu-

tion, of our civil and religious liberty, are represented as fanatics and be-
wildered enthusiasts. But histories incomparably more authentic than Mr.
Hume's, (nay, spite of himself even his own history) confirm by irrefragable
evidence the aphorism of ancient wisdom, that nothing great was ever
achieved without enthusiasm. For what is enthusiasm but the oblivion and
swallowing-up of self in an object dearer than self, or in an idea more vivid?"
(1972, 23)

Coleridge's picture sorts well with our understanding of Hume's theatrical
detachment. After all, Hume defines the mind as "a kind of theatre." In Book
1 of the *Treatise of Human Nature,* he ends his long reverie of an increasingly
self-obliterating "philosophical melancholy" with a newfound sociability of
dining, conversation, and backgammon that made his earlier passions seem
"cold, and strain'd, and ridiculous" (T 253, 269). And after all, Jerome Christensen begins his book on Hume's career with the sentence "The theatrical
dream of being all things to all men received its theoretical justification in the
moral and political philosophy of eighteenth-century Britain" (1987, 3). In this
familiar picture, Hume's theatricality stands against enthusiasm and absorption—not, in Michael Fried's (1980) sense, as one aesthetic mode trumping
another within a single work of art, but as a collision between different world-
views or conceptual schemes.

This chapter tells three versions of a single story with two linked pairs of
binaries: irony and absorption, and true and false beliefs. My thesis, in its most
abstract form, is that the dangerous proximity of true to false belief causes the
line between irony and absorption to blur. In a paradigmatic example from
Book 1 of the *Treatise,* Hume distinguishes true beliefs from fictional beliefs
that *feel* true. On the first page he jauntily announces that "it will not be very
necessary to employ many words in explaining this distinction. Every one of
himself will readily perceive the difference between feeling and thinking." Yet
six hundred pages later we find him struggling, in the absence of reasons for
this distinction, to justify our making it. He finally admits that we have no rule
(i.e., no reason) to distinguish between true and false beliefs, between beliefs
that are ordinary (dependent on sensory input) and those that are visionary
(achieved without it) (T 123).[2] His journey has taken him deep into the epistemology of poetic forms, and his jauntiness has been tempered by episodes
of delusional melancholy in his writing closet. Hume's reluctant assertion that
true beliefs feel true just because they do makes the line between theatrical detachment and fanatical absorption (to adapt Coleridge's terms) seem both
thin and impermeable. Indeed, there is biographical evidence for the proxim-

ity of irony and absorption: Hume's pose of detachment grew out of melancholic abjection, and his systematic theory of belief becomes more interesting when we apprehend its origins there, as well as in his feelings about religion. Because it is important to have a working sense of the theory itself, I begin by renarrating it in such a way that its relevance to my other examples emerges.

What distinguishes my belief that I am sitting in a red chair in a dark room, writing with a black pen and drinking coffee, from your belief that you are about to be struck down by God because the luck has been breaking your way for a little bit too long? Nothing properly *distinguishes* them, you say, because they can't be compared. Yours is not so much a belief as a sense of anxiety. Perhaps your anxiety is based on belief: it may be caused by your first axiom of life (which happens to be the same as the Buddha's) that "life is suffering" or by your suspicion that you are somehow worthless. My belief, by contrast, is a simple mental state consisting of impressions such as the redness of the chair, the flow of ink, the crook of my finger. I believe in the room, the chair, and the pen because I am an animal whose nervous system has evolved to deliver such information about the world as the spacing of its shapes and the distribution of its colors. I have learned to rely on this information as a guide to the world because it has been reliable in the past.

Now what if, believing that God is about to strike you down, you conjure a vision of how it might happen? You describe God's agent in glorious Technicolor and grow incredibly agitated at the thought that it might be standing in the room with us now. Because we are friends, I have a stake in convincing you that God has not sent this vision to do battle with you. But I, a Humean, know that there is no real way to distinguish my beliefs on this point from yours. So I begin to feel melancholy; the room is spinning about, and I do not know who I am or where. Fortunately, nature intervenes to rid me of these speculations; I dine and play a game of backgammon. Restored to my equilibrium, I slip into my philosophical habits, confident that my beliefs are true and yours are false.

Where does my confidence come from? Not from any reasons that I can point to. On the contrary, I have just seen that my beliefs do not survive reflection and that the hunt for reasons is futile. Whatever you might say, my beliefs simply *feel* more true to me than yours do to you. But I no sooner invoke this criterion than I have to run back to my backgammon game before you can reply that your anxiety feels strong and vivid too. To prevent my slipping into doubt again, I adopt a pose of ironic detachment and dub myself a "man of letters."

Hume's earliest encounter with an irrationalist was an encounter with himself. I explore examples that press on the phenomenological feel of encounters between absorption and detachment, while I flesh out two aspects of Hume's view of how true beliefs are constituted. One is the notion of "vivacity," the other of confidence. Both aspects are perilously close to the convictions they mean to supplant. Vivacity, the only positive criterion Hume gives of a belief's falsity or truth, is especially related to the history of rhetoric—Ciceronian *energeia* and the like—and hence to fictionally intense moments.[3] This lineage is obviously problematic for Hume's case: nothing says that vivacity has to be linked to experience; indeed, many people—including Thomas Warton—have thought that the particular pleasure we get from repudiating experience is more vivid than ordinary experience. Warton's *Pleasures of Melancholy* (1747) is, among other things, an example of vivacity that consciously repudiates experience.

The second aspect of the Humean view of true belief, confidence, assimilates it even more clearly to false belief. In the picture Hume paints, the detachment of the man of letters stands against the absorption of the religious fanatic or the melancholic. The outlines of the Coleridgean picture of Hume transfer easily to a story from the late eighteenth century in which William Hayley, a man of letters, seeks to ironize William Cowper's religious abjection by enforcing self-consciousness on him. They transfer also to the older Hume's assertion of independence from his younger, depressed self. Yet Hume's assertion of freedom from absorption is puzzling, because true belief rests on fanatic grounds if true believers justify their beliefs by insisting that they know they are right.

An objection, which I grant in the case of Hume, might be lodged to my use of the term *fanaticism*, since it implies that one is committed to a particular project, not just that one lacks adequate reasons for one's commitments. Standing firm on sentiment is certainly not the same thing as actively adopting an irrational procedure, although in using the term *fanaticism*, I perhaps meant to convey my unease at the Humean position, from which in a slightly different context, one might say, "We both think we're right, but I have might on my side." Fanaticism, while incontinent, is not the wrong way to describe what Hume thinks he is defeating: Coleridge quite astutely decries the insulting tone of Hume's writings on religious belief.

The right question to ask is whether a lack of any absolute epistemological distinction between ordinary true belief and the varieties of false belief makes them identical, and the answer is, of course not. But the question can easily be turned around: what, in fact, separates them? Posing this question, it turns out, allows us to appreciate the relevance of Hume's theory to ongoing discussions of literature and belief. Two different but closely connected traditions come into play. The first is the Romantic/Bloomian/Rortian tradition, which understands beliefs as being relative to a conceptual scheme, their truth or falsity being relative to what counts as true or false within that scheme. Because, as Richard Rorty puts it, conscience and language are contingent, one set of beliefs is always liable to "redescription"—or to "translation"—into a new set of beliefs (1989, 30).[4] Human beings can be penetrated by new beliefs at any time; and for both Rorty and Bloom, there is something inherently literary about this situation. In the second, Romantic/Coleridgean tradition, which includes I. A. Richards and most recently Steven Knapp, moments of fictional and literary intensity are moments of "epistemological leisure," providing us with a holiday from rationality (1985, 151).

What a reading of Hume adds to these traditions is an on-the-ground, practical account of how to handle the burden of belief. Both Hume and William Hayley develop jovial, theatrical man-of-letters personae in response to the pain of being penetrated by beliefs that are potentially fanatical and absorbing. A question that I cannot directly face here is why Hume chooses literature, or more precisely, the literary life, as the term associated with ordinary belief. An adequate answer would depend on a massive exegesis of Hume's system, his sources, and his career. Perhaps he means to signal that, while periods of absorptive intensity go beyond rational belief, periods of ordinary belief also go beyond rationality. But the literariness of, or lack of rational ground for, ordinary belief does not make it any softer or more vulnerable to alteration. In fact, Hume's theory commits a person to phenomenological stubbornness: rather than soften your beliefs in the face of the fanatic, you cling to them with your own intensity. Facing a person swallowed up in his own vivid beliefs, you assert the immunity of your own beliefs to translation.

In 1734, when he was twenty-three and researching materials for his *Treatise*, Hume wrote an anonymous letter to Dr. John Arbuthnot asking his advice about a debilitating episode of depression. The letter is quite long, detailing Hume's physical complaints in terms very reminiscent of George Cheyne's case histories at the end of *The English Malady*, published the previous year.[5] Three-quarters of the way through the letter, Hume switches from describing his physical complaints to describing "how my mind stood all this time." His objective in writing the letter, he says, is to close "the small Distance betwixt me & perfect Health," a gap whose persistence he likens to the persistence of religious melancholia in autobiographical writings by certain French mystics, called the French Prophets:

I have notic'd in the Writings of the French Mysticks, & in those of our Fanatics here, that, when they give a History of the Situation of their Souls, they mention a Coldness & Desertion of the Spirit, which frequently returns, & some of them, at the beginning, have been tormented with it many Years. As this kind of Devotion depends entirely on the Force of Passion, & consequently of the Animal Spirits, I have often thought that their Case & mind were pretty parralel [*sic*], & that their rapturous Admirations might discompose the Fabric of the Nerves & Brain, as much as profound Reflections, & that warmth or Enthusiasm which is inseparable from them. (1932, 1:6–7)

Likening his "profound Reflections" to the "rapturous Admirations" of "our Fanatics here," Hume imagines that his postphilosophical coldness resembles their postreligious coldness. The French Prophets are important autobiographical figures for Hume: we can also detect traces of their presence in the scorn he expresses for his "cold and strain'd and ridiculous" philosophical melancholy in the *Treatise*.

Hume's letter to Dr. Arbuthnot forms part of the British cultivated elite's legacy of shock at a band of immigrant Huguenot refugees who fled religious persecution in the Cévennes, in southern France, between 1706 and 1708. The French Prophets, or "inspirés," were the first enthusiasts many English people had seen. Until then, *enthusiasm* had been a largely hypothetical term applied by writers like John Locke and Henry More to the millenarian excesses and violence of seventeenth-century religious wars. Hillel Schwartz (1980) documents the warm welcome given the prophets by Anglicans and dissenters, the former from a sense of political advantage and the latter from a sense of religious camaraderie. Schwartz has also described the growing revulsion toward the brand of prophecy practiced by the French refugees. In the warning words of a mainline French Protestant minister living in London, they offered "nothing but very violent and convulsive movements of the chest and head, with general prophecies of the destruction of Babylon and Antichrist, and some exhortations equally general to prayer and repentance, spoken in a manner very unworthy of the spirit" (Pierre Testas, quoted in H. Schwartz 1980, 76). These movements took place as the prophets slept; thus they claimed to be mere mouthpieces for the spirit, evacuated of any agency of their own. Eventually they were held to be insufficiently distinct from their papist persecutors, inasmuch as their attempts to convert matter into meaning and flesh into spirit were, from the point of view of English Protestants, absurd and frightening.

In the second and third decades of the eighteenth century, many writers were fascinated by the idea that some people could be inconsistently visited by the Spirit while remaining unconscious. British writers produced a huge number of tracts on religious melancholy. These tracts sought to distinguish true religious faith from the false inwardness practiced by the baffling prophets. Insisting that enthusiasts simply faked their passions, antievangelical writers sought to defend Protestantism from their excesses. Both orthodox and dissenting English Protestants held that the regimens of faith and prayer would cure religious melancholy, a special case of melancholia involving self-abnegation entailed by a loss of faith. In response to a request from a female parishioner that he codify his cure for it, the evangelical Robert Blakeway wrote to help her achieve "restoration of your Mind to its former self-satisfaction and quiet" (1717, 13). He described the panicky condition of the melancholic:

> Oh! what shall I do? Whither shall I fly? I dare not look up to Heaven, for there sits my Judge commanding down all his Vengeance upon me: Into his revealed word I dare not look, for there I read my condemnation and Doom; nor dare I run to the Grave for Rest and Shelter, for from thence I must be raised to her the wonderful sentence passed upon me; Oh that I had never been born, or could be now annihilated, & c! (19)

Blakeway recommended grace and the "paths of peace" in place of the "Austerities" of papist ritual: "pilgrimages, going bare-fac't, Hair-Shirts, Whips & c." (13). The papists, he thought, materially mortified the body rather than apply spiritual balm to false beliefs. Like many preachers offering therapy for religious melancholy, Blakeway did not specify the forms that his alternative "Confidence in, or Application of the Evangelical Promises to [the] self" might assume (17). Yet he starkly distinguished false beliefs from the true work of the Spirit. Like other evangelical and orthodox thinkers, Blakeway thought religious melancholics were antispiritual because their inwardness was generated inside them. Melancholy is typically a "Diseased Craziness, Hurt or Error of the Imagination, and consequently of the understanding" (4). Richard Baxter, another prolific preacher, contrasted religious melancholy to true acts of spirituality, which are the "inward Acts that are the Holiness of the Soul" (1716, 17).

This legacy helps place in context the famous sentences in the last paragraph of Hume's essay "Of Miracles," which suddenly swerves from attacking one form of revealed religion to characterizing Christianity *tout court* as internalized abstraction: "The Christian Religion not only was at first attended with miracles, but even at this day cannot be believed by any reasonable person without one. Mere reason is insufficient to convince us of its veracity; and whoever is moved by faith to assent to it, is conscious of a continued miracle in his own person, which subverts all the principles of his understanding, and gives him a determination to believe what is most contrary to experience" (E 131).

There is a peculiar blend of activity and passivity in these sentences: the religionist has exercised his power of "assent" and has achieved a highly self-reflective state of consciousness ("a continued miracle in his own person"), yet faith has "moved" him into this state.[6] Here Hume greedily reduces all religious belief to religious melancholy. His language is like the antienthusiastic pamphlets, particularly John Langhorne's strict Anglican *Letters on Religious Retirement, Melancholy and Enthusiasm* (1762), which describes enthusiasm as perpetual inward abstraction. Against the enthusiast's injunction to "pray always" and "without ceasing," Langhorne writes: "I need only observe that the mind of man, in this imperfect state, cannot by any means perpetually bear such an abstraction of thought, as the adoration of God requires" (1762, 84).

What is Hume's alternative to the religious melancholic's "abstraction of thought"? An immediately attractive candidate, often called Hume's "naturalism," is his positive psychology of the way our animal minds are conditioned to perform certain operations.[7] The mind, as Hume describes it, depends on the periodic spacing and succession of impressions and ideas deriving directly from the world. When Hume turns from the mind's working to its relationship to actual features of the world, he dabbles with extreme skepticism and so becomes subject to frequent bouts of melancholy. Yet naturalism is not Hume's alternative to absorptive melancholy; if anything, it is its predecessor, for his melancholy simply inherits the periodicity formerly associated with naturalistic spacing of perceptions. His language resembles descriptions of religious melancholia in the antienthusiastic pamphlets. Compare Blakeway's description of the phenomenology of religious melancholy to Hume's melancholic cry in the conclusion to Book 1 of the *Treatise:* "Where am I, or what? From what causes do I derive my existence, and to what condition shall I return? Whose favour shall I court, and whose anger must I dread? What beings surround me? And on whom have I any influence, or who have any influence on me? I am confounded with all these questions, and begin to fancy myself in the most deplorable condition imaginable, inviron'd with the deepest darkness, and utterly depriv'd of the use of every member and faculty" (T 269).

Hume breaks the grip of melancholy by coming back to the familiar comforts of custom, habit, and sociability. Yet like religious melancholy and unlike naturalism, custom and habit seem oddly immune to experience. Hume's early letter to Arbuthnot shows why. It ends with five questions; the last tacitly allows that his disease is primarily psychological: "I believe all proper Medicines have been us'd, and therefore I need mention nothing of them." In a remarkably simple and insightful reading of the letter, Hume's biographer, Ernest C. Mossner, argues that "in the very act of writing the letter, Hume may have come to the realization that all that could be done had been done" (1980, 86). Taken together, the questions and answers amount to a cathartic self-catechism. The last answer, in Mossner's reconstruction of Hume's internal dialogue, is a tautological credo: "No indeed; you are cured because you have the confidence that you are cured" (87).[8] That Hume should have discovered how easy belief could be, just as he was most afraid that the "small distance" between him and health might yawn open to reveal the lurking French Prophet within, was a stroke of luck.

According to Mossner's script, the beliefs that Hume established at twenty-three had a therapeutic or cathartic effect. In a brief autobiographical summary written much later, Hume describes as literary the process of detaching himself from his beliefs. "Seized very early with a passion for literature which has been the ruling passion of my Life, and the great source of my Enjoyments," he now finds himself in old age almost "more detached from Life" than it is possible for any person to be (1932, 1–7). This seeming contradiction and the Popean language of the ruling passion only reinforce that sense (after all, the people Pope describes as having a ruling passion are ruled by that passion, not detached in spite or because of it). Yet Hume describes a pose of detachment that is essentially ironic, as though he imagined the overcoming of his earlier fanatic self as the sort of journey an ironic narrator might undertake to shake free of a character (e.g., Pope and Philip, Duke of Wharton, whom Pope draws as an oblique self-portrait and then excoriates). A similar pose of detachment undergirds his writings on epistemological certainty, eloquence, and aesthetic belief. It would take an essay on each of these topics to explore Hume's idea that his "science of man" is literary and to study the history of the astonishing interest in Hume as a literary philosopher.

One way that the trope of detachment works is by analogy to Hume's naturalistic theories of mind. All experience, including that of self-consciousness, is, like ordinary sense impressions, the raw data of belief. The aggregate of experience is impressed on a system like the mind, yet it is bootstrapped up a few levels of generality until it becomes a purely formal operation. Thus Hume must establish the distinction between true and false by fiat, because from the ground of custom we make this distinction not reasonably but fanatically.[9] His early experience of depression leaves him with two fanatical options.

Either he can explore the phenomenology of "the most deplorable condition imaginable," or he can change his mind about being in such a condition. The second option allows Hume to reestablish an empiricist line (after an initial outlay to the fanatic's account); the first is literally unthinkable for an empiricist. Borrowing Thomas Nagel's famous question about bats, what is it like to be a religious melancholic? It must be like *something* to be one, but Hume's has grounded his system in custom so that he doesn't have to find out what.

The Pleasures of Melancholy

In the 1740s, only a few years after Hume had struggled to distinguish true from false belief, some English poets began to celebrate the pleasures of melancholy, a visionary emotion not connected to external sensory impressions. Marshall Brown (1991, 198) has catalogued "a line of melancholy prodigies" who dominated English poetry in the 1740s: Blair's "Grave," Young's "Night Thoughts," Hervey's prose poem "Meditations among the Tombs," Joseph Warton's "The Enthusiast," James Thomson's "Castle of Indolence," and Thomas Warton's *Pleasures of Melancholy.* These poems have their sources both in late-seventeenth- and early-eighteenth-century debates about religious melancholy and in Robert Burton's *Anatomy of Melancholy.* Burton had defined melancholy as a disorder of inwardness, wholly confined to the imagination: "feare and sorrow without a cause" (1989–94, 1:247). A psychological naturalist would find such an unmotivated emotion tantamount to false belief, but the charge would hardly be embarrassing. On the contrary, the very falseness, artificiality, and typicality of the visionary psychology leads some poets to embrace it.

Thomas Warton's *Pleasures of Melancholy* (1747), one of the most exuberant of these poems, begins by severely repudiating empiricist psychology. The narrator nurtures a patently contrived inwardness by replacing a realist mode of succession with an antirealist one. The poem critiques empiricism on two fronts, offering an alternative story about the mind's contents. As Warton tells it, literary history, not natural or divine history, has stuffed the mind, charging each image with an ambivalent (and erotic) pleasure.[10] The paradox of pleasing pain, converted into a source of epistemological power, is the key to the interiority Warton imagines for his narrator; indeed, it signals an affinity between his work and much of the melancholy poetry written in the 1740s (and published in Robert Dodsley's anthology, 1748–58).

Warton's debut poem is so full of paradox, in fact, that it seems to sign on to a literary canon through a bravura demonstration of one of the English tradition's best-known effects. At first the motivation for any image in the poem seems to be its place in a rapid oscillation between low and high, near and far, self and other:

> Mother of Musings, Contemplation sage,
> Whose grotto stands upon the topmost rock
> Of Teneriff, 'mid the tempestuous night,
> On which, in calmest meditation held
> Thou hearest with howling winds the beating rain.[11]

These opening lines are just the first in a string of double chiasms (contemplation is finally, after grotto/topmost rock, tempestuous night/meditation, held in contemplation).

Yet perhaps the poem's greatest paradox also unfolds in these lines: the poem thematizes inwardness, while replacing any imaginable eighteenth-century account of ideas with a new psychology of abstractions. First, Warton nullifies the empiricist account of ideas. The thoughts and images that emblematize and narratively extend the poet's internal life come, not through sensations or impressions, but through analogy, specifically through the paradoxical psychology of the "Mother of Musings," contemplation (as seems appropriate to a Burtonian poet, describing "fear and sorrow without a cause"). So distant is the narrator's poetic experience from perceptual experience that the point of any mental image is to produce its *opposite* rather than to imitate an impression or a perception. Nor does Warton favor a strictly idealist account: the personification of contemplation does not subsume representations under herself, as she would if the understanding were supposed to foster sense perception.[12] In Warton's invocation, which sets the terms of the analogy, concepts seek their own conceptual forms (contemplation can return to contemplating), but only by alternating with the images and representations farthest from them. Not only does mother contemplation hear the howling storm "in calmest meditation held" and "from the topmost rock / Of Teneriff," but she hears it only after she has been, paradoxically, deindividuated by self-reference.

The psychology of paradoxical images can be thought of as external-world skepticism. The impressions available to the poet as he describes his own sensory experience arise, not from conventional objects, but from highly ornamental literary ones: a passion is joined to a durative mental state; neither passion nor mental state derives from sensory impressions; and each is antithetically related to the other. For instance, the poet experiences "how fearful is it to reflect / That through the still globe's awful solitude, / No being wakes but me!" Yet such an experience, instead of perking him up, puts him to sleep; and sleep turns into an occasion to reject dreams in favor of literary sources of images:

> Nor then let dreams, or wanton folly born,
> My senses lead through flow'ry paths of joy;
> But let the sacred Genius of the night
> Such mystic visions send, as Spenser saw.

So obviously does the poet prefer emotions and reflections to sensory perceptions that he rejects even those liminal kinds of perceptions, like dreams, that an external-world skeptic might see as reason to doubt sensory perception in the first place.

I will return in a moment to what it means for the poet to have emotions like fear and pleasure without anything—even sense-defeating dreams—actually striking his senses. For now, it is worth noticing that an ideational vocabulary of literary images only amounts to a psychology appropriate to the poem's purpose: not just to sign on to, but to create an English poetic canon. The poem gives an account of the seventeen-year-old poet's place in literary history, which turns out, predictably, to depend, not on his imitation of, but on his opposition to, other English poets. It would be more precise to say that even his opposition registers as ambivalence. Robert J. Griffin (1995, 24–63) shows that Warton's conscious choice of "Spenser's wildly-warbling song" over "Pope's Attic page" actually masks a preference for certain aspects of himself to which he gave the name Spenser, and a suppression of other aspects of himself to which he gave the name Pope, even as he salvaged some aspects of Pope and called them Thomas Warton (his poet father).

Yet even his hope that "the sacred Genius of the night" might "such mystic visions send, as Spenser saw" rather than sensory perceptions or even dreams, marks a paradox. "Spenser" is once again an effect of Warton's desire to take his place at the end of the line. In his *Observations on the "Faerie Queene" of Spenser*, written a year before he revised *The Pleasures of Melancholy*, Warton attacked Spenser's epic as too "allegoric":

Spenser in the visionary dominions of Una's father has planted the Tree of Life, and Knowledge. . . .

The extravagancies of Pagan Mythology are not improperly introduced into a poem of this sort, as they are acknowledged falsities, or at best, if expressive of any moral truth, no more than the inventions of men. But he that applies the VISIONS OF GOD in such a manner, is guilty of an impropriety, which, I fear, amounts to an impiety.

If we look back from Spenser's age thro' the state of poesy in this kingdom, we shall find that it principally consisted in the allegoric species, and that this species never re-

ceiv'd its absolute consummation till it appear'd with new lustre in THE FAERIE
QUEENE. (1754, 226–27)

A young cleric might have written these words because he felt anxious about
the impropriety of his own gothicism.[13]

Later, widening the compass of his remarks, Warton asserts that, "if we take
a retrospect of English poetry from the age of Spenser," all of it is found to
have "principally consisted in visions and allegories" (1762, 2:101). In one
stroke, he makes Spenser less antithetical to his predecessors and reduces his
own uneasiness about "visions." Spenser's visions in his poems, like Warton's
visions of him, are not visions in any sensory way, but visions in virtue of his
structural place in the English canon. Seeing at all becomes practically indistinguishable from seeing other poets, or indeed from seeing *as* other poets.
And since this is a national line of descent, it begins with (and continues in
imitation of) the visions of God.

Warton's tendency to subordinate vision to re-vision, or seeing to seeing *as,*
reaches a climax in his revisionary account of Pope's "visionary maid"
Eloisa.[14] The interest in Pope's personification of melancholy in *Eloisa to
Abelard* (1717) partly lies in the way Pope converts Eloisa's visions into an index of typical subjectivity while abandoning the particular Eloisa. (In this respect, Pope turns out to resemble the abandoning Abelard himself, who loves
"Eloisa" in general without being able to consummate his love for the particular woman.) In Eloisa's monologue, the proximity of the visionary maid and
Black Melancholy—a female source for the secondary qualities of the objects
of perception—raises the issue of the self's relationship to its perceptual or
cognitive representations.

> Black Melancholy sits, and round her throws
> A death-like silence, and a dread repose:
> her gloomy presence saddens all the scene,
> Shades every flower, and darkens every green,
> Deepens the murmur of the falling floods,
> And breathes a browner horror on the woods.
> (TE 2:332–333)

There are two steps. First the scenes that aid Eloisa's meditation give way, when
she goes to sleep and renounces visions, to scenes influenced, if not wholly created, by her mood. It seems as if Eloisa's mood is going to determine what objects are available to her consciousness and thus allow her to be independent
of this strangely eroticized landscape reclining, quivering, and panting after
her. But in the second step, surprisingly, Eloisa disappears instead, leaving only

the precipitate of a female subjectivity behind. Far from gaining the independence to determine objects of consciousness, she fails even to gain a foothold against her own mood: Black Melancholy wipes her out of the picture.

Warton's response to Pope's personification links the poet's pleasure in abstractions to the theme of imitative visions:

> Ye youths of Albion's beauty-blooming isle,
> Whose brows have worn the wreath of luckless love,
> Is there a pleasure like the pensive mood,
> Whose magic wont to soothe your soften'd souls?
> O tell how rapturous the joy, to melt
> To Melody's assuasive voice; to bend
> Th'uncertain step along the midnight mead,
> And pour your sorrows to the pitying moon,
> By many a slow trill from the bird of woe
> Oft interrupted; in embow'ring woods
> By darksome brook to muse, and there forget
> The solemn dulness of the tedious world,
> While Fancy grasps the visionary fair:
> And now no more th'abstracted ear attends
> The water's murm'ring lapse, th'entranced eye
> Pierces no longer thro' th'extended rows
> Of thick-rang'd trees; 'till haply from the depth
> The woodman's stroke, or distant tinkling team,
> Of heifers rustling thro' the brake, alarms
> Th'illuded sense, and mars the golden dream.

Wharton reverses the order in which melancholy steals away and evacuates Eloisa's self. He makes it look as though "tinkling" heifers and ruddily masculine woodsmen break fancy's grasp on the "visionary fair" and distract the "abstracted ear" from the "water's murm'ring lapse." In Pope's lines, of course, the opposite happens: Idealist perceptions consume and evacuate real objects. Yet even if Warton wants his readers to consider the intrusion of sense perception upon idealism as violence (alarming the "illuded sense" and marring the "golden dream"), why does he figure such an intrusion as both a team of domesticated animals and a castrating woodsman? In part, the paired attitudes of the sensory intruders (submissive and dominant) simply repeat a dualism that Warton has developed all along in relation to the literary tradition. Warton has imagined his visionary insides as male poets, yet when he comes to imagine his insides as his closest source of influence (i.e., Pope), he recasts himself as one of Pope's female characters. His close relationship to the poetic line makes him undergo a conversion to an evacuated literary image, subordinated by gender. It is almost as though Warton oscillates between a yearning to take his place at the table of the great by repeating literary imitations, and a yearning to be served up at the table of the great as a (feminized) literary imitation.

The most important point about both kinds of imitations, the "abstracted thought" of Milton and the "abstracted ear" of Eloisa, is that they point to the special artificiality of the poet's inwardness. Not only does he imagine his mind as an abstract space whose images result from "visions" rather than vision, but the form of the empty inner space is always plugged up by an especially *formal* content. The poet's visual phenomenology alternates between positing sight as subsuming one's self under someone else's vision—becoming absorbed in the visions of male poets—and seeing as being, that is, becoming the image of an opaque yet emptied literary woman.

One of Warton's great achievements, then, is to convert his lowly status at the end of the poetic line, as well as the epistemological evacuation that accompanies it, into a source of pleasure. Ultimately, the pleasure of such an antisensual phenomenology depends on the greater ease and efficiency with which it resists the temporal losses entailed by ordinary perception. Ordinary (empiricist) notions of perception depend on the *succession* of images striking the mind; Warton's phenomenology depends on slowing down or stopping that succession. In their classic study *Saturn and Melancholy* (1964), Raymond Klibansky, Erwin Panofsky, and Fritz Saxl argue that the specifically "poetic" meaning of the word *melancholy* became synonymous in the English poetic tradition with a temporary mood rather than an enduring character trait: "The predicate 'melancholy' could be transferred from the person to the object that gave rise to his mood, so that one could speak of melancholy spaces, melancholy light, melancholy notes or melancholy landscapes" (217). Essentially, melancholy reflects on itself *as a means of* becoming (merely or distinctly) poetic. In Warton's case, however, the direction of the absorption is opposite to the one Klibansky and his colleagues imagine fits a literary relationship between moods and their objects. Here the poet tends to absorb a range of objects from the outside world through his melancholy, rather than to project his melancholy outward in an apotropaic scheme not to identify with it too closely (i.e., to turn it into an illness or pathogenic condition).

Thus, the poet's melancholy functions like an ordinary sensory organ, though with an important difference. Melancholy absorbs information and then so thoroughly suspends awareness of it that it is no longer recognizable as information. Warton continually refers to this process as the operation of his "pensive mind" and associates it finally with the "pleasures" of melancholy that he has written the poem to describe. For instance, in one passage he castigates a lone pilgrim for not properly sensing the pleasures of "sacred Night," "Murder" and "secret slaughter" that melancholy brings with her in her "gloom":

> What tho' they stay the pilgrim curseth oft,
> As all benighted in Arabian wastes
> He hears the wilderness around him howl
> With roaming monsters, while on his hoar head
> The black-descending tempest ceaseless beats;
> Yet more delightful to my pensive mind
> Is thy return, than blooming-morn's approach.

The contrast between the cursing pilgrim, who finds the "ceaseless beat" of the "black-descending tempest" tedious, and the poet, whose "pensive mind" finds all this delightful, only furthers Warton's excoriation of the senses. But why does he associate the horrors of sensory experience, not with the experience of murder or secret slaughter, but with a pilgrim insufficiently appreciative of wastelands? The pilgrim, a religious figure, is associated with sensory error. He resembles the poet in his ambivalence: they are both peripatetics. His refusal to commit to a unified sensory experience and his ambivalent desire to remain on the road to Mecca, however, take the form of an impulse toward the sources of sensory experience, not away from them. The poet's turn from the eye to the mind's eye is also marked by ambivalence, but it impels him *away from* sensory perception. The mind's eye imitates the body's eye in that it rapidly outlines images, oscillating quickly between two or more of them. But while the pilgrim's overidentification with his roving eye condemns him to wastelands, the poet's gesture gives him pleasure. Thus pleasure is already committed to the mind as a formal abstraction produced by the negation of objects. We have already seen how the concept of literary inheritance defeats anything as worldly as sensory perception. Now it looks as though "pleasure" is the name Warton gives to the literary process through which a melancholy feeling nonsensually extends and asserts its fixated, abstract self-reference.

Warton's poetic claim is that the pleasures of melancholy are the positive result of the denigration of sense perception. In the abstract, atemporal space left in the mind after the senses have been decommissioned, images from literary history arise and subsist. What causes them to do so is a person's structural place at the end of, in a paradoxically dominant and subordinate relationship to, a chain of literary imitations. Thus Warton puts in place what

William Jewett calls "the literary culture of fanaticism," which "acts out a truth that it also states in various covert ways—namely that there is more pleasure in writing than in sensory experience because pleasure (as distinct from say gratification) follows from a reflexive turn by which the mind, conceived of as a formal mechanism of abstraction, discovers or decrees its autonomy from the sensory infrastructure" (personal communication). We are reminded that a fascinating harvest of theory may still be gleaned from a once-powerful tradition of thought about the "dangers of the imagination/fiction."[15]

William Hayley, Man of Letters

In 1797, as though driven by Boswell's ghost, William Hayley, soon to be William Cowper's biographer, described for Cowper an "Ecstatic Vision" in which "I beheld the throne of God, whose splendor, though in excess, did not strike me blind; but left me power to discern, on the steps of it, two kneeling angelic forms" ("Second Memorial"). For many years Cowper, convinced that he was about to be struck down by God, had been severely depressed. He heard threatening voices that he thought came from Satan and from God, who tormented him personally: "[I] dreamed that in a state of the most insupportable misery I looked through the window of a strange room being all alone, and saw preparations making for my execution" (1979–86, 4:237). His resistance to his friends' protests, his ingenious dodges when confronted with the groundlessness of his feelings, and his tendency "to convert any message, however sanguine, into one of condemnation," led his friends to perform increasingly strained acts of therapy (King 1986, 274).[16] Even considering Cowper's cousin's attempt to build a pipeline into Cowper's room through which he could subliminally feed comforting voices while Cowper slept, Hayley's "Ecstatic Vision" must rank as one of the strangest of these acts:

A kind seraph seemed to whisper to me, that these heavenly petitioners were your lovely mother, and my own; both engaged in fervent supplications for your restoration to mental serenity, and comfort. I sprang eagerly forward to enquire your destiny of your mother. Turning towards me, with a look of seraphic benignity, she smiled upon me, and said: "warmest of earthly friends! moderate the anxiety of thy zeal, lest it distract thy declining faculties! and know, as a reward for thy kindness, that my son shall be restored to himself, and to friendship.

But the all-merciful and almighty ordains, that his restoration shall be gradual; and that his peace with heaven shall be preceded by the following extraordinary circumstances of signal honour on earth. He shall receive letters from Members of Parliament, from Judges, and from Bishops, to thank him for the service, that he has rendered to the Christian world by his devotional poetry. These shall be followed by a letter from the Prime Minister to the same effect; and this by thanks expressed to him, on the same account, in the hand of the King himself. Tell him, when these events take place, he may confide in his celestial emancipation from despair, granted to the prayers of his mother; and he may rest satisfied with this assurance from her, that his peace is perfectly made with heaven. Hasten to impart these blessed tidings to your favorite friend! said the maternal spirit; and let your thanksgiving to God be an increase of reciprocal kindness to each other!" ("Second Memorial")

In writing to Cowper, Hayley was, he said, obeying Cowper's mother, who had died when Cowper was six years old; Hayley's conscience may have pricked him, however, because he admitted that the vision may only be "the fruitless offspring of my agitated fancy." He added that "if any part of the prophecy shall soon be accomplished, a faint ray of hope will be turned into strong, luminous, and delightful conviction in my heart, and I trust in yours."

Over the next eight months, Hayley and Cowper's two cousins, John Johnson and Harriet Hesketh, set about fulfilling Cowper's mother's "prophecy." They wrote to Lord Thurlow; Lord Kenyon; William Wilberforce; Beilby Porteus, the evangelical bishop of London; and the bishop of Llandaff (and probably to many others) to send commendatory letters to Cowper and to make them look spontaneous. They formed a pact to keep Cowper's depression and their plans to cure it secret from their famous correspondents. When only Wilberforce and the bishops of London and Llandaff wrote back—Lord Kenyon apparently felt that such assurances to Cowper from a stranger would be inappropriate—Hayley, although disappointed, persisted. "How hard it is," he wrote to Hesketh, "to make great men do, what they ought to do with alacrity of heart and soul."[17] When, in February 1798, Hesketh entreated Hayley not to "apply to [Lord Kenyon] *any more*—you have done your part sufficiently, as far as respects this luminary of the law," Hayley's self-described "bold experiment" finally came to an end.

It was not successful. Each of the letters fell on deaf ears as Cowper magnificently converted kindly words into further evidence of his damnation.[18] It must be said, however, that Cowper's friends just as magnificently converted his dodges into evidence of their project's success. Johnson heard Cowper's response to the Wilberforce letter and encouraged Hayley not to be upset by it, "For I know he ponders it in his heart. . . . He has read the letter, with unusual attention: and I am certain, that he compares it with the prophecy in the Vision."[19] At points the conflict between Cowper and his circle of projectors broke into the open, and Cowper had to admit that his stubbornness was more than incomprehension. When the letter from the bishop of Llandaff arrived,

Johnson and Cowper happened to be reading Llandaff's *Apology for Christianity* together. "You may be sure," Johnson wrote to Hayley, "our poor friend was rather startled at the wonderful coincidence; and so in truth was I, and inwardly thankful to that kind providence, whose finger I discerned so plainly." Johnson then tried to insinuate the connection to Cowper by reminding him of Hayley's vision: "I therefore began . . . one day after dinner, as we were all using the finger-glasses.—'Miss Perowne (said I) don't you recollect something about a letter's coming to Mr. Cowper in the summer from Mr. Hayley, containing a wonderful vision, which he had lately had? . . . By the bye . . . I will go, and look for Mr. Hayley's letter.'—Mr. Cowper immediately called out 'No pray don't.' Johnny—'Because it strikes me, there is a kind of accomplishment of what is predicted'" ("Second Memorial").

Hayley was openly skeptical of the providential claims of project. He had intended, he wrote, to "invent" nothing more than a "large and complicated intellectual machine" for changing Cowper's beliefs. There are some puzzling aspects to Hayley's invention. When Hayley encountered Cowper and his companion, Mary Unwin, eight years earlier, they had been living in a community dominated by the evangelical preacher John Newton. In addition to participating in an evangelical life, Cowper and Newton had collaborated on a group of religious poems, the *Olney Hymns*. How, then, was Hayley able to convince the small group of evangelical Christians living around Cowper to lie, describing as "providential" a method of therapy that depended on Hayley as the catalyst of change? To ensure Harriet Hesketh's "tender Regard for the friendly ambition of the projector," he recounted the real origins of his project:

It arose from my very acute sense of our dear friend's sufferings, and my intense desire to relieve them. After reading his most affecting billet of despair, I fell into a deep meditation upon it; and while my eyes were covered by my hand, I seemed to behold something very like the vision, I have described. The images appeared so forcible to my own fancy, that I immediately resolved to make a bold, affectionate attempt to render them *instrumental,* if possible, (with the blessing of God and good angels) to the restoration of our invaluable friend."[20]

Perhaps because of Hayley's frank admission that he had devised his prophecy intentionally as a project, the group's initial acknowledgment of the mechanics of the fake vision gave way to a thoroughly sentimentalized version.[21] In part, this version was the result of a conscious expurgation of the published record. After Hayley's death, Johnson edited his memoirs, in which he directs the reader to a "full explication of the incident in another place"—by which

he means Hayley's *Life of Cowper,* since "The Second Memorial of Hayley's Endeavours to serve his Friend Cowper," from which I take the account of the incident, exists only in a manuscript copy handwritten by Hayley. And yet in the
Life of Cowper, Hayley says only that "several individuals" of "piety and learning" wrote to Cowper "in the benevolent hope that expressions of friendly
praise from persons who could be influenced only by the most laudable motives in bestowing it" could "re-animate the dejected spirit of a poet" (1803,
2:205–6).

The sentimentalizing of the fake vision may have been connected to Hayley's increasingly explicit fantasies of himself in a popular romantic identity.
(He started signing his correspondence with officials and family members
"hermit" and talked about building a "marine turret," or hermitage by the
sea).[22] Thus his memory may have suppressed his role as agent of Providence,
although Cowper understood Hayley's desire to assume such a role and even
humored him. On another occasion, Hayley claimed, Cowper gently supported Hayley's fantasies by investing him with a mystical healing power:

With a countenance of absolute distraction [Cowper] exclaimed: 'there is a wall of separation between me and my God.' I looked fixedly in his face, and answered, with equal
celerity and vehemence of expression, 'so there is, my friend, but I can inform you, I
am the most resolute mortal on earth for pulling down old walls, and by the living God
I will not leave a stone standing in the wall, you speak of.' He examined my features in-
tently for a few moments; and then, taking my hand most cordially, he said, with a
sweet appearance of recovered serenity: 'I believe you.' ("Second Memorial")

Hayley believed that Cowper attributed providential powers to him; when
he received Cowper's "affecting billet of despair," the temptation to act as a
providential agent again may have been strong in him. At the nadir of his depression, Cowper sent Hayley an unsigned letter that concludes, "Perfect Despair the most perfect that ever possessed any Mind has had possession of
mine you know how long, and knowing that, will not need to be told who
writes." Hayley partly justified his intervention by eliding any distinction between Cowper's agency and God's, noting that Cowper's "intimation of being
bidden to write to me did not allude to any human injunction for that purpose, but to some internal impulse on his wonderful mind."[23]

Writing retrospectively in the *Life of Cowper,* Hayley smoothed over the
disparity between Cowper's hope of providential intervention and the machinery of his fake vision to make the whole exchange look like seamless social benevolence. However, an evangelical reader of Cowper responded differently to Hayley's attempt to cure Cowper's melancholy through such means.

After Hayley's copyright on the *Life of Cowper* had run out, the Reverend T. S. Grimshawe undertook a full revision of it to "defend the honour of religion" from Hayley's cavalier approach (1835, 1:vii). "In no portion of [Hayley's *Life*] is this defect more visible than where he attributes the malady of Cowper to the operation of religious causes," Grimshawe wrote (5:318).

Grimshawe set out to construct an elaborate scaffold of interpretation around the weakening foundations of the narrative, at some points breaking into it to expostulate against Hayley and at other points suppressing unfavorable parts of the story. Cowper's evangelicalism could not be the cause of his illness, Grimshawe argued, "for what creed ever proclaimed the delusion under which Cowper laboured?" (5:312). On the contrary, "In proportion as [Cowper] forgot the heavenly Monitor, his peace vanished, his passions resumed the ascendancy, and he presented an unhappy compound of guilt and wretchedness" (5:305). Grimshawe ascribed Cowper's malady to nerves: "In this state religion found him, and administered the happy cure" (5:306). (By Cowper's own admission, however, happiness and strong religious feeling never went together, so it is hard to see exactly what Grimshawe meant.) Finally, Grimshawe concluded, Hayley's devaluing of the religious content of Cowper's beliefs to avoid "alarming his reader" is merely the last refuge for "literary and elegant" explanations of a failed secularism (1:vi).

Grimshawe was essentially correct about Hayley's project. The form of cognitive therapy Hayley invented was indeed a literary (and secularizing) approach to Cowper's disordered passions. Its very possibility depended on the idea that Cowper's friends could contribute new and different beliefs to his internal constitution. By helping himself to the authority of the poet's dead mother, Hayley had sought to introduce Cowper to the temporal authority of the political and religious leaders he contacted and thus to alter Cowper's beliefs by making them contingent upon their actions.

This tale might simply dramatize an encounter between the fanatic mind and a literary skeptic were it not that Cowper's irony about his beliefs is palpable throughout his writings. Cowper, although often racked by the certainty that his beliefs were false, never questions his experience of melancholia. His *Spiritual Diary* (1795), a series of mad, disjointed reflections written over a period of a few months, records an ambivalence in which false beliefs and intense feeling coexist as part of a necessary relationship to a mutilating God: "See now, O God, if this be a doom, if this a condition such as a creature of thine could have deserved to be exposed to. I know that thou thyself wast not without thy fears that I should incur it. But thou wouldst set me on the slippery brink of this horrible pit in a state of infatuation little short of idiotism,

204   THE SPECTATOR MORALITY OF THE ENLIGHTENMENT

and wouldst in effect say to me—Die this moment or fall into it, and if you fall into it, be it your portion for ever. Such was not the mercy I expected from Thee" (1979–86, 4:470).

Cowper acknowledges the disparity between his puny intentions and God's mighty ones, yet paradoxically he describes his *own* intentions as inscrutable ("a state of infatuation little short of idiotism") while magnificently ventrilo-quizing God's thoughts ("and wouldst in effect say to me"). Cowper's willful blindness to his own intentions makes him seem especially subject to God's control, even as he writes the script through which God controls him. Yet the irony in this position stems from the way Cowper makes himself an emblem or *type* (in the figural sense) of God's intentions: by insisting on the opacity of his own consciousness, Cowper generalizes himself until he is both the source and end of God's intentions. His irony is thus satiric, for when a giant script is written to catch a type of person, the person can do little, once caught, but conform to his or her type. (Various phenomenologically opaque figures in Pope's *Essay on Man* are particular victims of this kind of irony).

This complex oscillation between opacity and awareness as a means, not of avoiding, but of describing the inexorability of melancholia is Cowper's strat-egy even in his more lucid or "pathetic" poems. Late poems like "The Cast-away" (1799), though they represent the survival of an essentially religious per-spective on melancholia, take self-awareness to be part of the melancholic's condition:

> No voice divine the storm allay'd,
> No light propitious shone;
> When, snatch'd from all effectual aid,
> We perish'd, each alone;
> But I beneath a rougher sea,
> And whelm'd in deeper gulphs than he.[24]

The religious melancholic, comparing himself unfavorably to a drowning sailor, views his own melancholia with detachment, despite feeling it intensely. There is a gap between the general feeling of melancholia and the particular melancholic, yet the gap is motivated or opened only insofar as the latter iden-tifies with the former. This account goes part of the way toward explaining the failure of Cowper's irony to save him, as Hayley assumed it should, from en-thusiasm and melancholia. Hayley thought that adding new knowledge to Cowper's internal constitution would "re-animate" the poet's spirits, but he misread the two powerful traditions in eighteenth-century thought that we have sketched—Hume's and Warton's—both of which hold ordinary and ab-sorptive experience to separate untranslatable states of mind.

In our ordinary ways of talking about belief, we often switch between figures of distance (having, holding) and figures of identity (being possessed by), classifying our beliefs as states that we entertain and that grip us. We think that beliefs are either destroyed or revealed by skeptical inquiry, that beliefs are both the shining foundation of our identities and the first casualties of our self-knowledge. Mark Edmundson's fascinating book on how literary theory has disenfranchised poetry illustrates the habit of polarized thinking with a sketch that might find a home in any eighteenth-century gallery of character portraits:

> There's a particular kind of mind that assumes that the most unpalatable truth must be the essential truth, and proceeds from there. A votary of this doctrine, which has been called the reductive fallacy, fears deception above almost everything else, and in particular fears being taken completely unawares. So he prepares himself by thinking the worst and then too by expressing it—with the sad result that he sometimes tells others how to bring his ruin. Yet saying the worst, when it is done with some measure of ironic distance, with an awareness of what one is about, can be salutary for interpreting both literature and life. It gives you access to your most firmly held values and beliefs, those commitments that survive after fierce scrutiny. (1995, 214)

Edmundson is a romanticist by training and an intellectual associate of Richard Rorty, so it is perhaps not surprising to find him celebrating literary irony as an antidote to the reductive mind (fanaticism). Yet his assertion that "saying the worst . . . gives you access to your most firmly held . . . beliefs" presupposes that beliefs are merely the last survivors of "fierce scrutiny," rather than its products. Beliefs seem to be hard-won states of mind, residing either in the breach or just beyond the crest of battle. Holding beliefs does not mean holding them at arm's length; it means holding on for dear life.

For Hume, the preeminent eighteenth-century theorist of belief, believing is easier than reflecting on what we believe. Only vivacity produces true beliefs; reflection leads to doubt and thus tends to destroy belief. Hume's view that we just believe what we believe can be construed as antithetical to the tradition of liberal irony, magnificently invoked by Rorty and criticized most recently by Stanley Fish.[25] Adopting the English Romantic poets as his precursors, Rorty admits irony's power to take us behind our beliefs and realize their contingency, to "hold" them, as it were; Fish retorts that the liberal hope of finding a belief-free space behind our beliefs is doomed (Rorty 1989, 30).[26]

Strangely, although Hume put no stock in reflection, his writings on belief have been assimilated to the tradition of liberal irony.[27] And calling Hume a liberal ironist may not be such a bad way to describe important contours of his thought. As we have seen, Hume's special life project was to defeat fanaticism by cultivating detachment. Pressed to decide, Hume would choose irony

over absorption, although he might see the choice as tantamount to prefer-
ring sin over death. Yet Hayley is more clearly a man of letters and liberal ironist in the tradition of Rorty and Edmundson, who take seriously the tropes
of "access" (Edmundson's term), "rediscription" (Rorty's), and translation of
old beliefs into the language of new ones.

Differences between deep and shallow beliefs are a matter of degree rather
than kind, since we get access to our own beliefs or another's by revising them
down or up. In fact, the basic incredibility of the fanatic mind to the self-
announced "literary" mind issues in a solution that Hume would have found
uncomfortable: our deepest beliefs are produced by the collective stories we
tell ourselves. (In Rorty's terms, a literary ironist is "the sort of person who
faces up to the contingency of her most central beliefs and desires" [1989, xv]).
But preaching the values of contingency and redescription may mean pursuing a markedly imperialist translation policy, and thus really a nontranslation
policy. Hume, unlike Hayley, is quite up-front about his nontranslation policy. Access to others' beliefs is not necessary, because if others had the sorts of
beliefs we could share, we would have them as well. In other words, if we do
not feel the truth of our beliefs, they are not beliefs. Yet, as I argued at the out-
set, all this quickly leads Hume into Wartonian territory: there is nothing to
translate; there is only our oblique pleasure in beliefs whose truth is impossible to test.

Each of my examples highlights a process of reduction: one person encounters another mind, doubts that its beliefs are genuine, classifies it as
fanatic, but proceeds without genuine reasons and hence fanatically. This pes-
simistic paradigm applies most forcefully to Hayley and Hume, who are revealed to be—in some of their actions—fanatics of reason. Warton is another
story. A literary agnostic about belief, he opens up the mind of the religious
melancholic, rendered mute by pain and reason, to pleasurable exploration.
Pressing inward, he supplies imagistic content to the formal operation that
Hume had predicted could be found inside a fanatic. Hume's religious melancholic is "conscious of a continued miracle in his own person." Warton retains
the essential self-reflexiveness of this picture, crediting it to his personifications, and offers secular content as well, telling an elaborate story about English literature and his place in it. He finally rejects empiricist procedures, used
by Hume to test for the fanatic mind, that rest on the idea that a fanatic stuck
in the posture of formal self-reference is immune to the strong antiformalist
lure of the senses.

Each example also shows that when people operate without reasons for distinguishing their own (true) beliefs from the varieties of (false) belief they en-

counter, they make opaque the minds of the persons whose beliefs they have no independent way of confirming. In short, everyone is potentially a fanatic when we doubt their minds, which Hume thinks we are hard-wired to do because we lack access to their mental states. The only response is to remain jovial, literary, and detached to avoid suddenly discovering what other minds are like.

Notes

One Introduction

1. My understanding of what obligation entails has been shaped—I cannot put it too strongly—by the writings of Christine Korsgaard, especially *The Sources of Normativity* (1996) but also the final chapter of *Creating the Kingdom of Ends* (1993). Korsgaard argues that a certain way of conceiving of obligation—the Kantian way—is best, and she may well be right. But this book will argue that for Pope, Johnson, and Hume, obligation and its psychology is a serious, deep, and finally personal topic—one for which no theoretical account is adequate. All three may have been reassured by Kant's solution to their questions about what morality is.

2. Throughout this book I use variants on the phrase "the notion that things can be different, better, more perfect than they are" to describe the moral stance. The origin of this phrase, I realized only after I had used it too many times, is the very first paragraph of Christine Korsgaard's *Sources of Normativity* (1996).

3. This topic is addressed, for example, by the new field of social norms theory in law and economics. For a fascinating recent contribution, see Balkin 1998.

4. The most notable difference is the question of domain generality versus domain specificity: British associationists thought that all cognitive categories could be generated from a few simple laws of connection, contiguity, and resemblance, laws operating in what Steven Pinker wittily calls "connectoplasm" (1997, 112; Hirschfeld and Gelman 1994). Daniel Dennett traces the connections between evolutionary thinking and eighteenth-century naturalism through the powerful figure of Nietzsche (1995, 181–183).

5. One sign that the field is successful is that it is now fragmenting into camps with conflicting viewpoints. A recognizable divide now runs between sociobiology and evolutionary psychology. On one account, there is no real divide: the sociobiology of the 1970s and 1980s was roundly critiqued for its purportedly dubious political implications, and it reinvented itself in the 1990s as the more rhetorically savvy evolutionary psychology. But this story misses some substantive differences between the older and the newer versions. Both sociobiology and evolutionary psychology hold a view about what we might call the conceptual medium between biological substrate and cultural

manifestation. Sociobiology posited a mechanistic genetic medium, expressed in the form of sentences like "There are genes for x or y." Evolutionary psychology revises that sentence into "There are mental modules for x or y." Meanwhile, sociobiology now offers its own newer versions: "There is such a thing as gene-culture co-evolution; there are epigenetic rules for x or y." Debate continues about these formulations: each has some advantages; each lays itself open to (similar kinds of) doubts.

6. For an overview of the field of evolutionary ethics, see E. O. Wilson 1975; Singer 1981; and Pinker 1997.

7. An important book has recently revived the group-selectionist controversy: Sober and Wilson 1998.

8. Most evolutionary psychologists would reject Richard Dawkins's early assertion of human selfishness as much too reductive. Dawkins wrote, "Be warned that if you wish, as I do, to build a society in which individuals cooperate generously and un-selfishly towards a common good, you can expect little help from biological nature. Let us try to *teach* generosity and altruism, because we are born selfish" (Dawkins 1976, 3). Dawkins is clearly confusing (at least) two different senses of selfishness. He thinks that because our genes our selfish, we are selfish; but that assumption is obviously belied by the homely example of parental investment, in which genetic selfishness is perfectly compatible with intense self-sacrifice.

9. A host of books putting forth rival interpretations about the paradox have recently appeared. See, for example, Ridley 1996; Sober and Wilson 1998.

10. The outcry against Mandeville that has lasted, almost undimmed, from the eighteenth to the twentieth centuries might be taken as evidence in support of Alexander's suggestion. On the "Mandevillian Mistake," see Gordon 1997, 476–77.

11. Though Korsgaard cites the emerging paradigm of evolutionary ethics only to sidestep what she calls its third-person focus, she repeatedly claims to be presenting a theory of value with "biological origins." See Korsgaard 1996, 8, 14–16, 54–55, 157–60.

12. I borrow the phrase *anthropology of morals* from Gould (1998).

13. Consider the somewhat hyperbolic characterization of his project that Richard Alexander offers at the beginning of *The Biology of Moral Systems,* a project that seems to be to get people to wake up to the brute facts of their moral selves: "What this 'greatest intellectual revolution of the century' tells us is that, despite our intuitions, there is not a shred of evidence to support [a] view of beneficence, and a great deal of convincing theory suggests that any such view will eventually be judged false. This implies that we will have to start all over again to describe and understand ourselves, in terms alien to our intuitions, and in one way or another different from every discussion of this topic across the whole of human history" (1987, 3).

14. I am indebted to David Bromwich for this insight.

15. Aesthetic theory was in turmoil throughout the eighteenth century. As the century progressed, aesthetics itself was increasingly viewed not only as an instrument to order and classify other realms of human experience but also as the proper object of scientific knowledge in its own right. See Lipking (1970) for a fuller account.

16. The reasons that high culture emerged in eighteenth-century England are com-

plex and various. They include the desire, articulated by Addison and others, to posit a sphere in which to displace religious and political conflict, and a large economic surpluses that gave rise to a new trading class of urban merchants. Because for the first time in history there was a cadre of writers and thinkers committed to speculation about art as art, the disciplines of literary criticism, art criticism, connoisseurship, collecting, and philosophical aesthetics emerged in tandem. Artists were at once entrusted with an enormous mandate and put on the defensive by the proudly Philistine and probusiness climate of the Walpole government.

17. David Solkin uses the phrase "the power of the aesthetic" to describe the tradition of aesthetics inaugurated by Shaftesbury and Addison. For lucid and concise discussion of this tradition, see Solkin 1993, 7–12 and 220–24.

18. Recently, theorists have revived the idea of art's moral efficacy, from the Addisonian Richard Rorty, who thinks that liberal irony leads to democracy, to David Lloyd and Terry Eagleton, who think that Kantianism was responsible for the formation of abstract bourgeois subjects. Meanwhile, new historicists like D. A. Miller argue that novel reading is a "drill in the rhythms of bourgeois industrial culture" (1988, 83). Indeed, this new consensus about the "power of the aesthetic" inherits an older tradition of Horatianism. From the earliest new critics to now, each new generation of critics has elaborated on it in some way (for example, see R. Rorty 1996).

19. As Korsgaard (1996) points out, Hume's stance is slightly disingenuous, for while he is not an ideologue of virtue, as Shaftesbury was, he has much of the practical philosopher in him, especially in the essays he wrote for a general audience. He is interested in finding out what makes people sociable. For her critique of Hume's scientist of man persona, see p. 54.

20. The relationship between the normative impulse and actual norms is subtle and difficult to define. At one extreme, it calls for total demystification. I take the view that we are normative animals, and that normative animals are prone to self-deception, even to hypocrisy. When we call for things to be different or better, we often mean different or better for us; our norms are often self-justifying. And self-justifying norms, when groupish and exclusive, can become violent. This book will not address self-justification in the service of intergroup violence. But in its more rhetorical form, and practiced systemically by a dominant class in order to discount the suffering faced by subordinated peoples, self-justification can become ideology.

Solkin has a wonderful discussion of the claims to virtue by the self-described moralist Anthony Ashley Cooper, the 3rd Earl of Shaftesbury, whose moralism depends heavily on a "civic humanist" ideal "attached to the great landowner, whose independence qualified him to serve the state in two essential capacities: the exercise of leadership and the bearing of arms" (1993, 22). Arguing from a version of this ideal, Shaftesbury called for all kinds of things to be better (by which he meant more Roman) than they were—art, virtue, politeness, politics and so on. Solkin writes: "Of course the impressive civic edifice we have just been admiring is nothing more nor less than a marvelous piece of ideology. Under the spotless cover of an ostensibly autonomous subjectivity, Lord Shaftesbury's citizen-landowners were quite happy to depend on a ruthless legal and political system to ensure that they remained in private possession of their estates; and we should not need reminding that a hierarchy based on inequalities of class and gender was hardly a thing of beauty (or of public interest) from everyone's point of view (1993, 13).

21. Eagleton describes the aesthetic sphere as "a community of subjects now linked by sensuous impulse and fellow-feeling rather than by heteronomous law, each safeguarded in its unique particularity while bound at the same time into social harmony" (Eagleton 1990, 28).

22. Most readers will be aware that eighteenth-century philosophers typically saw this problem not as an abstract moral question but as a political issue about state organization. Kant memorably wrote: "The problem of organizing a state, however hard it may seem, can be solved even for a race of devils, if only they are intelligent. The problem is: 'Given a multitude of rational beings requiring universal laws for their preservation, but each of whom is secretly inclined to exempt himself from them, to establish a constitution in such a way that, although their private intentions conflict, they check each other, with the result that their public conduct is the same as if they had no such intentions'" (quoted by Arendt 1982, 36).

23. It is a commonplace of socialist rhetoric that any doctrine that emphasizes the innate selfishness of human beings (including the doctrine of reciprocal altruism, which I explore at length in chapter 4) is inherently Thatcherite or right-wing capitalist. This is a reduction of the way human interests conflict and intersect with group interests. The premise of socialism, after all, is that people subordinate their interests to the collective, not to reside permanently in a state of deficit and sacrifice, but to receive in return the benefits of public resources. Of course, this reduction has been promoted most vigorously by right-wing ideologues themselves. If we humans can be persuaded that we are innately selfish, we will immediately commit the naturalistic fallacy (deriving *ought* from *is*) and pursue our own interests without guilt. It was Margaret Thatcher, after all, who famously and polemically said, "There is no such thing as society. There are only families and there are individuals."

24. The recent work of Richard Wendorf (1996) on Sir Joshua Reynolds and his circle makes this wonderfully vivid. Particular works of art can represent the artist and his friends as especially virtuous, kind, and generous. The quest for status and power are usually among the secondary meanings of eighteenth-century works of art.

25. For a discussion of this concept, see Bernard Williams 1972, 1–12. Williams makes the case that there is no such thing as a true amoralist, because just perceiving someone else's reasons gets us off on the moral foot to begin with.

Two Formalism, Criticism, Obligation

1. For an exhaustive recent history of the eighteenth-century British material production of art, see Brewer 1997.

2. I am indebted to Howard Weinbrot for the information about Brooks's source.

3. I am indebted to Steven Knapp for this formulation (personal communication).

4. The notion that language escapes and takes on a life of its own became one of Pope's favorite conceits. Consider that amazing couplet from the "Epistle to Dr. Arbuthnot": "Poor Cornus sees his frantic wife elope/And curses wit, and poetry, and Pope." In this couplet Cornus's dullard perspective becomes normative precisely because he makes the mistake of thinking that Pope had something to do with his wife's eloping because of the similarity between his name and her action. (This point has been made brilliantly by Hunter 1969, 633). What Cornus fails to understand, of course, is that his own name caused his wife to elope: he understands that language caused something, but he fails to discern exactly what.

5. It will soon become clear that nothing of the account that follows could have been written without Maynard Mack's biography of Pope (1985). It was because of this book that I first became interested in Pope, and in writing this chapter I follow Mack very closely.

6. There are many examples of the way Pope's eighteenth-century enemies stress the paradox of his poetic refinement and bodily deformity. Perhaps the best known example was written and circulated by Colley Cibber, who imagines that he goes with Pope and an unnamed nobleman—a "tittering" Lord—to visit "a certain House of Carnal Recreation": "His Lordship's Frolick propos'd was to slip his little Homer, as he call'd him, at a Girl of the Game, that he might see what sort of Figure a Man of his Size, Sobriety, and Vigour (in Verse) would make, when the frail fit of Love had got into him" (1742, 47). So much a cliché was this connection that in their *Verses Addressed to the Imitator of the First Satire of the Second Book of Horace* (1733), Lady Mary Wortley Montagu and Lord Hervey made a point of arguing that Horace represents true refinement, while Pope only achieves the "crabbed numbers" of a "dull copi'st," which, as it happens, closely resembles his own deformed body (Montagu 1977, 266).

7. The evolutionary account of individual psychology is, paradoxically, more structuralist and relativist than even the most extreme social constructionism. Frank Sulloway's immense study, *Born to Rebel: Birth Order, Family Dynamics, and Creative Lives* (1996), makes this intellectual orientation clear. Why is it, he wondered, that on a continuum of authoritarianism and radicalism—in science, religion, and politics—eldest children tend to be more inclined to follow rules, while youngest children tend towards radicalism? Since there are almost certainly no genes for a tendency to identify with authority or genes for rebelliousness, there are at best optimal strategies when one is placed in a given relative position. The eldest child may perceive himself to be more valued by the parents and may expect to control more of parental resources; the youngest child may therefore perceive that he needs to strike out on his own at an early age. These optimal strategies are not conscious; they penetrate deep into the personality, even influencing creative choices. On the emerging evolutionary picture, the most intensely personal facts about us are relative to social position and condition.

8. My discussion of this passage is heavily indebted to Frank Stack (1985, 255–56).

9. Of course these lines celebrate intellectual independence rather than social skill. Of the proper names here, only Lyttleton is a living contemporary of Pope's; the rest represent often puzzlingly abstract principles.

10. I am indebted to Steven Knapp for these examples (personal communication).

11. Steven Knapp discusses this problem at length in chapter 3 of *Literary Interest* (1993).

12. Once while teaching Pope's character sketches, I tried to describe this familiar corner of our moral lives to the students, who expressed some doubt about whether such satiric reduction is a familiar social habit. So I ran a little experiment: I asked each of them to write down a five line description of someone they hated, protecting the person's identity by giving him or her an apt fictional name. A few people in the class, two or three, described hating somebody because the person had wronged them in some way—"the boss" or "the thief" were the names they chose. But the great majority of my students described such hateful and familiar types as "the suck-up," "the vain aristocrat," "the pretty boy," "Mr. competitive ambition," "the actress," and "Ms. lipstick and blue eye shadow." Some students were notably humorless in defense of their hatreds: in response to teasing from me about how one could possible *hate* a person for wearing lipstick and blue eye shadow, one student simply kept piling on more description: "well, but she wears mini-skirts, and she's heiress to a large fortune, and she drives a Mercedes" and so on, in a rising tone of moral outrage. Another student was more forthright in admitting that perhaps his own jealousy, rather than something "objectively true," motivated his hatred of "Mr. Competitive Ambition," but nevertheless insisted that "it is wrong" to so shamelessly put oneself forward.

Three   "To Virtue Only and Her Friends, a Friend"

1. March 1733. Quoted in Hammond 1984, 47.

2. See Hammond (1984) for very specific information about how the two men's interests dovetailed.

3. See Hammond (1984, 103) for an analysis of the power shifts in their friendship.

4. For a complete account of the influence of Bolingbroke's thought on Pope's poetry, see Hammond 1984; for a thorough study of Bolingbroke's thought itself, see Kramnick 1979.

5. Hammond puts the figure at two hundred and explicitly uses the phrase "poet of friendship" (1984, 1).

6. In an important pair of essays, "The Advancement and Reformation of Modern Poetry" (1701) and "The Grounds of Criticism in Poetry" (1704), Dennis attempted to "complete" Longinus's account of the sublime by pointing to specific sources in poetry (especially Milton). See Dennis 1939–43, 1:223.

7. For an intriguing political reading of Longinian notions of individuation, see

Lamb 1993, 545–67. Lamb's argument partly turns on the difficulty of just anybody's acting like Longinus; and against the spirit of the great eighteenth-century translator William Smith's rather more fanatical attempt to Christianize Longinus, Lamb's account of sublime political agency is assimilated to certain episodes in Longinus's own biography.

8. One nineteenth-century satirist likened Longinianism to insanity: "Those who talk rationally on other subjects, no sooner touch on this, than they go off in a literary delirium; fancy themselves, like Longinus, 'the great sublime they draw,' and rave like Methodists, of inward lights, and enthusiastic emotions, which, if you cannot comprehend, you are set down an un-illumined by the grace of criticism, and excluded from the elect of taste" (quoted in Monk [1935] 1960, 3).

9. We might think of Kant's account of the ambivalence of the imagination's "delight in the sublime" as part of a larger eighteenth-century concern with the aesthetic paradox of the pleasures of pain. In its characteristic form, the eighteenth-century aesthetic question of ambivalence focused on tragedy: Dryden, Addison, Burke, and Hume all wrote solutions to the paradox that tragedy produces pleasurable emotions through representations of painful events. Yet the Kantian version of the problem in its own right has appealed to a range of critics. For an account of the relationship between Kant's paradox and the eighteenth-century ambivalence toward personification, see Knapp 1985.

10. For an extended discussion of this passage, see Weiskel [1976] 1986, 39–41.

11. William Roberts in the *Bookworm* 4, 294; quoted Paul 1911, 45 n. 42.

12. The question of whether such literary imitations of aggression produce the effects of violence or minimize them has been a persistent one in writings about Longinus and imitation in neoclassicism. Howard Weinbrot has recently argued that while such aggression is central to Longinian literary theories, we should consider such aestheticized versions of aggression as "emulation": "Unlike actual bloody war for supremacy, neither head nor crown is lost in this miracle of benevolent combat. Indeed, properly nurtured such competition reduces rather than increases aggression." He also quotes Brossette from the *Oeuvres de M. Boileau Despreaux* (Geneva, 1716): "dans ce genre (i.e., imitation) on peut etre vaincu sans honte." See Weinbrot 1993, 100–110.

13. The charge in this case was that Dryden had maliciously misled Congreve.

14. The text of the Addison portrait is from *Minor Poems* (TE 6). The text is Pope's autograph, reprinted in *St. James's Journal* for 15 December 1722. Pope revised the sketch a number of times before it found its way into the "Epistle to Arbuthnot" in 1734, but the core lines on Addison are constant across the versions. This text is probably close to what Pope sent Addison himself. The portrait was later titled "Atticus"; this title does not figure into my exposition here.

15. On the spread of politeness, see Barker-Benfield 1992, esp. 61–64, 77–103; Pocock 1985; Woodman 1989; Langford 1989, esp. chap. 3; and Klein 1994, 3–14.

16. For a fascinating reading of this quotation, see Wendorf 1996, 14.

17. My sources throughout are Mack 1985; Ault 1949; Sherburn 1934; and Rosslyn 1990.

Four   Abstraction, Reference, and the Dualism of Pope's Dunciad

1. For reasons that will become clear in this chapter, I believe we can hazard a comparison between the *Dunciad* and the structure of metaphor as influentially (and controversially) described by Donald Davidson (1984). The relevant aspect of Davidson's account is his stark distinction between the meaning of a metaphor and its use. What metaphors mean is "what the words, in their most literal interpretation, mean, and nothing more" (245). Metaphors are therefore not ambiguous. Instead of a hidden or secondary meaning that it is the goal of interpretation to make explicit, metaphors contain a "hidden power" (264) that can push us to notice certain states of affairs and can thus accomplish or bring something off for the author in addition to the meaning it communicates (255). Throughout this chapter I intend my use of the terms *reference* and *meaning* to describe a distinction in Pope that loosely corresponds to Davidson's distinction between "hidden power" and "meaning."

2. In a chapter called "Disfigured Truth and the Proper Name," Deutsch takes up questions about the epistemological effects of Pope's naming practice in the *Imitations of Horace*. In a wonderful formulation, she inserts a third term into Pope's conflation of "reform" and "chastise" in his letter to Arbuthnot: "Pope reveals that his task is neither to reform, nor to chastise, but rather to enforce: the concept serves as a middle term which allows the satirist to execute a logical couplet equating the two previous definitions—reform and chastise—between which Arbuthnot had distinguished" (1996, 193). Enforcement, she writes, is analogous to Pope's desire to "touch" persons. I agree with Deutsch that "enforcement" is Pope's ideal, but the burden of this chapter is to show him finally skeptical about attaining it.

3. Two spirited cases of special pleading: (1) "My thesis will be that even in these apparently very personal poems, we overlook what is most essential if we overlook the distinction between the historical Alexander Pope and the dramatic Alexander Pope who speaks them" (Mack 1982, 57). (2) On Book IV: "If Pope had written the whole of the Dunciad in a mode of such complexity and such inclusive moral and intellectual implication, he would indeed have produced an ironic 'long poem'... that might rank with Paradise Lost in integrity of vision and design. And there are enough traces of this poem in earlier books to tempt us into believing that he really succeeded" (Brower 1959, 325–26).

4. Dustin Griffin writes: "Opera was already out of fashion when Pope attacked it in the *Dunciad,* and Walpole already fallen when the four-book version of the poem appeared in 1743. Cibber was in no real way discredited (in the eyes of his contemporaries, anyway) by Pope's attacks on him" (1990, 130).

5. D. Griffin writes: "Satire—in Greece, Rome, or Augustan England—did not bring down tyrants, or even discredit public figures, any more than it made people re-

form or laughed foolish fashions off the stage" (1990, 130). He proposes that we read satire as expressing complicated psychological attitudes about power: for an individual satirist, satire relieves burdensome feelings of bitterness. Writing the *Dunciad* may have helped Pope vent his spleen, but he could never have intended that it do so. At most, the poem's therapeutic effect could have provided balm for the sting of repeated verbal failures.

6. David Morris writes: "Satire, cut off from its former resources, came to seem almost antipoetic: transitory, local, limited, inessential, and eventually unintelligible" (1984, 215).Yet his very helpful discussion of personal satire in late Pope successfully reclaims it from its apparent triviality by linking it both to the traditions of formal verse satire and to pain as a serious dimension of ethical life.

7. For a brief but illuminating discussion of the "building-block" theory of meaning and reference, see Davidson, "Reality Without Reference" (1984, 219–20). Davidson cites early British empiricists as the clearest exponents of building-block theories.

8. On the relationship between our capacity to make metaphors—to abstract—and to learn language, see Quine (1979, 160).

9. Pace Paul De Man (1979, 19–20), who finds that Locke's examples of general terms are symptoms of an "ethical tension" related to the inescapable conclusion that in condemning figure, Locke must condemn language in general.

10. Elaborations of the Lockean semiotic by J. S. Mill, Gottlob Frege, Bertrand Russell, and John Searle, and criticisms of it by the Anglo-American "physicalists" Saul Kripke, Gareth Evans, and Keith Donellan, suggest that Locke should have been more aggravated than he was by the incommensurableness of words that are *causally* "true of" their bearers with words that are *figuratively* "true of" their bearers. At the fountainhead of Locke criticism, George Berkeley (1909) promoted the idea of a necessary opposition between particular and general by subjecting the mode—abstraction—by which one is supposed to yield to the other to a scorching skepticism in the spirit of Locke's own attacks on figure.

11. In this vein Vincent Carretta finds a political analogue in Pope's move to general satire in the late poem: "The emblematic and allegorical nature of the *New Dunciad* expresses Pope's shift back to a greater emphasis on practices rather than men. Particular men are not totally absent from the new poem, but the ones named are usually objects of praise, not blame: Chesterfield, Wyndham, Talbot, Murray, and Pulteney" (1983, 141).

12. At least this is the hypothesis of W. L. MacDonald (1951, 201). MacDonald correctly concludes his discussion of the *Dunciad* by noting that Warburton seems to have participated in Pope's personal satire when it suited his own needs, and that "apart from advising Pope to add the *New Dunciad* to the older poem, Warburton made no contribution toward an interpretation of the *Dunciad* as general satire" (211).

13. C. R. Kropf gives a succinct account of the literary strategies (including abstract pictorialism and definite descriptions) that Augustan authors used to avoid libel laws especially intended to encourage general rather than particular satire (1974, 159). I have

never found any evidence that Pope was seriously threatened with a libel suit. Even when libel laws were invoked against the publishers and sellers of Swift's poems, the cases quickly fell apart as John Fischer's painstaking research has shown (see Fischer 1986, 35–39, and 1989). In light of governmental disinterest, Pope was rather unceremoniously reduced to complaining to Arbuthnot that "to be uncensored and to be obscure is the same thing" (*Corr.* 3:419). Pope never lost hope that he had some practical interest in obscuring the names of the Dunces: he covered himself on his daily walks from Twickenham to Richmond with two pistols and a ferocious-looking Great Dane.

14. I am referring to Catherine Gallagher's recent work on fictional discourse in Charlotte Lennox's the *Female Quixote* (London, 1752). See Gallagher 1994, 165.

15. Realizing that some appeal to context is useful in determining the referents of proper names (how else could we distinguish amongst the various Aristotles?), Gareth Evans and others have filled out Kripke's hypotheses about rigid designation to include a "historical explanation" of the way proper names come to refer to people or objects in the absence of related identifying descriptions. Rather than being true of a bearer because an associated description is true of the bearer, a proper name is linked in a causal, historical chain back to the first person or object who fit its reference (Evans 1977, 197).

16. For Searle's explanation of, and objection to, Frege's theory of naming, see Searle 1972, 488–9.

17. This is consistent with empiricism generally; and in fact, Searle's view has been traced historically to the Lockean semiotic, which posits a metonymic relationship between general terms and their identifying descriptions. Locke's principle is that the meaning of a word is specified by giving a number of properties associated with it, and that the conjunction of these properties determines what things can be called by that word—the extension or sum of the connotations of a word determine its intension or denotative reference (that is, the "essence" of the term). Hilary Putnam describes Lockean reference this way: "On the traditional view, the meaning of say, 'lemon,' is given by specifying a conjunction of properties. For each of these properties, the statement 'lemons have the property P' is an analytic truth; and if $P_1, P_2, \ldots P_n$ are all of the properties in the conjunction, then 'anything with all of the properties $P_1, \ldots$, is a lemon' is likewise an analytic truth" (quoted in S. Schwartz 1977, 14). Kripke argues forcefully that statements like "Anything with all the properties $P_1, \ldots$, is a lemon" is not an analytic truth (1972, 74–75).

18. This chapter's narrow focus on representational changes internal to the *Dunciad* sequence itself has meant that I have not explored the potentially fascinating topic of the poem's generic affiliations with the scandal narrative.

19. Wimsatt's piece and Maynard Mack's "Wit and Poetry and Pope" (1949) from which this discussion is taken, are uncannily similar polemics published in the same year, and both are concerned with saving the reputation of Pope's poetry from nineteenth-century critics hostile to his late Renaissance metaphysical wit (and perhaps

also to his lack of Arnoldian disinterestedness). Both use proper names as evidence for Pope's attachment to metaphorical complexity.

20. Pat Rogers's writing on the *Dunciad* presents perhaps the clearest example of roman à clef thinking. He writes: "In 1730 one navigated by given features of the landscape, most of which played an obvious part in the religious, legal, or commercial life of the city. . . . Similarly, ones navigates the satire of Pope, Gay or Swift with the help of these conspicuous directional aids: now become moral landmarks, they carry special associations, broadly sociological or historical—which help to underpin the satire" (1972, 6).

21. I am indebted to Joshua Scodel for bringing these verses to my attention.

22. See, for example, Wasserman 1950; Youngren 1980.

23. My interpretation of the philosophical tradition of reference and of Pope's relation to it places me in disagreement with a different tradition, one that celebrates poetic language as mysteriously distinct from reference. Geoffrey Hartman writes: "Naming, like counting, is a strong mode of specification. It disambiguates the relation of sign to signified, making the proper term one end and the thing that is meant the other" (1970, 352).

Five   The Kindness of Strangers

1. For the most complete discussion of prudence in Johnson's text, see Basney 1990. Paul Alkon (1974) also stresses the opposition between the two terms.

2. I am adapting this definition from Thomas Nagel (1970, 36ff). Nagel makes clear that the two definitions of prudence that Johnson is working with—practical reason oriented toward the future and self-interest—are both still very much in play in contemporary moral philosophical discussions of the concept.

3. These prejudices became more pronounced later in his life. To cite a famous example, in the *Life of Milton* Johnson wrote "Milton's republicanism was, I am afraid, founded in an envious hatred of greatness, and a sullen desire of independence; in petulance impatient of control, and pride disdainful of superiority. He hated monarchs in the state and prelates in the church; for he hated all whom he was required to obey. It is to be suspected that his predominant desire was to destroy rather than establish, and that he felt not so much the love of liberty as repugnance to authority" Johnson (1967, 3:157). This topic is approached sensitively and intelligently by Frederic Bogel (1990, esp. 10).

4. Nagel is here attacking the notion that pure egoism is possible. His hostility to pure egoism derives from his view that desire alone cannot motivate a person, that motivations come from reasons, and reasons are inherently objective rather than subjective.

5. For a recent and highly readable argument about why morality consists in suspending our immediate interests in service of a broader social polity, see Stephen L.

Carter (1998). A typical sentence that could also serve as the thesis of the book is this: "Civility . . . teaches us to discipline our desires for the sake of others. So much in our world teaches us not to: politics in particular proposes that what life is for is to allow us to get what we want" (164–65). I agree with Carter that social rhetoric tends to emphasize that morality consists in self-denial for the sake of society, but like many evolutionary psychologists, I tend to see morality as being in our long-term self-interest rather than as a form of self-deprivation that we practice on behalf of other people. I also doubt very much whether politics and other social institutions teach us to be self-interested.

6. My summary partially paraphrases *Political and Personal Satires* (2:584–5).

7. Because there have been many excellent explorations of the problem of authorship in the *Life of Savage,* I am not going to take up that topic explicitly here. For the most recent and most complete, see Lipking 1998, 75–85. Nussbaum has recently argued that language, figure, descriptive power are the resources that men seek to control; Johnson's horror of Lady Macclesfield stems from his desire to usurp her procreative power: "The male narrator impersonates the reproductive body to give birth to Savage('s life)" (1995, 66).

8. See Isobel Grundy (1984, 26–27), Paul K. Alkon (1974), Helen Deutsch (1995), and Lawrence Lipking (1984) for an excellent sampling of recent criticism on the maxim as a feature of Johnson's prose style.

9. Another point of resistance has been the *Life of Savage*'s fictitious elements. Resistance takes the form of interpretation, which consists in pointing out disparities between the representation and what it represents. The disparities and errors of fact are conspicuous and important, as is the critical impulse to "expose" them. For critics and biographers, the work of exposure is motivated by the thought that facts exert a normative claim on literary texts. I want to raise, briefly, the possibility that such a thought may also be driven by a moralizing fantasies.

10. These mechanisms, especially the last one, have been discussed and critiqued in brilliant detail by Catherine Gallagher (1994, 168–74).

11. Michael Ruse gives this account of the sentimentalist's response to the rationalist, a response that we could imagine Savage making: "You might tell me that I have a moral obligation to stand on my head every Friday afternoon, but I am not going to take you very seriously until you strike some responsive chord within my breast" (1986, 241).

12. That Hume's theory of sympathy admits that humans tend to sympathize more easily with members of their own family than with nonrelatives has often been treated as a kind of scandal. But Hume is not a churchman or a moralist who is interested in scoring points by telling people that they ought to care for people at a distance as much as they do for their own families. Hume's theory purports to be descriptive, not normative. He is not a moralist arguing that people *should* love their children more than they love other people, but a student of human nature who finds that, on the whole, they do.

13. Without using the term, critics have made much of family thinking in the *Life of Savage*. Family thinking, according to Felicity Nussbaum's reading of the text, is Johnson's way of spreading and consolidating patriarchal authority. It is also a major ideological ploy of colonialism: "The crisis of authority over England's mothers is sometimes deflected onto its 'children'—the territories outside the mother country—and it has implications for women of all races and species.... The metaphors of mother country and the associations of maternity with nationhood elevate the woman to mythic heights, whereas in reality we find, for example, that women have less authority over birthing, since the female scientific profession of midwifery is somewhat displaced by male physicians (1995, 48).

14. The translation is Clarence Tracy's (quoted in Epstein 1986, 149).

Six   Pride's Reasons

1. For powerful reflections on this topic, see Dykstra 1996.

2. Annette Baier (1991, 17–18) has rendered a beautiful and convincing map nonetheless.

3. The term "pre-selected" is Baier's (1978, 29). I rely throughout this discussion on her very helpful summary of what is at stake in Hume's theory, as well as on her broader critique of Davidson's attempt to make sense of it.

4. Neu (1977) quotes the following passage from Passmore (1952) on the confusion between pride and the self, which is the object of pride: "A particularly important problem arises out of his description of the passions—which, after all, are only 'impression'—as having 'objects.' The fact is that Hume never really thinks out the relation between his epistemology and his theory of passions; sometimes 'the view' (whatever this is) 'fixes on ourselves,' when pride 'actuates us' (T 177); sometimes pride 'produces' the idea of the self (T, 287); sometimes pride is described as something which can never 'look beyond self' (T, 286). If what really happens is that pride 'produces' the idea of self, that idea will be its effect, not its object; if, on the other hand, pride itself views the self, this will involve a complete revision of Hume's epistemology. The consequences will be no less far-reaching if pride somehow provokes the mind to have an idea of itself; and in this case, too, that idea is in no sense the 'object' of pride, but only an idea which regularly occurs later than pride" (Passmore 1952, 126–27; quoted in Neu 1977, 27).

5. I am here adapting a diagram of Neu's (1977, 10), though simplifying it slightly.

6. See Neu (1977, 6–19) for an extended discussion of the difficulty of claiming that two absolute simples can be compared without the benefit of thinking about them.

7. I am drawing my account of an internal audience from Richard Wollheim, who has long been interested in the nature of certain iconic mental states. He believes that these iconic mental states can be most fruitfully understood by an analogy to the roles of audience, actor, and dramatist in the classical western theater. He writes: "How does this account of the theatre and its constitutive roles illuminate the nature of iconic

mental states? It does so by providing us with a way of describing what goes on in the mind when we entertain such states: for we can think of them as the work, the conjoint work, or internal counterparts to the three roles of the theatre. An iconic mental state, we can say, arises our of a collaboration, though not on equal terms, between an internal dramatist, an internal actor, and an internal audience. The purpose of this comparison is to get a clear description, it is not to get sound explanation. It has no explanatory force" (1984, 69).

8. Does Christensen mean "representation" in the technical Kantian sense of "impression"? If so, it is difficult to see where he gets the idea that impressions refer only to themselves—the part of Hume's epistemology that might justifiably be described as representationalist admits of no self-reflexivity.

9. This is the objection given by Passmore (1952; quoted in Neu 1977, 27).

10. In addition to the many eighteenth-century writers who, in discussing this problem, often practically refuse to distinguish between various forms of instrumentality, twentieth-century critics have been less than clear about which kind of instrumentality is at stake in their deployment of Hume's definition. For an account of how the doctrine of the "sympathetic imagination" fits all three kinds of instrumentality, see Wasserman 1947. For a deployment of Hume's definition that frankly slides between the first and third kind of instrumentality, see Jerome Christensen's brief discussion of acting theory, where he clearly prefers an analysis of actor/audience relations to an analysis of "how an actor forms his ideas": "The case of the theater does not threaten Hume's model of sympathy because that model is fully theatrical; the 'mind is a kind of theatre,' and the theater is that place designed to enable the free exchange of simulated feelings. Hume never shows any interest in the way an actor forms his ideas or any concern for the actual presence or absence of the feelings represented. If he had attended the problem, the ready and agreeable solution would have been that the actor, who is subject to the same mechanical operations of the spirit as everyone else, forms his ideas and his passions according to the same process of sympathy by which he then communicates them to his audience" (1987, 71–72).

11. Here is Garrick discussing the French actress Madame Clarion, and echoing Shaftesbury's interest in authors who "fill us full of false terrors": "Madame Clarion is so conscious and certain of what she can do, that she never, I believe, had the feelings of the instant come upon her unexpectedly: but I pronounce that the greatest strokes of genius have been unknown to the actor himself, till circumstances, and the warmth of the scene has sprung the mind as it were, as much to his own surprise, as that of the audience. Thus I make a great difference between a great genius and a good actor. The first will always realize the feelings of his character, and be transported beyond himself; while he other, with great powers and good sense, will give pleasure to an audience, but never

> . . . pectus inaniter angit,
> Irritat, mulcet, falsis terroribus implet,
> Ut Magus."   [quoting Horace, *Epistle* I.i]

(From *The Private Correspondence of David Garrick* [London, 1831] I:359; quoted in Wasserman 1947, 269).

The proximity of the theory of character in acting theory to the general tenets of neoclassical representation is striking. Compare Pope's humoral discussion of character in the Preface to the *Iliad* with that of Thomas Wilkes, writing in 1759. Pope writes: "Everyone has something so singularly his own, that no painter could have distinguished them more by their features, than the poet has by their manner. . . . The single quality of courage is wonderfully diversified in the several characters of the *Iliad*. That of Achilles is furious and intractable; that of Diomede forward, yet listening to advice and subject to command: that of Ajax is heavy and self-confiding. . . . The courage of Agamemnon is inspirited by love of empire and ambition" (TE 7: 7).

By contrast, Thomas Wilkes, *A General View of the Stage* (London, 1759), writes: "It has been the opinion of an eminent writer, 'that if a Player enters thoroughly into the nature and circumstances of his part, a proper action will necessarily follow;' but, if this assertion be true, there will then be no necessity of study or previous preparation, and genius, unassisted by art, is alone sufficient; but, in the mean time, where shall be fixed the standard of genius and perfection, since judgment and taste are so various? It is certain, as was before observed, that every passion and sentiment has a proper air and appearance, both of countenance and action, stamped upon it by Nature, whereby it is easily known and distinguished; every representation which comes short of, or exceeds it, is a departure from it. This every actor ought to be strictly acquainted with, else he may affix the most unnatural grimace and gesture to the most striking passages, and yet call it natural and just acting. I have met with many who were able to enter into all the spirit and fire of a character in idea, and yet, for want of sufficient knowledge and experience in the Drama, were never able to bring that idea into execution, because he wanted judgment to adjust both his voice and his action; mistaking rant for energy, and beating the air instead of keeping up a proper deportment" (108–9).

12. See Wilson 1990; Duerr 1965, 201–30; and Stone and Kahrl 1979, 29–45.

13. My understanding of the authoring and history of Gildon's text, and the context for this quotation, has been supplemented by Duerr (1965, 206).

14. See George Taylor (1972, 51–52); see also Downer (1943) for a sampling of such commentary, especially pertaining to Garrick's handling of the ghost scene in Hamlet.

15. For an extended version of this point, see Stone and Kahrl 1979, 30.

16. The stasis of the represented passions is suggested by Joseph Roach, who describes "the notion that the management of the face, limbs, and torso should conform to certain ideal patterns" as deriving from "the successful methodology of physics" (1985, 71).

17. On the broader cultural significance of this point, see Koffka 1942.

18. Hogarth used Lebrun's expressions in some of his best known figures of extreme emotion. The fifth painting of "Marriage a la Mode," "The Death of the Earl,"

shows Earl Squanderfield in a state of "extreme pain" after having been stabbed by his wife's lover. For Lebrun's specific influence on Hogarth's painting, see Alan T. McKenzie's introduction to Lebrun (1734), vii-viii.

19. Edgar Wind intriguingly relates Burke's observation to two seemingly disparate eighteenth-century traditions, both of which Hume opposed. The first is Joshua Reynolds's defense of copying or imitation on the grounds of the surprise a spectator will experience at recognizing an allusion to a style or work. He quotes Reynolds: "It must be remembered, that as this great style itself is artificial in the highest degree, it presupposes in the spectator, a cultivated and prepared artificial state of mind" (Discourse XV). The other is religious enthusiasm. He quotes Hume: "So congenial to the human mind are religious sentiments, that it is impossible to counterfeit long these holy fervours, without feeling some share of the assumed warmth. And, on the other hand, so precarious and temporary, from the frailty of human nature, is the operation of these spiritual views, that the religious ecstasies, if constantly employed, must often be counterfeit, and must be warped by those more familiar motives of interest and ambition, which insensibly gain upon the mind" (*The History of England* 6, chap. 4). See Wind 1986, 21.

20. This technique has been interpreted as Garrick's comic "syncopation," which his own theory suggested ought to be mastered before an actor could become a tragedian. In that sense, it has been argued, Garrick's Hamlet shows the residue of his comic training—a mixing of styles and effects that explains the subject matter of such paintings as Reynolds's "Garrick between Tragedy and Comedy." See Wind 1986, 35–6.

21. In *An Essay on Acting* (1744), one of his few reflections on his technique, Garrick compares what it is like to be mentally absorbed in two of his most famous characters, the low character of Abel Drugger in Ben Jonson's *Alchemist,* and the high character of Macbeth:

"I shall now, as relative to my present subject, describe in what manner the two abovemention'd characters ought to be mentally and corporeally agitated, under the different circumstances of the dagger, and urinal; and by that shall more fully delineate what is meant by passions and humours. When Abel Drugger has broke the Urinal, he is mentally absorb'd with the different ideas of the invaluable price of the urinal, and the punishment that may be inflicted in consequence of a curiosity, no way appertaining or belonging to the business he came about. Now, if this, as it certainly is, the situation of his mind, how are the different members of the body to be agitated? Why thus,— his eyes must be revers'd from the object he is most intimidated with, and by dropping his lip at the same time to the object, it throws a trembling languor upon every muscle, and by declining the right part of the head towards the urinal, it casts the most comic terror and shame over all the upper part of the body, that can be imagin'd; and to make the lower part equally ridiculous, his toes must be inverted from the heel, and by holding his breath, he will unavoidably give himself a tremor in the knees, and if his fingers, at the same time, seem convuls'd, it finished the compleatest low picture of grotesque terror that can be imagin'd by a Dutch painter.—Let this be compar'd with the modern copies, and then let the town judge.—Now to Macbeth.—When the murder of Duncan is committed, from an immediate consciousness of the fact, his ambition is ingulph'd at that Instant, by the Horror of the Deed; his Faculties are intensely riveted to the murder alone, without having the least consolation of consequential advantages, to comfort him in that exigency. He should at that time, be a moving statue, or indeed a petrify'd man; his eyes must speak, and his tongue be metaphorically silent; his ears must be sensible of imaginary noises, and deaf to the present and audible voice of his wife; his attitudes must be quick and permanent; his voice articulately trembling, and confusedly intelligible; the murderer should be seen in every limb, and yet every member, at that instant, should seem separated from his Body, and his Body from his soul: this is the picture of a compleat regicide, and as at that time the orb below should be as hush as death; I hope I shall not be thought minutely circumstantial, if I should advise a real genius to wear cork heels to his shoes, as in this scene he should seem to tread on air, and I promise him he will soon discover the great benefit of this (however seeming trifling) piece of advice." (1744, 7–9)

22. Hill's 1750 version of the treatise *The Actor* was a translation of Pierre Rémond de Sainte-Albine's 1747 treatise *Le Comédien*. The version he published 1755, after extensive revision, contains many of the same ideas, but is rewritten to respond more directly to many contemporary stage performances. In *Le Paradoxe sur le Comédien*, Diderot is responding to a 1769 French translation of Hill's later work called *Garrick; ou Les Acteurs Anglais*. See Duerr 1962, 231.

23. This is the question Kant will consider, responding to Hume at the beginning of section 16 of the "Transcendental Deduction" section of the *Critique of Pure Reason*, where he addresses the problem of the analytic unity of apperception with the statement, "It must be possible for the 'I think' to accompany all of my representations."

24. For these suggestions, see McIntyre 1989; Ardal 1966, esp. 44–46; and Penelhum 1976.

25. Hume first introduced "impressions of reflexion" early in Book 2, to describe a special case in which we can "copy" our impressions (especially such impressions as fear, hope, and desire) from antecedent ideas (T 6). So one can remember an experience that made one feel afraid and have the same feeling of fear again.

Seven   Jovial 'Fanatics

1. In the *Treatise of Human Nature*, Hume declares that "this operation of the mind, which forms the belief of any matter of fact, seems hitherto to have been one of the greatest mysteries of philosophy; tho' no one has so much as suspected, that there was any difficulty in explaining it" (quoted in Mossner 1980, 77).

2. Hume flatly contradicts himself in the appendix to the *Treatise:* "We shall afterwards have occasion to remake both the resemblances and differences betwixt a poetical enthusiasm and a serious conviction. In the mean time I cannot forbear observing, that the great difference in their feeling proceeds in some measure from reflexion

and general rules" (T 631). Yet he never goes on to characterize these general rules or to say how they differentiate "poetical enthusiasm" from "serious conviction."

3. For a fuller account of the relationship between Hume's concept of vivacity and the history of rhetoric, see Dykstra 1996.

4. I borrow the term *translation* from the writings of W. V. O. Quine and his student, Daniel C. Dennett. Rorty, I take it, borrows it as well, using *redescription* to mean roughly what they mean by *translation*. For a discussion of his and Quine's views of translation, see Dennett 1987.

5. The proximity of Hume's to Cheyne's case histories might be the only countervailing evidence against the convincing view of Mossner (1943) that Hume intended his letter to go to Arbuthnot, instead of Cheyne, the other famous Scottish doctor in London.

6. Even more strongly than his antienthusiast contemporaries, Hume seems to voice a "gesture of astonishment," a cry of amazement against the ineffability of religious belief (Gaskin 1993, 340). He describes a religious melancholic taking intense pleasure from his absorption in a nonempirically derived inwardness. Detaching people from the pleasure they take in their own beliefs requires the verbal equivalent of a slap.

7. "Naturalism" refers to the many discoveries Hume makes in his scientific persona, not, as is sometimes assumed, to any extratheoretical sense that the self can be stabilized through its commitment to habit and custom. The term was first used by Hume's twentieth-century commentators (e.g., Norman Kemp Smith) to rebut his nineteenth-century commentators (e.g., T. H. Green). The issue at hand was whether Hume's philosophical system is purely skeptical and destructive, as the Victorians thought, or had a positive component. Naturalism, rather than skepticism, Kemp Smith and others argued, was the predominant mode of Hume's philosophical system.

8. Indeed, Mossner (1943) believes that the letter served its purpose in the composition and was never sent.

9. John Sitter (1982), similarly interested in the persistence of the topic of belief in Hume's writings, connects it to Hume's literary style.

10. I am indebted to Marshall Brown for the observation that the trope of pleasing pain is a common erotic one. Thus Warton can be seen as an important early contributor to the conflation or reduction of aesthetic to erotic pleasure that so dominates current (post-Freudian) thinking about aesthetic pleasure.

11. T. Warton 1747. This edition contains no page or line numbers.

12. Similarly, Frances Ferguson attacks empiricist psychology for its dependence on procedures of induction: "The operation of the senses would, in the terms of the Burkean account, be self-annihilating if it operated efficiently. One would continually be experiencing and acting out (producing the physical symptoms of one's experiences) in a series of sensations that would themselves be overtaken by whatever sensation came next. The inefficiency of sensation, however, emerges in its own misfiring, its inability to separate an experience from an image of an experience" (1992, 55).

13. For a fuller version of this account, see Lipking 1970, 355–56.

14. Pope's Twickenham editors point out that there is precedent in both Virgil and Dryden for the ambiguity of "visionary": a maid seeing visions, a maid seen in visions.

15. Elaine Scarry (1995) repudiates the central assumptions of this tradition by pointing out that, in fact, people experience a visual impression of an object much more intensely than they imagine or remember it: "When we speak in everyday conversation about the imagination, we often attribute to it powers that are greater than ordinary sensation. But when we are asked to perform the concrete experiment of comparing an imagined object with a perceptual one—that is, of actually stopping, closing our eyes, concentrating on the imagined face or the imagined room, then opening our eyes and comparing its attributes to whatever greets us when we return to the sensory world—we at once reach the opposite conclusion: the imagined object lacks the vitality and vivacity that enable us to differentiate the actual world present to our senses from the one that we introduce through the exercise of the imagination." Yet Scarry then rehabilitates a literary version of this tradition by claiming the "remarkable fact that this ordinary enfeeblement of images has a striking exception in the verbal arts where images somehow do acquire the vivacity of perceptual objects" (1995, 1–2).

16. On 31 August 1797 Harriet Hesketh wrote to John Johnson to proclaim "how amazing it is, that such repeated proofs, as He [Cowper] has had of the Fallacy of all his dreadful alarms, respecting his own safety, do not convince him, that he *has nothing to fear*" (BL Add. MSS 30, 803, B).

17. Hayley to Hesketh, 27 August 1797, BL Add. MSS 30, 803 A.B.

18. When Wilberforce's letter arrived, Cowper found a persecuting pun in his name: "The outside tells me, I am to be taken away by force, and the inside will tell me the time when." Cowper assimilated other letters to the nefarious purposes of his satanic God-figure. Of the bishop of London's letter Cowper said, "Never was such a letter written, never was such a letter read to a man so overwhelmed with despair, as I am—It was written in *derision*—I know, and am sure of it." Indeed the bishop, ignorant of the letter's purpose, had written sentences that could only seem designed to provoke a stronger melancholic reaction: "That love [of God] you must possess as surely in as full extent as any human Being ever did." Cowper replied: "Not an atom of it" (quoted in King 1986, 276).

19. Johnson to Hayley, 24 August 1797. BL Add. MSS 30, 803, A. B.

20. Hayley to Hesketh, 6 August 1797, BL Add. MSS 30, 803.

21. In her reply to Hayley, Hesketh slyly asked the head mechanic's permission to write to an acquaintance of hers in order to procure another letter: "But this affair must be so absolutely your own, and the whole machine so governed and guided by you, that I dare not take the smallest step without your approbation and shall therefore beg a few lines, as soon as possible, to say if you approve my plan" (1 September 1797, BL Add. MSS 30, 803).

22. BL Add. MSS 30, 803, A. B.

23. Hayley responded to Cowper's letter of 20 June 1797, the complete text of which reads as follows: "Ignorant of every thing but my own instant and impending Misery, I know neither what I do when I write nor can do otherwise than write because I am bidden to do so. Perfect Despair the most perfect that ever possessed any Mind has had possession of mine you know how long, and knowing that, will not need to be told who writes" (quoted in *Cowper's Letters*, 200).

24. The text is that of Hayley's *Life of Cowper*, which contains the first printing of the poem.

25. For an excellent summary of the main components of liberalism, as attacked by the non-Marxist antiliberal tradition (of which Fish is only the latest proponent), see S. Holmes 1993.

26. For Fish's critique of Rorty's position, and of what he calls critical self-consciousness generally, see Fish 1994, esp. chaps. 10 and 13.

27. There is a long tradition, beginning with John Stuart Mill, of calling Hume a literary philosopher and an ironic one. In the last few decades, literary critics have paid ceaseless attention to the ironic features of his style; when they have discussed his philosophy at all, they have assimilated his thinking to his supposed rhetorical detachment. See Price 1965; Sitter 1982; Richetti 1983; Box 1990. Christensen (1987) is unique both in paying close attention to some features of Hume's thinking and in criticizing Hume for being insufficiently skeptical about presence, and hence insufficiently ironic.

Works Cited

Abbreviations

Corr. Pope, Alexander, 1688–1744. *Correspondence.* 5 vols. Edited by George Sherburn. Oxford: Clarendon Press, 1956.

E Hume, David. 1975. *Enquiries Concerning Human Understanding and Concerning the Principles of Morals.* Edited by L. A. Selby-Bigge; 3d ed. Peter H.
Nidditch. Oxford: Clarendon Press.

T Hume, David. [1978] 1987. *A Treatise of Human Nature.* Edited by L. A.
Selby-Bigge; 2d ed. Peter H. Nidditch. Oxford: Clarendon Press.

TE *The Twickenham Edition of the Poems of Alexander Pope.* 1939–69. Edited
by John Butt. 11 vols. London: Methuen. New Haven: Yale University Press.

Vol. 1 *Pastoral Poetry and An Essay on Criticism.* Edited by E. Audra and
Aubrey Williams. 1961.

Vol. 2 *The Rape of the Lock and Other Poems.* Edited by Geoffrey Tillotson. 1940.

Vol. 3 (i) *An Essay On Man.* Edited by Maynard Mack. 1950.

Vol. 3 (ii) *Epistles to Several Persons (Moral Essays).* Edited by F. W. Bate-
son. 1951.

Vol. 4 *Imitations of Horace, with An Epistle to Dr. Arbuthnot and The
Epilogue to the Satires.* Edited by John Butt. 1939.

Vol. 5 *The Dunciad.* Edited by James Sutherland. 1953.

Vol. 6 *Minor Poems.* Edited by Norman Ault and John Butt. 1954.

Vol. 7 *The Iliad of Homer Books I–IX.* Edited by Maynard Mack. 1967.

Vol. 8 *The Iliad of Homer Books X–XXIV.* Edited by Maynard Mack.
1967.

Vol. 9 *The Odyssey of Homer Books I–XII.* Edited by Maynard Mack.
1967.

Vol. 10 *The Odyssey of Homer Books XIII–XXIV.* Edited by Maynard
Mack. 1967.

Vol. 11 *Index.* Edited by Maynard Mack. 1969.

References

Aaron, Richard I. 1968. *The Theory of Universals*. Oxford: Clarendon Press.

Addison, Joseph. [1974] 1988. *Cato. The Beggars Opera and Other Eighteenth-Century Plays*. Edited by David Lindsay.

Addison, Joseph, and Richard Steele. 1965. *The Spectator*. Edited by Donald F. Bond. Oxford: Clarendon Press. 5 vols.

Alexander, Richard D. 1987. *The Biology of Moral Systems*. Hawthorne, N.Y.: Aldine de Gruyter.

Alkon, Paul K. 1974. "The Intention and Reception of Johnson's *Life of Savage*." *Modern Philology* 72:139–50.

Ardal, Pall S. 1966. *Passion and Value in Hume's Treatise*. Edinburgh: Edinburgh University Press.

Arendt, Hannah. 1982. *Lectures on Kant's Political Philosophy*. Edited with an interpretive essay by Ronald Beiner. Brighton, Sussex: Harvester Press Ltd.

Ault, Norman. 1949. *New Light on Pope*. London: Methuen.

Axelrod, Robert. 1984. *The Evolution of Cooperation*. New York: Basic Books.

Baier, Annette C. 1978. "Hume's Analysis of Pride." *Journal of Philosophy* 75 (1): 27–40.

———. 1991. *A Progress of Sentiments: Reflections on Hume's Treatise*. Cambridge: Harvard University Press.

Baier, Kurt. 1965. *The Moral Point of View: A Rational Basis of Ethics*. New York: Random House.

Balkin, J. M. 1998. *Cultural Software: A Theory of Ideology*. New Haven: Yale University Press.

Barker-Benfield, G. J. 1992. *The Culture of Sensibility: Sex and Society in Eighteenth-Century Britain*. Chicago: University of Chicago Press.

Barnett, Louise K. 1992. "Johnson's Mother: Maternal Ideology and the *Life of Savage*." *Studies on Voltaire and the Eighteenth Century* 304:856–59.

Barrell, John. 1986. *The Political Theory of Painting from Reynolds to Hazlitt 'The Body of the Public.'* New Haven: Yale University Press, 1986.

Basney, Lionel. 1990. "Prudence in the *Life of Savage*." *English Language Notes* 28 (2): 17–24.

Bate, Walter Jackson. 1977. *Samuel Johnson*. New York: Harcourt Brace Jovanovich.

Baxter, Richard. 1716. *The Signs and Causes of Melancholy, with Directions suited to the Case of those who are afflicted with it*. Collected out of the works of Mr. Richard Baxter . . . by Samuel Clifford. London.

Berkeley, George. 1909. *A Treatise concerning the Principles of Human Knowledge*. Edited by Thomas J. McCormack. Chicago: University of Chicago Press.

Betterton, Thomas. 1741. *The History of the English Stage, from the Restauration to the*

Present Time. Including the Lives, Characters and Amours, or the most Eminent Actors and Actresses. London.

Blakeway, Robert. 1717. *An Essay towards the Cure of Religious Melancholy, in a Letter to a Gentlewoman afflicted with it.* London.

Bloom, Harold. 1982. *Agon: Towards a Theory of Revisionism.* New York: Oxford University Press.

Bogel, Frederic V. 1990. *The Dream of My Brother: An Essay on Johnson's Authority.* English Literary Studies Monograph Series 47. British Columbia: University of Victoria Press.

Boswell, James. 1934. *Life of Johnson.* Edited by George Birkbeck Hill. 6 vols. Oxford: Clarendon Press.

———. 1956. *Boswell in Search of a Wife, 1766–1769.* Edited by Frank Brady and Frederick Pottle. New York: McGraw-Hill.

Bowers, Toni O'Shaughnessy. 1992. "Critical Complicities: Savage Mothers, Johnson's Mother, and the Containment of Maternal Difference." *The Age of Johnson: A Scholarly Annual* 5:115–46.

Box, M. A. 1990. *The Suasive Art of David Hume.* Princeton: Princeton University Press.

Boyce, Benjamin. 1962. *The Character-Sketches in Pope's Poems.* Durham: Duke University Press.

Boyer, Abel. 1695. *Characters of Virtues and Vices of the Age.* London.

Bragge, Francis. 1708. *A Practical Treatise of the Regulation of the Passions.* London.

Brewer, John. 1997. *The Pleasures of the Imagination: English Culture in the Eighteenth Century.* New York: Farrar Straus and Giroux.

Bromwich, David. 1989. *A Choice of Inheritance: Self and Community from Edmund Burke to Robert Frost.* Cambridge: Harvard University Press.

Brooks, Cleanth. 1947. *The Well-Wrought Urn: Studies in the Structure of Poetry.* New York: Cornwall Press.

Brower, Reuben A. 1959. *Alexander Pope: The Poetry of Allusion.* Oxford: Clarendon Press.

Brown, Laura. 1985. *Alexander Pope.* Oxford: Basil Blackwell.

Brown, Laura, and Felicity Nussbaum, eds. 1987. *The New Eighteenth Century.* New York: Methuen.

Brown, Marshall. 1991. *Preromanticism.* Stanford: Stanford University Press.

Brownell, Morris R. 1977. *Alexander Pope and the Arts of Georgian England.* Oxford: Clarendon Press.

Budgell, Eustace. 1714. *The Moral Characters of Theophrastus.* London.

Burke, Edmund. 1958. *A Philosophical Enquiry into the Origin of our Ideas of the Sublime and Beautiful.* Edited by James T. Boulton. Notre Dame: University of Notre Dame Press.

Burt, Stephen. 1998. "'The Cat Concert Under the Window': Ten Years of the Best American," *Times Literary Supplement.* May 22.

Burton, Robert. 1989–94. *The Anatomy of Melancholy.* Edited by Thomas C. Faulkner, Nicolas K. Kiessling, and Rhonda L. Blair. 3 vols. Oxford: Clarendon.

Butler, Judith. 1997. *The Psychic Life of Power: Theories in Subjection.* Stanford: Stanford University Press.

Byron, George Gordon. 1898–1904. *The Words of Lord Byron.* Edited by R. E. Prothero and E. H. Coleridge. 13 vols. London.

Carretta, Vincent. 1983. *The Snarling Muse: Verbal and Visual Political Satire from Pope to Churchill.* Philadelphia: University of Pennsylvania Press.

Carter, Stephen L. 1998. *Civility: Manners, Morals, and the Etiquette of Democracy.* New York: Basic Books.

Cary, John. 1717. *An Essay Towards Regulating the Trade and Employing the Poor of this Kingdom.* London.

Cassirer, Ernst. 1955. *The Philosophy of the Enlightenment.* Translated by Fritz Koelln and James Pettegrove. Boston: Beacon Press.

Cibber, Colley. 1742. *A Letter from Mr. Cibber to Mr. Pope.* London.

———. 1968. *An Apology for the Life of Colley Cibber, with An Historical View of the Stage during his Time.* Edited by B. R. S. Fone. Ann Arbor: University of Michigan Press.

Chandler, James. 1984. "The Pope Controversy: Romantic Poetics, and the English Canon." In *Canons,* edited by Robert von Hallberg, 197–225. Chicago: University of Chicago Press.

Cheyne, George. 1773. *The English Malady; or, A treatise of nervous diseases of all kinds, as spleen, vapours, lowness of spirits.* London.

Christensen, Jerome. 1987. *Practicing Enlightenment: Hume and the Formation of a Literary Career.* Madison: University of Wisconsin Press.

Coleridge, Samuel Taylor. 1972. *The Collected Works of Samuel Taylor Coleridge: Lay S ermons.* Edited by R. J. White. London: Routledge and Kegan Paul.

Colomb, Gregory C. 1992. *Designs on Truth: The Poetics of the Augustan Mock-Epic.* University Park: Pennsylvania State University Press.

Cosmides, Leda, and John Tooby. 1992a. "The Psychological Foundations of Culture." In *The Adapted Mind: Evolutionary Psychology and the Generation of Culture,* edited by J. Barkow, L. Cosmides, and J. Tooby, 19–136. Oxford: Oxford University Press.

———. 1992b. "Cognitive Adaptations for Social Exchange." In *The Adapted Mind,* edited by J. Barkow, L. Cosmides, and J. Tooby, 163–228. Oxford: Oxford University Press.

Cowper, William. 1979–86. *The Letters and Prose Writings of William Cowper.* 5 vols. Edited by James King and Charles Ryskamp. Oxford: Oxford University Press.

Crews, Frederick. 1997. *The Memory Wars: Freud's Legacy in Dispute.* New York: New York Review of Books.

Daly, Martin, and Margo Wilson. 1988. *Homicide.* New York: Aldine de Gruyter.

Danto, Arthur C. 1986. *The Philosophical Disenfranchisement of Art.* New York: Columbia University Press.

Davidow, Lawrence Lee. 1977. "Pope's Verse Epistles: Friendship and the Private Sphere of Life." *Huntington Library Quarterly* 40:151–70.

Davidson, Donald. 1980. "Hume's Cognitive Theory of Pride." In *Essays on Actions and Events.* Oxford: Clarendon Press.

———. 1984. *Inquiries into Truth and Interpretation.* Oxford: Clarendon Press.

Dawkins, Richard. 1976. *The Selfish Gene.* Oxford: Oxford University Press.

Deleuze, Gilles. 1991. *Empiricism and Subjectivity: An Essay on Hume's Theory of Human Nature.* Translated by Constantin V. Boundas. New York: Columbia University Press.

De Man, Paul. 1979. "The Epistemology of Metaphor." In *On Metaphor,* edited by Sheldon Sacks. Chicago: University of Chicago Press.

Dennett, Daniel C. 1987. *The Intentional Stance.* Cambridge: MIT Press.

———. 1995. *Darwin's Dangerous Idea: Evolution and the Meanings of Life.* New York: Simon and Schuster.

Dennis, John. 1696. *Letters upon Several Occasions: Written by and between Mr. Dryden, Mr. Wycherley, Mr., Mr. Congreve, and Mr. Dennis.* London.

———. 1721. *Original Letters, Familiar, Moral and Critical.* London.

———. 1939–43. *The Critical Works of John Dennis.* Edited by Edward N. Hooker. 2 vols. Baltimore: Johns Hopkins University Press.

De Quincey, Thomas. 1968. *The Collected Writings of Thomas De Quincey.* 14 vols. Edited by David Masson. Edinburgh: A. and C. Black, 1889–90. New York: AMS Press.

Descartes, René. 1989. *The Passions of the Soul.* Translated by Stephen Voss. Introduction by Genevieve Rodis-Lewis. Indianapolis: Hackett Publishing Company.

Deutsch, Helen. 1995. "'The Name of an Author': Moral Economics in Johnson's Life of Savage." *Modern Philology* 92:328–45.

———. 1996. *Resemblance and Disgrace: Alexander Pope and the Deformation of Culture.* Cambridge: Harvard University Press.

Diderot, Denis. [1774] 1957. *The Paradox of Acting.* Translated by Walter Herries Pollock. Introduction by Lee Strasberg. New York: Hill and Wang.

Dodsley, Robert, ed. 1748–58. *A Collection of Poems.* 3 vols. London: Printed for R. Dodsley.

Downer, Alan S. 1943. "Nature to Advantage Dressed: Eighteenth-Century Acting." *PMLA* 58:1002–37.

Duerr, Edwin. 1962. *The Length and Depth of Acting*. New York: Holt, Rinehart and Winston.

Dussinger, John A. 1970. "Style and Intention in Johnson's *Life of Savage*." *English Literary History* 37 (4): 564–80.

Dykstra, Scott. 1996. *Wordsworth's Realism*. Ph.D. dissertation. University of California, Berkeley.

Eagleton, Terry. 1990. *The Ideology of the Aesthetic*. Cambridge: Basil Blackwell.

Edmundson, Mark. 1995. *Literature Against Philosophy, Plato to Derrida: A Defence of Poetry*. Cambridge: Cambridge University Press.

Elledge, Scott, ed. 1961. *Eighteenth-Century Critical Essays*. 2 vols. Ithaca: Cornell University Press.

Empson, William. 1964. "Wit in the Essay on Criticism." In *Essential Articles for the Study of Alexander Pope*, edited by Maynard Mack. Hamden, Conn: Archon Books.

Epstein, William H. 1986. "Patronizing the Biographical Subject: Johnson's Savage and Pastoral Power." In *Johnson After Two Hundred Years*, edited by Paul J. Korshin. Philadelphia: University of Pennsylvania Press.

Erskine-Hill, Howard. 1981. "Alexander Pope: The Political Poet in His Time." *Eighteenth- Century Studies* 15 (2): 123–48.

Evans, Gareth. 1977. "The Causal Theory of Names." In *Naming, Necessity and Natural Kinds*, edited by Stephen P. Schwartz. Ithaca: Cornell University Press.

Ferguson, Frances. 1992. *Solitude and the Sublime: Romanticism and the Aesthetics of Individuation*. New York: Routledge.

Fischer, John I. 1986. "The Government's Response to Swift's 'An Epistle to a Lady.'" *Philological Quarterly* 65:35–59

———. 1989. "The Legal Response to Swift's 'The Public Spirit of the Whigs.'" In *Swift and His Contexts*, edited by John I. Fischer. New York: AMS Press.

Fish, Stanley. 1994. *There's No Such Thing as Free Speech, And It's a Good Thing Too*. Oxford: Oxford University Press.

Fried, Michael. 1980. *Absorption and Theatricality: Painting and Beholder in the Age of Diderot*. Chicago: University of Chicago Press.

Fry, Paul H. 1983. *The Reach of Criticism: Method and Perception in Literary Theory*. New Haven: Yale University Press.

Gallagher, Catherine. 1994. *Nobody's Story: The Vanishing Acts of Women Writers in the Literary Marketplace, 1670–1820*. Berkeley: University of California Press.

Gardner, Alan H. 1940. *The Theory of Proper Names: A Controversial Essay*. Oxford: Oxford University Press.

Garrick, David. 1744. *An Essay on Acting.* London.

———. 1831–32. *The Private Correspondence of David Garrick,* edited by James Boaden. 2 vols. London.

Gaskin, J. C. A. 1993. "Hume on Religion." In *The Cambridge Companion to Hume,* edited by David Fate Norton. Cambridge: Cambridge University Press.

Gerrard, Christine. 1994. *The Patriot Opposition to Walpole: Politics, Poetry, and National Myth, 1725–1742.* Oxford: Clarendon Press.

Gildon, Charles. 1710. *The Life of Mr. Thomas Betterton.* London.

Ginsborg, Hannah. 1991. "On the Key to Kant's Critique of Taste." *Pacific Philosophical Quarterly* 72:290–313.

Goldgar, Bertrand. 1976. *Walpole and the Wits: The Relation of Politics to Literature, 1722–1742.* Lincoln: University of Nebraska Press.

Gordon, Scott Paul. 1997. "Disinterested Selves: *Clarissa* and the Tactics of Sentiment." *English Literary History* 64 (2): 473–502.

Gould, Stephen Jay. 1997. "Evolution: The Pleasures of Pluralism," *New York Review of Books.* 26 June, 47–52.

———. 1998. "Let's Leave Darwin Out of It." *New York Times,* 29 May, Op-Ed.

Greene, Donald. 1988. "An Anatomy of Pope-bashing." In *The Enduring Legacy: Alexander Pope Tercentenary Essays,* edited by G. S. Rousseau and Pat Rogers, 241–81. Cambridge: Cambridge University Press.

Griffin, Dustin. 1990. "Venting Spleen." *Essays in Criticism.* 40 (2): 124–35.

Griffin, Robert J. 1995. *Wordsworth's Pope: A Study in Literary Historiography.* Cambridge: Cambridge University Press.

Grimshawe, Rev. T. S., ed. 1835. *The Works of William Cowper, His Life and Letters, by William Hayley esq., Now first completed by the introduction of Cowper's private correspondence.* 8 vols. London.

Grunbaum, Adolf. 1984. *The Foundations of Psychoanalysis: A Philosophical Critique.* Berkeley: University of California Press.

Grundy, Isobel. 1984. "Samuel Johnson: Man of Maxims?" In *Samuel Johnson: New Critical Essays,* edited by Isobel Grundy. London: Vision Press.

Guerinot, J. V. 1969. *Pamphlet Attacks on Alexander Pope 1711–1744.* London: Methuen.

Guardian, The. 1982. Edited by John Calhoun Stephens. Lexington: University Press of Kentucky.

Gunn, Thom. 1985. *The Occasions of Poetry: Essays in Criticism and Autobiography.* San Francisco: North Point Press.

Guyer, Paul. 1979. *Kant and the Claims of Taste.* Cambridge: Harvard University Press.

Habermas, Jurgen. 1989. *The Structural Transformation of the Public Sphere: An Inquiry into a Category of Bourgeois Society.* Translated by Thomas Burger. Cambridge: MIT Press.

Hamilton, William D. 1964. "The Genetical Evolution of Social Behavior. *Journal of Theoretical Biology* 7:1–52.

Hammond, Brean S. 1984. *Pope and Bolingbroke: A Study of Friendship and Influence.* Columbia: University of Missouri Press.

Harte, Walter A. 1730. *An Essay on Satire, particularly on the Dunciad. To which is added, A Discourse on Satires, Arraigning persons by name. By Monsieur Boileau.* London.

Hartman, Geoffrey. 1970. *Beyond Formalism.* New Haven: Yale University Press.

Hawkins, Sir John. 1787. *The Works of Samuel Johnson, LL.D. Together with His Life and Notes on His Lives of the Poets.* 11 vols. London.

Hayley, William. 1803. *The Life and Posthumous Writings of William Cowper, Esq.* 3 vols. London.

———. "The Second Memorial of Hayley's Endeavours to Serve his Friend Cowper—Containing a Minute Account of Devices Employed to Restore his Dejected Spirits." 26 July 1809. British Library Add. MSS 8887.

———. 1809. "Two Memorials." British Library Add. MSS 30, 803, A.B.

———. 1823. *Memoirs of the Life and Writings of William Hayley.* Edited by John Johnson. 2 vols. London.

Heywood, Thomas. 1612. *An Apology for Actors.* London.

Hertz, Neil. 1985. *The End of the Line: Essays on Psychoanalysis and the Sublime.* New York: Columbia University Press.

Hill, Aaron. 1753. *The Works of the Late Aaron Hill, Esq.* 4 vols. London.

Hill, John. 1750. *The Actor: Or a Treatise on the Art of Playing.* London.

Hirschfeld, Lawrence, and Susan Gelman. 1994. "Toward a Topography of Mind: An Introduction to Domain Specificity." In *Mapping the Mind: Domain Specificity in Cognition and Culture,* edited by L. Hirschfeld and S. Gelman, 3–35. Cambridge: Cambridge University Press.

Hobbes, Thomas. 1991. *Leviathan.* Cambridge: Cambridge University Press.

Holmes, Richard. 1993. *Dr. Johnson and Mr. Savage.* New York: Pantheon Books.

Holmes, Stephen. 1993. *The Anatomy of Antiliberalism.* Cambridge: Harvard University Press.

Horne, Thomas A. 1978. *The Social Thought of Bernard Mandeville: Virtue and Commerce in Early Eighteenth-Century England.* London: Macmillan.

Hrdy, Sarah Blaffer. 1997. "Fitness Tradeoffs in the History and Evolution of Delegated Mothering with Special Reference to Wet-Nursing, Abandonment, and Infanticide," in *Human Nature: A Critical Reader,* edited by Laura Betzig. New York: Oxford University Press.

Hume, David. 1932. *The Letters of David Hume.* Edited by J. Y. T. Grieg. 2 vols. Oxford: Clarendon Press.

Hunter, J. Paul. 1969. "Satiric Apology as Satiric Instance: Pope's Arbuthnot." *Journal of English and Germanic Philology* 68 (4): 625–47.

———. 1996. "Form as Meaning: The Case of the Couplet." *The Eighteenth Century: Theory and Interpretation* 37 (3): 257–70.

Jay, Martin. 1993. "Name-Dropping or Dropping Names? Modes of Legitimation in the Humanities." In *Force Fields: Between Intellectual History and Cultural Critique.* New York: Routledge.

Johnson, Mark. 1996. "How Moral Psychology Changes Moral Theory." In *Mind and Morals: Essays on Cognitive Science and Ethics,* edited by Larry May et al. Cambridge: MIT Press.

Johnson, Samuel. 1967. *Lives of the English Poets.* Edited by George Birbeck Hill. 3 vols. New York: Octagon Books.

———. 1971. *An Account of the Life of Mr. Richard Savage, Son of the Earl Rivers.* Edited by Clarence Tracy. Oxford: Clarendon Press.

Jones, Emrys. 1980. "Pope and Dulness." In *Pope: Recent Essays by Several Hands,* edited by Maynard Mack and James A. Winn. Hamden, Conn.: Archon Books.

Kant, Immanuel. 1952. *Critique of Judgment.* Translated by James Creed Meredith. Oxford: Clarendon Press.

———. 1981. *Grounding for the Metaphysics of Morals.* Translated by James W. Ellington. Indianapolis: Hackett Publishing Company.

Keats, John. [1978] 1982. *Complete Poems.* Edited by Jack Stillinger. Cambridge: Belknap Press..

Kenny, Anthony. 1964. *Action, Emotion, and Will.* London: Routledge and Kegan Paul.

Kernan, Alvin. 1993. "Plausible and Helpful Things to Say about Literature in a Time when all Print Institutions are Breaking Down." In *English Inside and Out: The Places of Literature Criticism,* edited by Susan Gubar and Jonathan Kamholtz. New York: Routledge.

King, James. 1986. *William Cowper: A Biography.* Durham: Duke University Press.

Kitcher, Philip. 1985. *Vaulting Ambition: Sociobiology and the Quest for Human Nature.* Cambridge: MIT Press.

Klein, Lawrence E. 1994. *Shaftesbury and the Culture of Politeness: Moral Discourse and Cultural Politics in Early Eighteenth-Century England.* Cambridge: Cambridge University Press.

Klibansky, Raymond, Erwin Panofsky, and Fritz Saxl. 1964. *Saturn and Melancholy: Studies in the History of Natural Philosophy, Religion and Art.* London: Nelson.

Knapp, Steven. 1985. *Personification and the Sublime: Milton to Coleridge.* Cambridge: Harvard University Press.

———. 1993. *Literary Interest: The Limits of Anti-Formalism.* Cambridge: Harvard University Press.

Koffka, Kurt. 1942 "The Art of the Actor as a Psychological Problem." *American Scholar* 2:315–26.

Korsgaard, Christine. 1993. *Creating the Kingdom of Ends*. Cambridge: Cambridge University Press.

———. 1996. *The Sources of Normativity*. Cambridge: Cambridge University Press.

Kramnick, Isaac. 1979. *Bolingbroke and His Circle: The Politics of Nostalgia in the Age of Walpole*. Cambridge: Harvard University Press.

Kripke, Saul A. 1972. *Naming and Necessity*. Cambridge: Harvard University Press.

Kropf, C. R. 1974. "Libel and Satire in the Eighteenth Century." *Eighteenth-Century Studies* 8 (2): 153–68.

Lamb, Jonathan. 1993. "Longinus, the Dialectic, and the Practice of Mastery." *English Literary History* 60 (3): 545–67.

Langer, W. 1973. "Infanticide: A Historical Survey." *History of Childhood Quarterly* 1:353–65.

Langford, Paul. 1989. *A Polite and Commercial People: England 1727–1783*. Oxford: Clarendon Press.

Langhorne, John. 1762. *Letters on Religious Retirement, Melancholy, and Enthusiasm*. London.

Lebrun, Charles. 1701. *Conference of Monsieur Le Brun, Chief Painter to the French King . . . Upon Expression, General and Particular*. Translated by John Smith. London.

———. 1734. *A Method to Learn to design the Passions*. Introduction by Alan T. McKenzie. Augustan Reprint Society, 200–201. Los Angeles: William Andrews Clark Memorial Library, 1980.

Lichtenberg, Georg Christoph. 1938. *Lichtenberg's Visits to England*. Edited and translated by Margaret L. Mare and W. H. Quarrell. Oxford: Clarendon Press.

Lindsay, David, ed. 1988 [1974]. *The Beggar's Opera and other Eighteenth-Century Plays*. Selected by John Hampden. London: Everyman's Library, J. M. Dent and Sons.

Lipking, Lawrence. 1970. *The Ordering of the Arts in Eighteenth-Century England*. Princeton: Princeton University Press.

———. 1984. "Samuel Johnson and the Meaning of Life." In *Harvard English Studies* 12, edited by James Engell. Cambridge: Harvard University Press.

———. 1998. *Samuel Johnson: A Life of the Author*. Cambridge: Harvard University Press.

Lloyd, David. 1989. "Kant's Examples." *Representations* 28:34–54.

———. 1990. "Analogies of the Aesthetic: The Politics of Culture and the Limits of Materialist Aesthetics." *New Formations* 10.

Locke, John. [1975] 1988. *An Essay concerning Human Understanding*. Edited by Peter H. Nidditch. Oxford: Clarendon Press.

Longinus. 1965. "On the Sublime." *Classical Literary Criticism*. Edited by T. S. Dorsch. London.

Lyttleton, George. 1760. *Dialogues of the Dead*. London.

MacDonald, W. L. 1951. *Pope and His Critics: A Study in Eighteenth Century Personalities*. London: J. M. Dent and Sons.

MacIntyre, Alasdair. 1984. *After Virtue: A Study in Moral Theory*, 2d ed. Notre Dame: University of Notre Dame Press.

Mack, Maynard. 1949."'Wit and Poetry and Pope': Some Observations on his Imagery." In *Pope and His Contemporaries: Essays Presented to George Sherburn*, edited by James L. Clifford and Louis A. Landa. Oxford: Clarendon Press.

———. 1982. *Collected in Himself: Essays Critical, Biographical, and Bibliographical on Pope and Some of His Contemporaries*. Newark: University of Delaware Press.

———. 1985. *Alexander Pope: A Life*. New York: W. W. Norton.

Magnusson, Lars. 1994. *Mercantilism: The Shaping of an Economic Language*. New York: Routledge.

Mandeville, Bernard. 1989. *The Fable of the Bees*. Edited by Philip Harth. London: Penguin Classics.

Manning, Susan L. 1991. "'This Philosophical Melancholy': Style and Self in Boswell and Hume." In *New Light on Boswell: Critical and Historical Essays on the Occasions of the Bicentenary of The Life of Johnson*, edited by Greg Clingham. Cambridge: Cambridge University Press.

Mao, Douglas. 1996. "The New Critics and the Text-Object." *ELH* 63:227–54.

May, Larry, Marilyn Friedman, and Andy Clark, eds. 1996. *Mind and Morals: Essays on Cognitive Science and Ethics*. Cambridge: MIT Press.

McCrea, Brian. 1990. *Addison and Steele Are Dead: The English Department, Its Canon, and the Professionalization of Literary Criticism*. Newark: University of Delaware Press; London: Associated University Presses.

McIntyre, Jane L. 1989. "Personal Identity and the Passions." *Journal of the History of Philosophy* 27 (4): 545–57.

McKeon, Michael. 1987. *The Origins of the English Novel 1600–1740*. Baltimore: Johns Hopkins University Press.

McLaughlin, Brian P., and Amelie Oksenberg Rorty, eds. 1988. *Perspectives on Self-Deception*. Berkeley: University of California Press.

Memoirs of the Life and of his Grace Philip, Late Duke of Wharton. 1731. By an Impartial Hand. London.

Miller, D. A. 1988. *The Novel and the Police*. Berkeley: University of California Press.

Mithen, Steven. 1996. *The Prehistory of the Mind: The Cognitive Origins of Art and Science*. London: Thames and Hudson.

Monk, Samuel H. [1935] 1960. *The Sublime: A Study of Critical Theories in Eighteenth-Century England*. Ann Arbor: University of Michigan Press.

Montagu, Lady Mary Wortley. 1977. *Essays and Poems and Simplicity, A Comedy*. Edited by Robert Halsband and Isobel Grundy. Oxford: Clarendon Press.

Morris, David B. 1984. *Alexander Pope: The Genius of Sense*. Cambridge: Harvard University Press.

Mossner, Ernest Campbell. 1943. "Hume's Epistle to Dr. Arbuthnot, 1734: The Biographical Significance." *Huntington Library Quarterly* 7:135–52.

———. 1980. *The Life of David Hume*. 2d ed. Oxford: Clarendon Press.

Nagel, Thomas. 1970. *The Possibility of Altruism*. Princeton: Princeton University Press.

Neu, Jerome. 1977. *Emotion, Thought and Therapy: A Study of Hume and Spinoza and the Relationship of Philosophical Theories of the Emotions to Psychological Theories of Therapy*. London: Routledge and Kegan Paul.

Nicholson, Colin. 1994. *Writing and the Rise of Finance: Capital Satires of the Early Eighteenth Century*. Cambridge: Cambridge University Press.

Noggle, James. 1996. "Skepticism and the Sublime Advent of Modernity in the 1742 Dunciad." *The Eighteenth Century: Theory and Interpretation* 37 (1): 22–41.

Noxon, James. 1973. *Hume's Philosophical Development*. Oxford: Clarendon Press.

Nussbaum, Felicity. 1995. *Torrid Zones: Maternity, Sexuality, and Empire in Eighteenth-Century English Narratives*. Baltimore: Johns Hopkins University Press.

Passmore, J. A. 1952. *Hume's Intentions*. Cambridge: Cambridge University Press.

Paul, H. G. 1911. *John Dennis: His Life and Criticism*. New York: Columbia University Press.

Penelhum, Terence. 1976. "Self-Identity and Self-Regard." In *The Identities of Persons*, edited by A. O. Rorty, 253–80. Berkeley: University of California Press.

Piers, Maria. 1978. *Infanticide*. New York: W.W. Norton.

Pinker, Steven. 1997. *How the Mind Works*. New York: Norton.

Pocock, J. G. A.1985. *Virtue, Commerce, and History: Essays on Political Thought and History, Chiefly in the Eighteenth Century*. Cambridge: Cambridge University Press.

"Political and Personal Satires." 1873–1954. In *Catalogue of Prints and Drawings in the British Museum*, Division 1. London: Trustees of the British Museum, 11 vols. Vols. 1–4 prepared by Frederic George Stephens and Edward Hawkins; vols. 5–11 prepared by Mary Dorothy George.

Pope, Alexander.1742. *The New Dunciad: As it was Found in the year MDCCXLI. With the Illustrations of Scriblerus and Notes Variorum*. London.

———. 1751. *The Works of Alexander Pope, Esq*. Edited by William Warburton. 9 vols. London.

———. 1871–89. *The Works of Alexander Pope*. Edited by W. Elwin and W. J. Courthope, 10 vols. London.

———. 1935. *Pope's Own Miscellany.* Edited by Norman Ault. London: Nonesuch Press.

———. 1936. *The Prose Works of Alexander Pope.* Vol. 1: *The Earlier Works, 1711–1720.* Edited by Norman Ault. Oxford: Basil Blackwell.

———. 1986. *The Prose Works of Alexander Pope.* Vol. 2: *The Major Works, 1725–1744.* Edited by Rosemary Cowler. Hamden, Conn.: Archon Books.

Price, John Vladimir. 1965. *The Ironic Hume.* Austin: University of Texas Press.

Quine, W. V. O. 1979. "A Postscript on Metaphor." In *On Metaphor,* edited by Sheldon Sacks. Chicago: University of Chicago Press.

Richetti, John. 1983. *Philosophical Writing: Locke, Berkeley, Hume.* Cambridge: Harvard University Press.

Ridley, Matt. 1996. *The Origins of Virtue: Human Instincts and the Evolution of Cooperation.* New York: Viking.

Roach, Joseph. 1985. *The Player's Passion: Studies in the Science of Acting.* Newark: University of Delaware Press.

Rogers, Pat. 1972. *Grub Street: Studies in a Subculture.* London: Methuen.

———.[1972] 1980. *Hacks and Dunces: Pope, Swift and Grub Street.* London and New York: Metheuen.

Rogerson, Brewster. 1953. "The Art of Painting the Passions." *Journal of the History of Ideas* 14: 68–94.

Rorty, Amelie Oksenberg. 1988. "The Deceptive Self: Liars, Layers, and Lairs." In *Perspectives on Self-Deception,* edited by Brian P. McLaughlin and Amelie O. Rorty. Berkeley: University of California.

Rorty, Richard. 1989. *Contingency, Irony, and Solidarity.* Cambridge: Cambridge University Press.

———. 1996. "The Inspirational Value of Great Works of Literature." *Raritan: A Quarterly Review* 16 (1): 8–17.

Rosslyn, Felicity. 1990. *Alexander Pope: A Literary Life.* London: Macmillan.

Ruffhead, Owen. 1769. *The Life of Alexander Pope, Esq. Compiled from Original Manuscripts; With a Critical Essay on His Writings and Genius.* London.

Ruse, Michael. 1986. *Taking Darwin Seriously: A Naturalistic Approach to Philosophy.* Oxford: Basil Blackwell.

Savage, Richard. 1962. *Poetical Works.* Edited by Clarence Tracy. Cambridge: Cambridge University Press.

Scarry, Elaine. 1995. "On Vivacity: The Difference between Daydreaming and Imagining-Under-Authorial-Instruction." *Representations* 52:1–26.

Schneewind, J. B. 1992. "Autonomy, Obligation, and Virtue: An Overview of Kant's Moral Philosophy." In *Cambridge Companion to Kant,* edited by Paul Guyer, 309–41. Cambridge: Cambridge University Press.

Schwartz, Hillel. 1980. *The French Prophets: The History of a Millenarian Group in Eighteenth-Century England*. Berkeley: University of California Press.

Schwartz, Stephen. 1977. "Introduction." In *Naming, Necessity and Natural Kinds*, edited by Stephen Schwarz. Ithaca: Cornell University Press.

Searle, John R. 1958. "Proper Names." *Mind: A Quarterly Review of Psychology and Philosophy* 67:166–73.

Selby-Bigge, L. A. 1897. *British Moralists*. 2 vols. Oxford: Clarendon Press.

Shaftesbury, Anthony Ashley Cooper, 3rd Earl of. [1711] 1964. *Characteristics of Men, Manners, Opinions, Times*. Edited by John M. Robertson. Indianapolis: Bobbs-Merrill.

Sherburn, George. 1934. *The Early Career of Alexander Pope*. Oxford: Clarendon Press.

Shklovsky, Victor. 1965. "Art as Technique." In *Russian Formalist Criticism: Four Essays*, edited by L. T. Lemon and M. J. Reis. Lincoln: University of Nebraska Press.

Singer, Peter. 1981. *The Expanding Circle: Ethics and Sociobiology*. New York: Farrar, Straus and Giroux.

Sitter, John. 1982. *Literary Loneliness in Mid-Eighteenth-Century England*. Ithaca: Cornell University Press.

———. 1991. *Arguments of Augustan Wit*. Cambridge: Cambridge University Press.

Smith, Adam. 1982. *The Theory of Moral Sentiments*. Edited by D. D. Raphael and A. L. Macfie. Indianapolis: Liberty Fund.

Smithers, Peter F. 1968. *The Life of Joseph Addison*. 2d ed. Oxford: Clarendon Press.

Smuts, Barbara B. 1997. "Social Relationships and Life Histories of Primates." In *The Evolving Female: A Life-History Perspective*, edited by Mary Ellen Marbeck, Alison Gallaway, and Adrienne L. Zittlman, 60–68. Princeton: Princeton University Press.

Sober, Elliott, and David Sloan Wilson. 1998. *Unto Others: The Evolution and Psychology of Unselfish Behavior*. Cambridge: Harvard University Press.

Solkin, David. 1993. *Painting for Money: The Visual Arts and the Public Sphere in Eighteenth-Century England*. New Haven: Yale University Press.

Spence, Joseph. 1966. *Observations, Anecdotes, and Characters of Books and Men*. Edited by James M. Osborn. 2 vols. Oxford: Clarendon Press.

Stack, Frank. 1985. *Pope and Horace: Studies in Imitation*. Cambridge: Cambridge University Press.

Stephanson, Raymond. 1997. "'Epicoene Friendship': Understanding Male Friendship in the Early Eighteenth-Century, with Some Speculation about Pope." *Eighteenth-Century: Theory and Interpretation* 38 (2): 151–70.

Stephen, Sir Leslie. [1880] 1888. *Alexander Pope*. New Edition. London: MacMillan.

Stone, George Winchester, and Kahrl, George M. 1979. *David Garrick: A Critical Biography*. Carbondale: Southern Illinois University Press.

Strachey, Lytton. 1925. *Pope: The Leslie Stephen Lecture for 1925.* Cambridge: Cambridge University Press.

Sulloway, Frank. 1979. *Freud, Biologist of the Mind: Beyond the Psychoanalytic Legend.* New York: Basic Books.

———. 1996. *Born to Rebel: Birth Order, Family Dynamics, and Creative Lives.* New York: Pantheon.

Swift, Jonathan.1963. *The Correspondence of Jonathan Swift.* Edited by Harold Williams. 5 vols. Oxford: Clarendon Press.

Taylor, Gabriele. 1985. *Pride, Shame, and Guilt: Emotions of Self-Assessment.* Oxford: Clarendon Press.

Taylor, George. 1972. "'The Just Delineation of the Passions': Theories of Acting in the Age of Garrick." In *The Eighteenth-Century English Stage,* edited by Kenneth Richards and Peter Thomson. London: Methuen.

Tillotson, Geoffrey. 1966. *Pope and Human Nature.* Oxford: Clarendon Press.

Trivers, Robert L. 1971. "The Evolution of Reciprocal Altruism." *Quarterly Review of Biology* 46:35–56.

———. 1974. "Parent-Offspring Conflict." *American Zoologist* 14:249–64.

Virgil. 1983. *Aeneid.* Translated by Robert Fitzgerald. New York: Vintage Classics.

Warton, Joseph. 1756 and 1782. *An Essay on the Genius and Writings of Pope.* 2 vols. London.

Warton, Thomas. 1747. *The Pleasures of Melancholy.* London.

———. 1754. *Observations on the "Faerie Queene" of Spenser.* London.

———. 1755. *The Pleasures of Melancholy.* 2d ed. London.

———. 1762. *Observations on the "Faerie Queene" of Spenser.* 2d ed.. 2 vols. London.

Wasserman, Earl R. 1947. "The Sympathetic Imagination in Eighteenth-Century Theories of Acting." *Journal of English and Germanic Philology* 46:264–72.

———. 1950. "The Inherent Values of Eighteenth-Century Personification." *PMLA* 65:435–63.

Weinbrot, Howard D. 1969. *The Formal Strain: Studies in Augustan Imitation and Satire.* Chicago: University of Chicago Press.

———. 1982. *Alexander Pope and the Traditions of Formal Verse Satire.* Princeton: Princeton University Press.

———. 1993. *Britannia's Issue: The Rise of British Literature from Dryden to Ossian.* Cambridge: Cambridge University Press.

Weiskel, Thomas. [1976] 1986. *The Romantic Sublime: Studies in the Structure and Psychology of Transcendence.* Baltimore: Johns Hopkins University Press.

Wendorf, Richard. 1996. *Sir Joshua Reynolds: The Painter in Society.* Cambridge: Harvard University Press.

Wharton, Family of. 1727. *Whartoniana: or, Miscellanies, in Verse and Prose. By the*

Wharton Family, and Several Other Persons of Distinction. 2 vols. London: E. Curll.

Wharton, Philip Duke of. 1723. *The True Briton.*

Williams, Aubrey L. 1955. *Pope's* Dunciad: *A Study of its Meaning.* Baton Rouge: Louisiana State University Press.

Williams, Bernard. 1972. *Morality: An Introduction to Ethics.* New York: Harper and Row.

———. 1993. *Shame and Necessity.* Berkeley: University of California Press

Williams, George C. 1966. *Adaptation and Natural Selection.* Princeton: Princeton University Press.

Wilson, E. O. 1975. *Sociobiology: The New Synthesis.* Cambridge: Harvard University Press.

———. 1998. *Consilience: The Unity of Knowledge.* New York: Knopf.

Wilson, James Q. 1993. *The Moral Sense.* New York: Free Press.

Wilson, Michael. 1990. "Garrick, Iconic Acting, and the Ideologies of Theatrical Portraiture." *Word and Image* 6:368–94.

Wimsatt, William K. 1949. "Rhetoric and Poems: the Example of Pope." *English Institute Essays 1948.* New York: Columbia University Press.

———. 1954. *The Verbal Icon: Studies in the Meaning of Poetry.* Lexington: University of Kentucky Press.

Wind, Edgar. 1986. *Hume and the Heroic Portrait: Studies in Eighteenth-Century Imagery.* Oxford: Clarendon Press.

Winn, James Anderson. 1977. *A Window in the Bosom: The Letters of Alexander Pope.* Hamden, Conn.: Archon Books.

Wollheim, Richard. 1984. *The Thread of Life.* Cambridge: Harvard University Press.

———. 1993. "Art, Interpretation, and Perception." In *The Mind and Its Depths*, 132–43. Cambridge: Harvard University Press.

Wood, Gordon S. 1982. "Conspiracy and the Paranoid Style: Causality and Deceit in the Eighteenth Century." *William and Mary Quarterly* 39 (3): 401–41.

Woodman, Thomas. 1989. *Politeness and Poetry in the Age of Pope.* Rutherford, N.J.: Farleigh Dickinson University Press.

Wordsworth, William. 1974. "Essay upon Epitaphs." In *Wordsworth's Literary Criticism*, edited by W. J. B. Owen. London: Routledge and Kegan Paul.

Wright, Robert. 1994. *The Moral Animal: Evolutionary Psychology and Everyday Life.* New York: Viking.

———. 1996. "The Earthling," *Slate Magazine.* 29 June.

Youngren, William H. 1980. "Conceptualism and Neoclassic Generality." *ELH* 47:705–40.

Index

DATE DUE